The Development of British Tactical Air Power, 1940–1943

Matthew Powell

The Development of British Tactical Air Power, 1940–1943

A History of Army Co-operation Command

Matthew Powell
Cwmbran, United Kingdom

ISBN 978-1-137-54416-2   ISBN 978-1-137-54417-9 (eBook)
DOI 10.1057/978-1-137-54417-9

Library of Congress Control Number: 2016947263

© The Editor(s) (if applicable) and The Author(s) 2016
The author(s) has/have asserted their right(s) to be identified as the author(s) of this work in accordance with the Copyright, Designs and Patents Act 1988.
This work is subject to copyright. All rights are solely and exclusively licensed by the Publisher, whether the whole or part of the material is concerned, specifically the rights of translation, reprinting, reuse of illustrations, recitation, broadcasting, reproduction on microfilms or in any other physical way, and transmission or information storage and retrieval, electronic adaptation, computer software, or by similar or dissimilar methodology now known or hereafter developed.
The use of general descriptive names, registered names, trademarks, service marks, etc. in this publication does not imply, even in the absence of a specific statement, that such names are exempt from the relevant protective laws and regulations and therefore free for general use.
The publisher, the authors and the editors are safe to assume that the advice and information in this book are believed to be true and accurate at the date of publication. Neither the publisher nor the authors or the editors give a warranty, express or implied, with respect to the material contained herein or for any errors or omissions that may have been made.

Cover image © Antony Nettle / Alamy Stock Photo

Printed on acid-free paper

This Palgrave Macmillan imprint is published by Springer Nature
The registered company is Macmillan Publishers Ltd. London

For my grandmother Roseann Fraser

Introduction

Although the First World War ended with the existence of an independent air force in Britain, the majority of the work undertaken in the air during the war had been in aiding the British Expeditionary Force (BEF) to defeat Germany. One of the major developments in air power that came out of the First World War was in its application at the strategic level, through attacks on the German homeland. These attacks had been limited in both scale and damage done but they sowed the seeds for how the Royal Air Force (RAF) would look to develop air power in the future. During the interwar period, army support tasks, such as close air support, battlefield air interdiction and artillery spotting and reconnaissance were relatively neglected in comparison to the thinking on how to apply air power at the higher levels of war.

At the outbreak of the First World War in 1914, the newly created Royal Flying Corps (RFC) was not held in high regard by the army authorities who were to control its missions.[1] Aircraft, however, were to prove their use in the earliest campaigns of the war when they were initially used in a reconnaissance role. As the accuracy of aircraft reports were verified they were relied upon more and more in this function, and in spotting for artillery,[2] so much so that new aircraft designed by the RFC were constructed with army co-operation in mind.[3] They were able to provide 'invaluable sources of intelligence from as early as 19 August [1914]' and were able to detect the famous gap between the German First and Second Armies into which the BEF advanced, attacking and halting the German advance.[4] This was confirmed by further air reconnaissance that 'revealed that von Kluck's [the German First Army Commander] change of plan had left his right flank exposed, [and] an opportunity presented itself for counter-attack'.[5] This counter-attack manifested itself in the 'Miracle of the Marne'. Hyde has described the priorities assigned to the RFC as 'first[ly] reconnaissance and secondly fighting'.[6] Air power was employed in both tactical and strategic roles by both the British and the German air forces by the end of conflict.[7]

One of the first major uses of tactical air power during the First World War had been the interdiction operations conducted by the Second and Third Wings RFC on 10 March 1915 at Neuve Chappelle. During this operation, German reserves moving around the Lille–Menin–Courtrai area were bombed as they made their way up to the front lines.[8] The first operational order for the use of close air support for troop movements was at the Battle of Arras in April 1917.[9] Aircraft of the RFC were detailed to attack 'obstacles in the path of the advancing infantry'.[10] The opening of the third Battle of Ypres saw further refinement of close air support in the attacks made at Arras. Peter Simkins writes that 'RFC single-seater squadrons were detailed to give direct help to the infantry by making low-level attacks on German positions and troop concentrations with machine guns and 25lb Cooper bombs'.[11]

As the First World War descended into a mire of trench warfare, the RFC was able to conduct observation and reconnaissance missions over static front lines, giving the relatively inexperienced Corps time and opportunity to improve operational effectiveness.[12] The role the RFC was expected to play also increased as the conditions of static warfare allowed greater accuracy for the spotting of artillery shots.[13] This role in particular was to teach the RFC (and subsequently the RAF) the importance of denying the enemy the freedom to conduct similar reconnaissance and artillery support tasks themselves. This prevented the German air force from discovering troop concentrations prior to an attack and from conducting effective reconnaissance for their own offensive actions.[14]

In improving successful tactical operations, the RFC developed communication techniques to correct the fall of shot whilst aircraft were still in the air.[15] One of these was the Central Wireless Station, 'established in late 1916 as part of the efforts to improve the standard air-artillery co-operation. These provided a logical solution to the problem of directing attack aircraft against targets encountered by corps machines'.[16] Observation was of vital importance to higher commands who found themselves out of touch with the tactical situation of battles they were responsible for conducting. 'The senior RFC officer in the field would be expected to have a headquarters

[HQ] close to that of the general headquarters [GHQ]' in order to provide the Commander-in-Chief (C-in-C) with timely tactical information.[17] Aerial reconnaissance had improved to such an extent that 'by the end of 1917, photographic reconnaissance was in the need of only small refinement, mainly in the field of producing more efficient and effective cameras'.[18]

As more tactical air support operations were conducted, more experience was gained and assimilated quickly within the RFC, a remarkable feat when it is remembered that no official thinking or guidelines existed for pilots tasked with ground support operations.[19] Despite this lack of official doctrine, the ground attack role gathered pace during 1916 and when compared to the German air force, the support provided was 'generally effective, not least in terms of delivery of fire-power in lieu of artillery'.[20] Recent research has noted, however, that despite the lack of any official guidance the RFC's training manuals did discuss tactical methods and demonstrate the aggressive nature of the Corps.[21] Aircraft from 21 Squadron were used in both interdiction and close air support roles during the opening phase of the Somme offensive in 1916.[22] Jordan has argued that this form of support lacked any real effectiveness, aside from comparisons against the German air force, until 1917—'when ground attack missions involved the delivery of bombs in a manner far different from the speculative raids that had been carried out previously'.[23] Further to this, Jordan claims that due to the limited technological development of bombs the Germans found these raids were a 'source of inconvenience ... rather than providing a devastating blow'.[24] Close air support operations, due to their nature of low altitude attacks against ground troops firing back, as well as the close co-operation required with friendly ground troops, meant that the results obtained 'were disappointing when compared with the losses sustained'.[25] This was one of the factors that hampered development of this kind of offensive operation during the interwar years.

Even with the formation of the RAF as an independent air force, there was little change in the focus of operations, although there was a public outcry for air attacks to be conducted against German territory after air raids over Britain in 1917.[26] The use of aircraft to attack the British civilian population by the German air force shattered the illusion the British public had about the immunity they took for granted.[27] An Independent Force (IF), headed by the future Chief of the Air Staff (CAS), Sir Hugh Trenchard was created to fulfil this role. At this time, Trenchard was more in favour of aircraft conducting a tactical rather than an independent strategic role. However, with the end of the First World War and the independence of the RAF at stake, he saw the benefits an independently led and organised air force could bring.[28] He also understood the potential impact that aircraft could have when used in a strategic capacity.[29]

The RAF in 1918 was a force equipped to conduct a variety of army co-operation missions with a reasonable degree of success although the casualty rates for missions such as close support were still restrictively high with losses running up to thirty per cent.[30] Between July 1916 and 11 November 1918 the RAF, including the IF, 'destroyed or brought down 7,054 enemy aircraft, dropped 6,942 tons of bombs, flew over 900,000 hours (nearly 103 years), and fired over 10½ million rounds at ground targets'.[31] They were experienced in close air support missions in both an offensive and defensive situation.[32] Interdiction roles had been widely developed and were seen to be highly effective in preventing the flow of *matériel* and reinforcements along enemy supply routes. It was in this role that the RAF was the most effective during the last major offensives launched by the German army in the spring of 1918.[33] An article published by the *Journal of the Royal United Services Institute* (*JRUSI*) in 1934 went as far as to argue that the strategical [*sic*] operations conducted had been of 'high value'.[34] The war, however, had not continued long enough after the formation of the IF for these strategic bombing missions to have any real and noticeable effect,[35] but a platform had been built, one from which it would be possible to improve the RAF's ability to support the army in the field in areas from tactical air support to artillery spotting.

When investigating the impact of aircraft on the battlefield in support of the Third Army in the last one hundred days of the First World War, Jonathan Boff states that 'news brought by contact patrols ... was generally only 24 minutes out of date'. Of more interest to a study of this nature is the conclusion he puts forward that 'no single doctrine applied [to air support controls and procedures] across all the British armies'.[36] This conclusion can have a significant impact on the interpretation of events of the interwar period, especially when taken against the counter-arguments put forward by David Jordan: 'By the end of the First World War, the BEF and the RAF had developed an extremely high degree of cooperation [*sic*] that added considerably to the potency of the BEF as the war drew to a close'.[37] Jordan has further enforced Richard Hallion's views on the doctrine applied by the RFC in the First World War. This included different aircraft being employed in different roles on the battlefield such as the use of Sopwith Camels 'operating at medium altitudes for protection of reconnaissance, liaison, artillery spotting, and ground-attack flights'.[38] As can be seen, whether or not the RAF had a single unified doctrine for the support of ground troops by aircraft is still subject to much intense debate, as is whether the writings of the RFC and RAF can actually be considered doctrine in the first place.

The relative neglect of air power at the tactical and operational levels of war soured relations between the RAF and the army in Britain. This situation was not fully resolved until 1944 when the RAF was able to demonstrate what it had learned in offensive operations against the Germans on the European continent. The RAF's tactical knowledge was based on two things—experiments conducted in Britain, and the refinement of key aspects of these experiments in operations against the enemy in the Western Desert between 1942 and 1943. The development of an Army Co-operation Command (ACC) was at the heart of this learning process in Britain and it was vital to transforming the understanding of the army of the operational-level impact of tactical air power. It also developed concepts that transformed warfare and which were applied by British forces in many different theatres during the Second World War.

There has been an increase in the interest in tactical air power evolution by historians over the past two decades, with a particular emphasis on the developments made in both a single and joint service context during the Second World War. Research has also been conducted on how tactical air power was developed from humble origins in 1914 to an advanced state in 1918. Despite the interest shown in tactical air power development in the Second World War, there has been little focus on the organisation created by the RAF in 1940 to further its development in Britain—the Army Co-operation Command mentioned above. One the major factors for this lack of interest is that as a non-operational command, ACC could only develop ideas in theory and through experimentation. Once this stage of the ideas development process had been completed, ACC's work ceased and it was continued by operational commands of the RAF. For example,

The focus of the majority of these studies has been on the developments made by the RAF's WDAF under Air Marshal Sir Arthur Tedder and Air Vice-Marshal Sir Arthur 'Mary' Coningham. That the focus has been in this area is not surprising. Ideas about how to provide impromptu air support for ground forces were further refined by the WDAF in operations against the enemy. It was also in this desert theatre that new aircraft were developed, for example the Hurri-bomber, to provide close air support. Focusing on the WDAF and its work in overseas theatres has overshadowed the achievements of Army Co-operation Command—this book will redress this current imbalance.

It has been argued that very little was done to develop tactical air power during the Second World War,[39] but the work of the ACC, undertaken in difficult circumstances and without support from the RAF as a whole, did much to transform thinking on the subject. This book will shed new light on the topic by focusing not only on ACC as a stand-alone command but also by placing the organisation within its historical and geographical context. It will demonstrate the full role played by ACC in developing the tactical air support method that would form part of the basic system used in north-west Europe and Italy.

One of the major grievances of the army from 1918 until the creation of Army Co-operation Command in late 1940 was the lack of a specialised higher command formation within the RAF to work with the army to develop further the air support systems that had been created through the hard work of the First World War. The formation that did deal with army support was located at the Group (No. 22 Group) and not Command level. The lack of such a formation became even more pronounced when the RAF created formations based on a mono-role structure in 1936.[40] There were also fundamental disagreements between the two services over the nature of air support that should be provided. When the lessons of the First World War were codified by the RAF, the fundamental principle identified was that control of the air over the battlefield was the key to providing any form of air support. Once this had been achieved, the RAF felt that battlefield air interdiction, the use of air power to seal off the battlefield from enemy reserves and *matériel*, should be utilised. The army believed that aircraft should be used primarily in a close air support role, to attack enemy forces engaged with or in close proximity to friendly troops. They further felt that they should have their own organic air force available to provide this form of air support as and when they felt it was required.[41]

This fundamental disagreement appeared almost as soon as the fighting on the Western Front had finished. The lack of focus on support for land forces occurred for a number of reasons that will be explored in more depth in the following chapter, but they can be briefly stated as follows: there was a fundamental disagreement between the RAF and the army over the nature of air support that should be provided; the RAF was fighting for its very existence; the economic and political situation facing the governments of the interwar period meant that the development and rearmament of the services was politically difficult; and the state of the aviation industry meant the development of specialist army co-operation aircraft was low on the list of priorities given the strategic situation of the mid to late 1930s.

In an effort to prevent itself from being disbanded (with an inevitable return to the pre-April 1918 situation of an RFC attached to the army and a Royal Naval Air Service (RNAS) attached to the Royal Navy, the RAF emphasised an application of air power that only it, as an independent air service, could provide. It was also felt by many in the Air Ministry that the application of air power at a strategic level, targeting an enemy homeland, could prevent a repeat of the carnage of the Western Front in the First World War. This emphasis on the strategic application of air power, however, would inevitably lead to disagreements between the RAF and the army. The latter felt that without the necessary and in their view 'correct' form of air support in future conflicts against a first-rate continental opponent, they would find themselves at a severe disadvantage.[42]

The fundamental argument that will be put forward in this book is that Army Co-operation Command aided the development of tactical air support to a greater extent than has previously been recognised by historians in this field. ACC was helped in this success through the work of staff officers who had experienced the difficulties of conducting air support in France in 1940—key problems in how to conduct impromptu air support were highlighted and guided ACC's thinking in this area. The Command also fostered good relations between RAF and army officers at the lower command levels. These good relations allowed trials and experiments to be conducted between ACC and certain parts of the army, such as the School of Artillery. This was further helped by the fact that the commander of ACC, Air Marshal Sir Arthur 'Ugly' Barratt, was a former artillery officer.

The book is laid out as follows. Chap. 1 explores the development of close air support in Britain during the interwar period from the doctrinal base left at the end of the First World War. It starts with analysis of the joint work by the RAF and army in furthering a common intellectual basis through training exercises conducted in Britain. The annual reports of these training exercises are used to demonstrate the state and development of thinking in this area. The problems faced by the RAF in this period between the world wars further highlight the reasoning for the relative neglect of tactical air power. The role of the RAF in policing the empire forms the final section in this chapter. Contemporary reports of the use of air power around the empire are drawn upon to demonstrate how the RAF operated in these areas both independently and with ground forces.

Chapter 2 examines how the doctrine created during the interwar period was applied during the first major operation of the Second World

War in France and Belgium in 1940. This chapter also looks at how agencies created to conduct this support were formed and then re-formed in various guises prior to being engaged on active operations. One of these was the Air Observation Post (Air OP) Squadron and the beginnings of its development are discussed in this chapter as they provide the context required when the organisation's further development is analysed (frequently in subsequent chapters). Finally, the chapter considers the reports written by Lord Gort, C-in-C of the BEF, and Barratt who commanded the RAF in the immediate aftermath of the fighting in France, to contextualise the atmosphere in which army co-operation was created.

Chapter 3 examines the investigations launched in Britain after the fighting in France. Extreme pressure was applied to the RAF to change its attitude towards army co-operation, primarily from the army itself. The work undertaken to improve the RAF's ability to conduct air support in the field, work continued by the ACC, is reviewed. This is followed by an examination of the creation of ACC itself, in order to keep the chronological nature of the book, including how it was created and the RAF's motivations for doing so.

Chapter 4 explains how ACC went about fulfilling its role through 1941. It considers the changes made by the Command's head, Barratt, to allow the Command to function as efficiently and effectively as possible. Barratt's position, as well as his relationships with others in the RAF, is also scrutinised in this section as it further highlights the position of the Command. This is an aspect of ACC that has not been analysed in literature currently available on tactical air power development in Britain during the Second World War. Also in this chapter, the role of ACC working with the army to develop the Air OP Squadron is studied as it highlights what the Command was capable of when allowed a freer rein in its role. Exercises held throughout the year to prepare both the army and the RAF to conduct air support operations is also subject to analysis. To highlight the strategic context within which ACC was working, the steps taken in preparation to conduct anti-invasion operations are also discussed. Aircraft requirements for conducting both the exercises and anti-invasion measures form the final part of the chapter. The major events of the Middle East in 1941 are also mentioned to demonstrate the setbacks and developments taking place overseas in active operations against the *Wehrmacht*.

Chapter 5 continues the examination of the work undertaken by ACC throughout 1942. The major battles in the Middle East and Barratt's visit to the theatre are analysed. The development of the idea to use fighters, and as a result, the creation of Fighter Command, in tactical air support operations when the army returned to the continent are also examined. From this, the separate ideas put forward by Air Commodore Henry Thorold and Air Vice-Marshal John Slessor, working in isolation regarding what form an army air support organisation should take to support operations against the continent, are compared. These proposals led to formal discussions taking place and there was great debate between the army and the RAF over where this new formation was to be placed within the RAF's Command structure.

Chapter 6 examines the work of ACC until its disbandment in the middle of 1943. The development of the communications system used by land forces to call for air support is examined, as is the role played by the commander during the exercise that tested the army air support group idea, as well as the developments that occurred in the thinking regarding the conduct of army air support as a result. The chapter examines both the actual disbandment of ACC and the subsequent creation of the 2nd Tactical Air Force (TAF). This section concludes by examining the role played by ACC in the development of army air support in Britain between 1940 and 1943, highlighting the difficulties faced by the Command from its inception to its demise, and includes a discussion of RAF attitudes towards this aspect of British air power.

Notes

1. Andrew Whitmarsh, 'British Army Manoeuvres and the Development of British Military Aviation, 1910–1913', *War In History*, 14: 3 (July, 2007), p. 325.
2. See also Robin Higham, *Air Power: A Concise History* (St. Martin's Press: New York, 1972).
3. David Jordan, *The Army Co-operation Missions of The Royal Flying Corps/Royal Air Force 1914–1918*, unpublished PhD Thesis, University of Birmingham, Great Britain, 1997, p.14. See also Malcolm Cooper, *The Birth of Independent Air Power: British Air Policy in the First World War* (Allen & Unwin: London, 1986).
4. John Buckley, *Air Power in the Age of Total War* (University College London Press: London, 1999), p. 48.
5. Ralph Barker, *A Brief History of the Royal Flying Corps in World War I* (Constable and Robinson: London, 2002 [Constable & Co.: London, 1995]), p. 45.
6. H. Montgomery Hyde, *British Air Policy between the Wars, 1918–1939* (Heinemann: London, 1976), p. 23.

7. Williamson Murray, 'The Influence of Pre-war Anglo-American Doctrine on the Air Campaigns of the Second World War', in Horst Boog (ed.), *The Conduct of the Air War in the Second World War: An International Comparison* (Berg Publishers: New York and Oxford, 1992), p. 237.
8. Hilary St. George Saunders, *Per Ardua: The Rise of British Air Power 1911–1939* (Oxford University Press: London, New York and Toronto, 1944), p. 54.
9. David Jordan, 'War in the air: the fighter pilot', in John Bourne, Peter Liddle and Ian Whitehouse (eds), *The Great World War 1914–45 Vol. I: Lightning Strikes Twice* (HarperCollins: London, 2000), p. 87.
10. Lee Kennett, 'Developments to 1939', in Benjamin Franklin Cooling (ed.), *Case Studies in the Development of Close Air Support* (Office of Air Force History, United States Air Force: Washington, D.C., 1990), p. 18.
11. Peter Simkins, *Air Fighting 1914–18: The Struggle for Air Superiority over the Western Front* (Imperial War Museum: London, 1978), p. 62.
12. Jordan, *The Army Co-operation Missions*, p. 90.
13. Buckley, *Air Power*, p. 47.
14. Jonathan Boff, 'Air/Land Integration in the 100 days: The Case of Third Army', *Air Power Review*, 12: 3 (Autumn, 2009), pp. 77–88.
15. Simkins, *Air Fighting, 1914–18* p. 13.
16. Jordan, *The Army Co-operation Missions*, p. 315.
17. Neville Parton, *The Evolution and Impact of Royal Air Force Doctrine: 1919–1939* (unpublished PhD Thesis, University of Cambridge, Great Britain, 2009), p. 6.
18. Jordan, *The Army Co-operation Missions*, p.134. Cf. H. A. Jones, *The War in the Air: Being the Story of The part played in the Great War by the Royal Air Force Vol. IV*, (Imperial War Museum: London, 1928), chapters 7 and 8.
19. David Ian Hall, *Strategy for Victory: The Development of British Tactical Air Power, 1919–1943* (Praeger Security International: London and Westport, Connecticut, 2008), p. 2.
20. David Jordan, 'The Royal Air Force and Air/Land Integration in the 100 days, August–November 1918', *Air Power Review*, 11: 2 (Summer, 2008), pp. 17–18.
21. James Pugh, *The Conceptual Origins of the Control of the Air: British Military and Naval Aviation, 1911–1918* (PhD Thesis, University of Birmingham, 2012), pp. 174–5.
22. Jordan, *The Army Co-operation Missions*, p. 220.
23. Ibid. p. 216.
24. Ibid., pp. 222–3.
25. The National Archives (TNA), AIR 10/5547, Air Historical Branch (AHB) Narrative: Air Support (AP 3235), 1955.

26. This public outcry was responsible in itself for the creation of an independent RAF, as the British public had never been threatened on this scale previously. R. A. Mason, 'The British Dimension', in Mark K. Wells (ed.), *Air Power: Promise and Reality* (Imprint Publications: Chicago, 2000), p. 12. Also see Alfred M. Gollin, 'England is No Longer an Island: The Phantom Airship Scare of 1909', *Albion: A Quarterly Journal Concerned with British Studies*, 13: 1 (Spring, 1981), p. 43. Alfred Gollin, *The Impact of British Air Power on the British People and their Government, 1909–1914* (Stanford University Press: Stanford, California, 1989).
27. Tami Davis Biddle. *Rhetoric and Reality in Air Warfare: The Evolution of British and American Ideas about Strategic Bombing, 1914–1945* (Princeton University Press: Princeton, New Jersey, 2002), p. 24.
28. David Jordan and Gary Sheffield, 'The British Army and Air Power', in Peter W. Gray (ed.), *British Air Power* (The Stationery Office: London, 2003), p. 71. See also R. A. Mason, *Air Power: An Overview of Roles* (Brassey's: London, 1987).
29. Phillip S. Meilinger, 'Trenchard, Slessor, and Royal Air Force Doctrine before World War II', in Phillip S. Meilinger (ed.), *The Paths of Heaven: The Evolution of Air Power Theory* (Air University Press: Maxwell Alabama, 1997), p. 41.
30. Jordan, 'The Royal Air Force', p. 15. Peter C. Smith, *Close Air Support: An Illustrated History, 1914 to the Present* (Orion Books: New York, 1990), p. 8.
31. TNA AIR 8/13, British Air Effort during the War, Chapter 2 Co-operation with the Army, 1 January 1919.
32. Cf. Malcolm Cooper, 'Blueprint for Confusion: The Administrative Background to the Formation of the Royal Air Force', *Journal of Contemporary History*, 22: 3 (July, 1987), p. 441. Part of the argument of this book is that even after it became an independent force the RAF remained overwhelmingly committed to army co-operation work 'functioning as the RFC before it as a tactical ancillary of the service from which it had sprung'.
33. Jordan, *The Army Co-operation Missions*, pp. 281, 283 4
34. Oliver Stewart, 'Air Forces in the Great War: Some Strategical Lessons', *JRUSI*, 79 (February/November, 1934), p. 293.
35. Maurice Dean, *The Royal Air Force and Two World Wars* (Cassell: London, 1979), pp. 3–4.
36. Boff, 'Air/Land Integration', pp. 82–3.
37. Jordan, 'The Royal Air Force', p. 28. Cf. Jordan, *The Army Co-operation Missions*.
38. Richard P. Hallion, *Strike from the Sky: The History of Battlefield Air Attack, 1911–1945* (Smithsonian Institution Press: Washington and London, 1989), p. 23.

39. Simon Coningham, 'The Battle of Amiens: Air-Ground Co-operation and its Implications for Imperial Policing', in Gary Sheffield and Peter Gray (eds), *Changing War: The British Army, The Hundred Days Campaign and the Birth of the Royal Air Force* (Bloomsbury: London and New York, 2013), p. 223.
40. Alistair Byford, 'Fair Stood the Wind for France? The Royal Air Force's experience in 1940 as a case study of the relationship between policy, strategy and doctrine', *Air Power Review*, 14: 3 (Autumn/Winter, 2011), p. 41.
41. Sebastian Cox, 'The Air/Land relationship—an historical perspective 1918–1991', *Air Power Review*, 11: 2 (Summer, 2000), p. 1.
42. Neville Parton, 'The Development of Early RAF Doctrine', *The Journal of Military History* 72: 4 (October, 2008), pp. 1170–1.

Acknowledgments

This book owes much to the advice and guidance I have received throughout my academic career from many historians. Dr Peter Gray, Senior Research Fellow at the University of Birmingham, commented on the drafts that formed this book, and it is through his advice and suggestions that this work has taken the configuration that it has, both in the embryonic planning and further in the details. Many others have provided invaluable advice, support and friendship during the writing of this book. Dr James Pugh, Teaching Fellow at the University of Birmingham, has provided a friendly yet critical sounding board for the ideas, arguments and presentation within the text, and his comments and suggestions have improved both the form and interpretation. Dr Douglas Ford, Lecturer at the Baltic Defence College, provided invaluable advice for the master's thesis that first sparked my interest in tactical air power and Army Co-operation Command in general. I have been more than fortunate in having the opportunity to work with Emily Russell and Angharad Bishop at Palgrave Macmillan—their advice, support and patience have proved invaluable.

The support of the staff at the National Archives at Kew, the Imperial War Museum, the Liddell Hart Centre for Military Archives at King's College London and the Royal Air Force Museum, Hendon, whose tireless work ensures that historians are able to access the required information with speed and ease, is graciously and readily acknowledged. I also wish to thank the library staff of the University of Birmingham, who spent time searching for lost books and providing great help and direction to a new research student unfamiliar with the layout of yet another new library, and the staff of the library at Cardiff University who allowed me, through the SCONUL system, to access works held by them.

My family and friends have been a constant source of inspiration and support. Theresa and Darren Saban graciously gave me their home for research trips to London, and Callum Saban provided the necessary distraction after long days buried in archival papers. Gavin Jones was a constant source of support and help throughout my PhD studies and the writing of the book and provided vital advice in its presentation. Finally, I want to thank my parents, without whose help and support this project would have been inconceivable from the outset; my partner Jenna Manship, whose love, support and patience have allowed this project to be completed despite being absent both physically and mentally for great periods of time and my grandparents, particularly my late grandmother, Roseann Fraser, whose tales of living near the English Channel during the Second World War first sparked my interest in history, especially air power studies. This book is dedicated to her.

Cwmbran
28 October 2015

Matthew Powell

Contents

1 Army Co-operation at Home and Abroad — 1

2 Tactical Air Power and the Battle of France, 1940 — 43

3 The Creation of Army Co-operation Command — 83

4 The Work of Army Co-operation Command, 1941 — 119

5 The Beginning of the End of Army Co-operation Command, 1942 — 161

6 The End of Army Co-operation Command, 1943 — 197

Conclusion — 227

Appendix: Directive to AOC-in-C Army Co-operation Command — 233

Bibliography — 235

Index — 257

Abbreviations

A Air SC	Army Air Support Control
AASC	Army Air Support Control
AASF	Advanced Air Striking Force
AASG	Army Air Support Group
ACAB	Allied Central Air Bureau
ACAS	Assistant Chief of the Air Staff
ACC	Army Co-operation Command
ACM	Air Chief Marshall
AFV	Armoured Fighting Vehicle
AHB	Air Historical Branch
Air OP	Air Observation Post
ALO	Air Liaison Officer
AOC	Air Officer Commanding
AOC-in-C	Air Officer Commanding-in-Chief
ASC	Army Support Control
ASSU	Air Support Signals Unit
AVM	Air Vice Marshall
BAFF	British Air Forces in France
BEF	British Expeditionary Force
C2	command and control
C3	command, control and communication
CAS	Chief of the Air Staff
CID	Committee of Imperial Defence
C-in-C	Commander-in-Chief
CIGS	Chief of the Imperial General Staff
COS	Chiefs of Staff
CSBC	Close Support Bomber Control

DCAS	Deputy Chief of the Air Staff
DMC	Directorate of Military Co-operation
GHQ	general headquarters
GOC-in-C	General Officer Commanding-in-Chief
HQ	Headquarters
IF	Independent Force
IWM	Imperial War Museum, London
JRUSI	Journal of the Royal United Services Institute
MORU	Mobile Operations Room Units
OTU	Operational Training Unit
PRG	Photographic Reconnaissance Group
RAF	Royal Air Force
RAFM	Royal Air Force Museum, Hendon
RFC	Royal Flying Corps
RHA	Royal Horse Artillery
RNAS	Royal Naval Air Service
R/T	radio telegraphy
SASO	Senior Air Staff Officer
TNA	The National Archives (PRO, UK)
US	United States
VCAS	Vice Chief of the Air Staff
WDAF	Western Desert Air Force
W/T	wireless telegraphy
ZOAN	Zone d'Opérations Aériennes Nord

CHAPTER 1

Army Co-operation at Home and Abroad

The British military establishment ended the First World War with a newly created independent air force that had yet to test fully its hopes and ideas for the application of air power at all levels of war. Lessons learned and ideas on how best to apply air power in any future conflict would have to be developed in the operational vacuum of the interwar period as there was no longer a hostile first-class European military power against which to conduct operations. Britain was also militarily, economically and socially unable to undertake such a conflict for the foreseeable future.[1] The development of air power, as well as the very existence of the RAF as an independent force, was at a critical juncture in 1918. The decisions taken in the first years after the First World War were instrumental in how the RAF utilised air power until the end of the Second World War.

The experience of the First World War allowed the newly formed RAF to develop its ideas in a more coherent fashion and the fundamental principles were codified by Trenchard. These were (1) maintenance of initiative through offensive operations; (2) the concentration of force; (3) the command and control (C2) of aircraft being centralised (which would increase the concentration of force), and (4) the gaining and retention of air superiority.[2] The most important of these principles, which was to both drive and guide the theoretical thinking about the application of air power, was the fundamental need to gain, at the very least, local air superiority. Through the gaining of air superiority, other air power missions could be conducted, such as close air support, battlefield air interdiction and strategic bombardment. Apart from the gaining of air superiority, these principles were fundamentally at odds with how the army thought air support should be provided, although there was disagreement as to what air superiority entailed. The army felt that the primary role of the RAF in air support was to attack front line positions as and when required.[3] The army had become accustomed to a force dedicated almost solely to the support of its troops despite the creation of IF. For almost the entirety of the First World War, Trenchard saw the best role for aircraft as support for the army, and so it is not unreasonable to think that the army believed that this would continue with him as CAS.

Much has been claimed about the development of the army co-operation role by the RAF during the interwar period. Some have gone so far as to claim that very little was done in this area, and that what was done was almost an insignificance. Simon Coningham has argued that 'despite the concept of air-ground co-operation being largely ignored by both the RAF and the Army in Great Britain, the RAF was flexible and tactically acute enough to resurrect it when necessary to its imperial operational objectives'.[4] Richard Muller has argued that 'The perception that close air support was a costly luxury and an aberration would dominate the next quarter-century and contributed materially to the RAF's failure to advance its close-support practises during the inter-war period.'[5] This chapter will demonstrate, however, that this is not the case and that whilst it was not an overriding priority for the RAF before 1939, much good work was done. It will also highlight the developments that were made in army co-operation ideas across the British Empire and investigate the difficulties faced by all the services, with particular reference to the RAF, during the very difficult interwar period—financial stringency, the disarmament movement supported by the general public and the political class of Britain, and the difficulties caused by the need to rearm and reinvigorate the British aircraft industry. This will provide the necessary historical context for an analysis of the army co-operation exercises, the developments that emerged from them and how they were applied during the Battle of France in 1940.

Many of the issues encountered during the army co-operation missions in the Second World War had already been experienced in the exercises of the interwar period and it was here that ideas were first put forward to resolve them. These exercises, as well as the results arising from their theoretical development, will be highlighted in greater detail in this chapter. The ideas that emerged from these exercises helped to form the theoretical basis developed by Army Co-operation Command and allowed it to transform the thinking on tactical air power in Britain. The development of army co-operation, in its many facets, was, on the face of it, the most logical path for the RAF to follow, based on their experiences in the First World War. This option, however, placed the very existence of the RAF as an independent force in grave danger as it would, and indeed did, lead to calls from the senior services to return to the pre-1918 establishment of an RNAS and RFC.

It was partly due to this potential disbandment that the RAF looked to develop ideas that involved the projection of air power at the strategic, rather than the tactical, level of war. Due to the inconclusive results of the strategic bombardment missions conducted by the RAF towards the end of the First World War, they could express their ideas about its impact with a greater freedom of imagination.[6] The RAF were able to stave off calls for their disbandment, and increase their funding relative to the Royal Navy and army by stressing the potential impact of air power at this level of war on the enemy home population. This, they argued, could only be achieved by an independent air force and was enhanced by the lack of an early warning system that would allow for the interception of hostile bomber aircraft.[7] The monies available to the governments of the interwar period, however, were not enough to allow the RAF to build up an air force that was both equipped to conduct large-scale operations immediately and able to create the necessary establishments to allow them to develop their in-house education and training. Trenchard was forced to make this decision very soon after the end of the First World War, and he chose to use the limited funds available to build up the intellectual and physical framework of the RAF through institutions such as the RAF College at Cranwell, which could be added to when required and the necessary funds became available.[8]

Army co-operation was never a priority for the RAF at this time but it is incorrect to say that they simply forgot how to support the army. By November 1918, the RAF was relatively adept at army co-operation. One issue made apparent during the Hundred Days offensives, however, was how to provide the myriad of army co-operation missions during semi-mobile warfare. Aspects of army co-operation that had functioned well during the static trench warfare phase of the First World War, such as artillery spotting, began to see a drop off in efficiency as the C2 system for controlling aircraft found it difficult to keep pace with the advancing artillery batteries for which they were expected to spot. More direct support of land troops, such as through close air support, was inherently dangerous given its close proximity to both the ground and enemy forces.[9] This potential increase in danger was misinterpreted by the RAF in the early interwar period in order to provide the necessary reasoning not to concentrate on this aspect of air power, allowing a focus on its strategic application instead.

The figures used by the RAF to highlight the risk to both pilot and machine in conducting these missions was based on one single action in support of ground troops at the Battle of Amiens where casualties were particularly high. Alistair McCluskey has described the experience gained at Amiens as providing 'a critical point of reference that directly influenced the development of British air–land battle in the interwar period and its subsequent conduct in the Second World War'.[10] With the RAF's change of attitude towards this form of air power, however, the status of army co-operation and the pilots in the relevant squadrons dropped significantly. This caused a large turnover in personnel that hampered the training and development of these squadrons. An army co-operation squadron was no longer a base from which a promising junior officer could launch a career. Whilst there are isolated examples, of people who did work within army co-operation and rise to senior rank, such as Trafford Leigh-Mallory and John Slessor they are the exception rather than the rule. Charles Carrington, an army officer seconded to Bomber Command during the Second World War, noted in his memoirs that those involved in army co-operation work 'did not win favour or reward' in the interwar period.[11]

The arguments over both the form of air support and the numbers required to provide it began almost as soon as the First World War had ended and thoughts had turned to the next possible conflict. These arguments and the development of army co-operation before 1939 must be seen against the difficult economic circumstances that prevailed in terms of monies available to the governments of the day to equip and expand the three services.[12] The instrument used to restrain military spending at this time was the Ten-Year Rule, which stated that the services should base their spending plans on the assumption that Britain would not be involved in any major war against a first-class power for ten years.[13] It is not the intention of this book to delve into the debate about the Ten-Year Rule as this sits outside of its scope.[14] However, the policy had a major impact on relations between the three services and was a major source of friction as the newly established RAF looked to cement its place in the British military establishment.[15]

When the rule was first introduced in 1919 by Winston Churchill, it was a sound assessment of the European strategic situation. When it was continued on an annual rolling basis in the 1930s, the strategic situation had changed dramatically for Britain.[16] The reduction in monies available did not only impact on the services themselves—the RAF, which relied upon private industry for the supply of its airframes and engines, implemented procurement policies that kept as many manufacturers as possible in business.[17] One advantage that the Rule gave Britain was that it had not overly invested in a large air force composed of wooden biplanes that became obsolete with the development of all-metal monoplanes and was in a better position than it might have been when the decision was taken to rearm in the mid-1930s.[18]

The arguments between the services, partly as a result of the Ten-Year Rule, led the government to investigate the roles that were undertaken by each of them, and through the interim report of the Committee on National Expenditure under Sir Eric Geddes, came to the conclusion that there was 'serious overlapping and duplication within the three services'.[19] This was seized upon by the War Office and there was a strong push to have all of the military functions of the RAF transferred to the War Office, thereby giving them operational control of all army co-operation squadrons within the RAF.[20] This move was, however, firmly blocked by Geddes in his final conclusions when he suggested that of the cuts to the service budgets recommended, the RAF should take the least, and those that were necessary should be made in army and naval co-operation squadrons. Geddes' report made the further claim that adhering to the War Office's demands would not result in any substantial saving and that the RAF should be given responsibilities abroad.[21] The Air Staff, and in particular Trenchard, saw this as the best opportunity the RAF would have to lay permanent foundations for the service that would settle the arguments over its independence for good, and no time was wasted in building on the Geddes report. The RAF requested from their sister services a period of grace, during which they would be given the opportunity to conduct overseas responsibilities as laid down in the Geddes report. They also highlighted the savings that could be made if the army and Royal Navy relinquished the co-operation roles, avoiding the overlap that Geddes had highlighted.[22]

It was partly for these reasons that the RAF could not develop as both a tactical and a strategic air power. The RAF's status as one of the very few independent air forces in the world was used early on by the army and

Royal Navy in an attempt to have it disbanded. This would have placed Britain at a serious disadvantage compared with other major nations, as its land forces would not receive the support they felt was required when compared to foreign armies. In 1921, the Chief of the Imperial General Staff (CIGS), General Sir Henry Wilson, responded to a memorandum written by the Lord President of the Council, Sir Henry Balfour, to the Committee of Imperial Defence (CID) on the continuing independence of the RAF. In this response Wilson argued that

> Mr Balfour's … suggestion that unless the Royal Air Force be kept completely separate and independent of the Army and Navy we shall be at a serious disadvantage compared with foreign nations I am quite unable to understand. Neither France, America nor Japan, to quote only the greatest Naval and Military powers, have adopted such a policy.[23]

In response to this attack on the fundamental existence of an independent air force, the Air Staff argued that the organisation of the British military establishment should 'conform to the requirements of British imperial strategy, not to the methods adopted by Foreign Powers whose circumstances are entirely different to our own'.[24] The army was looking to return to a pre-First World War situation and based their ideas of how this should be on the geo-political situation facing other major nations and not that faced by Britain.[25]

The army at this time was also fearful of the implications caused by the loss of their own air service and the potential lack of aerial support if they were involved in another continental conflict. One of the major flashpoints for the army was how seriously they felt the RAF was taking the training of its forces to provide this support. This was especially troubling to the army given the ideas of independent application of air power at the strategic level emanating from the RAF since the First World War had ended. The War Office did not believe that the RAF saw army co-operation as a 'specialised branch of Air Force work'.[26] The army felt that a greater priority should be accorded to air support and a conference was organised to discuss this very matter. It was during staff exercises involving both the army and RAF that it had first been noticed that there was a great deal of ignorance of army co-operation matters.[27] In preparation for the conference the Air Staff highlighted that efforts were being made to train 'all young officers in the Air Force regarding the formations and organisations of their sister services whether or not the duties of co-operation will fall to these officers'.[28] That the RAF was having to highlight how far they were willing to go in terms of training all officers in at least understanding how the army and Royal Navy worked at the most basic level highlights how keenly they felt the pressure of the accusations. Whilst co-operation with its sister services was a key aspect of the education given to potential senior officers at Andover, it was done through the prism of RAF thinking on the fundamental principles of air power.[29]

The result of the conference appeared to be a blow to the RAF and its ambitions of independent air operations. They had agreed that they would place more emphasis on co-operation with the army, but for most of the interwar period this was to be a cosmetic change and not one that altered the fundamental *modus operandi* of the service. The RAF also highlighted the great difficulties that they would face in trying to implement these changes. The army had requested that two squadrons be attached to Aldershot Command to allow the army to conduct training that would increase the efficiency of both services' abilities to conduct air support operations and temper the expectations of troops and officers regarding the limitations of this support. The RAF agreed to this in principle, but stated that it would not be possible to do this until at least 1925, and could only be done if the expansion of the RAF, which had been proposed in 1923, came to fruition.[30] The expansion programme of 1923 was a reaction to the growing threat of France and its expanding air force, combined with the soured diplomatic relations caused by differing British and French policies regarding Germany and reparations payments required under the Versailles Treaty. It has been argued that one of the reasons why the British government focused on the development of air power was to meet this potential threat, one exacerbated by Air Staff fears of the possible impact a bombing campaign could have on Britain.[31] The RAF's response to the French air menace also shaped 'the Air Staff's views on operational requirements' of new aircraft.[32]

The Air Staff also hotly refuted the army's claim that they had not been taking their responsibilities regarding the development of army co-operation officers and squadrons seriously enough, highlighting that a specialist school existed within the RAF for just such training. What they failed to mention, however, was that after completing their specialist training, these officers were not being sent to army co-operation squadrons.[33]

A second conference was held in February 1923 during which the RAF highlighted the fundamental issue that would plague the practical development of army co-operation until 1938 and was more important than inter-service rivalry, economic stringency or problems in gearing up the aviation industry for full production. This was the strategic vacuum that existed in Britain for most of the interwar period—the army was unsure what operations it would undertake, where in the world it would operate or to what extent ground forces would be deployed:

> What war are the General Staff and the Air Staff going to train for? How can that training be co-ordinated so as to be able to meet any war that we have to consider probable … If it is decided that the war is in the nature of a European war, what, broadly speaking, are the views of the Staffs as to how that war will develop?[34]

Whilst a flexible approach had always been at the heart of British strategic thinking, the lack of any potential first-class enemy hampered this process. Without answers to these fundamental principles, the RAF was faced with the difficulty of trying to develop workable operational principles for a conflict that could see a large-scale BEF deployed on the European continent to face a major power in a long and protracted conflict. It could also have to develop ideas that would be suited to a theatre of war with poor communications in a strategic sideshow and supporting a small-scale expeditionary force. Operational principles that were suited to one would not be suitable for the other. This strategic confusion for most of the inter-war period was caused largely by the lack of any potential enemy that could drive operational thinking—the British services lacked anything to guide and develop such a strategy, resulting in little enthusiasm from either service for the development of co-operation procedures and tactics.

David Ian Hall has placed most of the blame for this relative lack of development of tactical air power on the army's unwillingness to compromise over operational control of their own separate air arm.[35] This argument, however, does not take into account the RAF's actions during the interwar period, and the fact that they looked upon co-operation with the army and Royal Navy as something that had to be endured. The RAF went out of their way to make it appear as if they were taking the development of co-operation with their sister services seriously on the surface but actually did little to facilitate it to any great degree. Their ideas on air support were driven by the thinking that aircraft in a close support role were a poor substitute for artillery on the ground, which was fundamentally divergent from army ideas.[36]

The RAF began the development of its doctrinal thinking on army co-operation prior to any of the co-operation exercises being conducted, relying instead on its experience of the First World War and the codifications of the principles of air power that had emerged from it to guide them. The first *Manual of Combined Naval, Military and Air Operations* was published in 1925, and this doctrinal manual placed emphasis on the idea that gaining and maintaining air superiority over an area of operations was the first and foremost role of the RAF. This had to be achieved before the RAF would be able to conduct any other role, including army air support. This idea was fundamentally misunderstood by the army throughout the entire interwar period and into the Second World War, and would cloud their judgement on how best to develop army co-operation. The RAF warned in the manual that, without air superiority, operations might fail before ground troops had a chance to influence events. This point was reinforced in the then Wing Commander Slessor's work on army co-operation during the First World War and how to apply it in future conflicts—*Air Power and Armies*.[37] This book was based on the lectures he delivered while teaching at the army's staff college at Camberley. Whilst Hall is correct to a degree that they 'represent a serious attempt to instil in air and army officers an understanding of how air power was likely to affect the problems of air and land warfare', they are an isolated example of this.[38]

The manual, however, did make one concession that appears unusual given the perilous state of the RAF as an independent force in 1925. This was that any squadron placed under the operational control of a land commander could not be used to gain or maintain air superiority without the express permission of that commander. It would be strange for a land commander to refuse this permission given that they should be well aware of the fundamental importance of air superiority. This concession must be seen as the RAF looking to placate an army increasingly frustrated by the lack of development of air support for their forces. The concession made by the RAF meant that the army could be sure of at least some aircraft that would always be available to conduct air support regardless of the air superiority situation faced. The manual also stated that, 'It is only by the closest liaison between the staffs of all three commands that the RAF units can be used to the best advantage and with a minimum of interference and wasted effort.'[39] This demonstrates that developments firmly established in the interwar period would have to be relearned in active operations, for example in the Western Desert during the Second World War.

The RAF's next doctrinal publication was their war manual, published in 1928. In this book, there was an entire chapter dedicated to army co-operation and how the RAF would look to conduct it. The discussion began again with the importance of gaining and maintaining air superiority to allow army co-operation missions to be conducted as efficiently as possible, but there was also a development in thinking more clearly about what aspect of tactical air support the RAF could best provide for land forces. This would cause the greatest disagreements between the RAF and army in an application of military resources context. For the RAF, the correct form of air support was that of battlefield air interdiction, with an emphasis on targets that were outside of artillery range. The close support role that the army wanted the RAF to perform was seen by the RAF as being an aerial extension of artillery and in their eyes a waste of precious resources—they did not want aircraft to be used as supplementary artillery or as a replacement for it. It was conceded in the war manual, however, that, in the case of a grave emergency, aircraft could be used in a close support role. The manual does not give any examples of what might constitute such an emergency, and given the lack of emphasis on training in this role in general it is doubtful how much of an effect aircraft could have had if they were required.

The thoughts developed in the war manual were not simply based on the type of air support and how it was best conducted; it also looked at the types of aircraft then available within the RAF that were best suited to conduct it. The manual recommended that fast single-seater fighters were best employed in a close support role. Two-seater fighters, then widely used within the RAF, were unsuited to such a role and should only be deployed when the target was of such vital importance that it required these aircraft to be diverted from their usual duties. The manual was at pains to point out that the use of aircraft in this role should be limited due to the potential cost to and exhaustion of pilots. When making the decision whether or not to order a close support attack on well-entrenched positions, commanders were instructed to consider the potential cost in casualties against the results that could be achieved.[40] An amended version of the war manual was published in 1935 but this new edition made no real addition to the fundamental thinking about how to conduct air support operations.[41]

The final authoritative publication by the RAF during the interwar period was the second edition of their *Manual of Army Co-operation* published in 1937. That such a topic would form the basis for the RAF's final doctrinal publication is surprising when it is considered just how little the RAF as a whole cared for this aspect of air power. This is most cogently explained by the fact that, as the least favoured aspect of air power, it had been left until last and it was based largely on the army co-operation exercises that had taken place between 1927 and 1934. The manual raised an important point that had hampered the discussions and development of tactical air power for the majority of the interwar period and concerned the composition of the force that was to provide such support. As mentioned above this was greatly dependent upon what conflict the army was preparing to fight. With the increasingly fluid geo-political situation of the 1930s creating confusion for politicians, the role of the army could not be confirmed and the RAF could not prepare a force to support them. If the role of the army was confirmed, the governments of the day would face demands for increased expenditure from the army.[42] As much as it could have not been known at the time that war would break out in September 1939, finalising the role of the army as late as 1937 gave both the army and RAF little time to overhaul their thinking on tactical air power, or alter the production of aircraft to manufacture more variants that could conduct an air support role in any form. The average lead time for the production of an all-metal, stressed skin monoplane fighter aircraft was five years; for a medium or heavy bomber it was eight years. With the focus on the production of fighter and bomber aircraft there was no spare capacity in the British aircraft industry that would allow new army co-operation aircraft to be produced.[43]

The manual also detailed communication procedures and how aircraft were to be used both in the approach phase of an operation as well as when ground forces were in contact with the enemy. The manual looked to give doctrinal guidance on as many different roles as the RAF could possibly be called upon to conduct in an air support capacity. In order to fulfil these wide-ranging roles, up-to-date intelligence of enemy movements would be required to plan operations. To provide RAF commanders with this necessary intelligence, Air Liaison Officers (ALOs) placed at army headquarters would allow army co-operation squadrons to be fully informed of friendly and hostile intentions. They would also provide these squadrons with artillery fire plans and direct squadrons whilst they were in the air based on the most recent intelligence and operational requirements.[44]

Throughout the interwar period, and despite it not being a priority, the RAF put in a lot of good work to gain a basic understanding of how to conduct air support missions in the post-1918 world. This understanding is clearly demonstrated through the ideas emanating from its doctrinal publications. The argument that the RAF ignored this aspect of air power or did very little to develop it further during the interwar period is not supported by the evidence presented here. Many of the methods utilised by both Army Co-operation Command and the WDAF to improve the application of tactical air support in the Second World War can be traced back to the army co-operation reports and doctrinal publications of the interwar period. One of the most important methods was the co-location of headquarters, which allowed both services to work together with greater ease according to the wider military plan. This had been highlighted first by Army Co-operation Command when codifying trials conducted in the wake of the Battle of France in 1940.

Whilst there was good work done in developing the ideas that would allow the RAF to successfully apply close air support and battlefield air interdiction in active operations, the main focus for the RAF was in the more traditional air support missions of artillery spotting and general reconnaissance.[45] There are also further examples of the RAF conducting air support training in Germany with the British Army of the Rhine. In one particular exercise, close air support training was conducted with great success when aircraft fired tennis balls upon a brigade in the field. This was achieved without a single shot being fired back.[46] It is fair to say, however, that in relative terms the use of air power at the tactical level was neglected when compared to the time and effort that was put into the development of a strategic air capability and fighter defence of Britain.[47] In order to ensure its survival as an independent force, the senior commanders of the RAF felt it was necessary to emphasise the need for an independent role. This led to the relative neglect of the application of air power at the tactical and operational levels. Trenchard, and the Air Staff as a whole, saw an independent air force as essential to fighting and winning a future conflict against a first-class enemy.

Despite this relative neglect many developments were made in army co-operation exercises held during this period at a brigade and division level. The results, conclusions and recommendations that emerged from these training exercises were published in annual reports. They highlighted the problems faced by those conducting the exercises—through analysis of the repetition of recommendations from year to year, how little the training achieved in the periods between the exercises can be evaluated. As is to be expected of theoretical ideas many of the conclusions and recommendations would have to be modified in the light of operational experience during the course of the Second World War. The exercises provided little guidance in terms of the tactical application of air support, but they did bring to light the difficulties that might be faced in terms of organisation of headquarters and C2 challenges. The 1927 army co-operation report stated that 'RAF commanders should point out to commanders of the formations under whose orders they are working the importance of their selecting headquarters in relation to possible landing grounds.' It further recommended that in order to know fully the requirements of the formations they were co-operating with they should keep in the closest contact with them. The report does not, however, state whether the air HQs were placed near airfields or army HQs.[48] Another issue that arose during the 1927 exercises was that of having to issue separate orders to RAF formations that were based upon the orders of the senior army commander and again demonstrated the importance of the co-location of headquarters. The report stated that

> In the event of late arrival of army operation orders, it is possible that it may prove difficult to issue a squadron operation order in writing early enough before operations take place. In such a case it is probable that the RAF commander will have attended a meeting at divisional or other headquarters. If this had occurred, he should have received sufficient instruction to enable him to hold a conference of his subordinate commanders and to issue verbal orders and instructions, supplemented, if necessary, by a table of work for the following day.[49]

If air and land headquarters were located as close together as possible this would allow orders to be created and disseminated more efficiently, as time would not be lost in travel to and from the meetings in which plans for operations for the following day were being discussed. This idea originally emerged in the First World War when the RFC was an army formation.

One final issue emerged from the 1927 army co-operation exercises, and that was the use of fighter aircraft in a close support role. This had been a major function of fighter aircraft in the First World War, but had resulted in heavy casualties when used against prepared positions and troops that had not come under a preliminary artillery bombardment or infantry action. This was a role that the RFC/RAF could conduct comfortably but was seen as exposing pilots to unnecessary danger. The RAF had looked to limit the time available to pilots in fighter squadrons to practice this role and this lack of practice was clear to see in how the attacks were conducted. As well as the lack of practice time available to these pilots, the army's view towards tactical air power is also demonstrated. The army felt that close air support was the correct and, indeed, only real form of air support required and that it was being utilised in situations where artillery bombardment was not a suitable alternative.[50] This further demonstrates that the army were beginning to lose sight of the operational level impact that tactical air support could have as their focus was simply on resolving the tactical problems faced by ground forces in contact with the enemy.[51] The report concluded that pilots

> Generally did not understand the principle of attacking troops on the ground. [This was] due to the small amount of practice which has been afforded them.[52]

The 1928 army co-operation report clarified how fighter aircraft were to be best used in a close support role—there had been little improvement in their deployment since the 1927 report twelve months earlier. Fighter squadrons were still being employed against 'unshaken troops', and this further demonstrates the lack of operational level thinking being employed by the army in utilising fighter squadrons. The 1928 report looked to address this issue, advising that

> The use of fighter squadrons should ... be directed towards harassing a retirement or carrying on a pursuit after the exhaustion of the pursuing troops. Low flying attacks [close air support] should never be launched unless information points to the existence of a definite and suitable objective.[53]

The emphasis on fighter squadrons being used to pursue retiring, or possibly retreating, troops, was an attempt by those charged with planning and conducting these missions to have an operational level effect after a success had been gained at the tactical level. That the conclusions reached in the previous years' reports had either been ignored or not acted upon raises questions over how seriously these exercises were being taken by those who held senior command positions in both the army and RAF. The reports as a whole, however, do demonstrate the level of thinking that was being applied to create an intellectual framework for the theoretical application of air support well before it would be necessary to test the system in active operations against hostile enemy action.

The 1928 report also highlighted the problems associated with the high turnover of staff within army co-operation squadrons. This led to a huge loss of personnel with experience of planning and conducting these missions, as well as having an in-depth understanding of how the army functioned and what they expected of air support. If the turnover of staff continued at the rate it was in the late 1920s, the training afforded to pilots would always be of a basic and rudimentary nature and could never progress beyond this level if new staff were continually having to undergo basic training. The report itself rather understates just how big a problem this was and would continue to be, simply stating that the high turnover was 'affecting the training of squadrons'.[54] It was still to be a major issue highlighted a year later in the 1929 army co-operation report.[55]

The lack of resolution of this fundamental issue for the expansion of an air support capability within the RAF brings to light even further the status of army co-operation and the RAF's general attitude to it during the interwar period. For an ambitious career officer within the RAF, an army co-operation squadron was not a place to stay long given its overall perception by those who held sway over promotions. It was a burden to be endured for as short a time as possible.[56] The 1929 report also demonstrates a more confident RAF, having survived the attempts of the army and Royal Navy to have it disbanded, making more of its independent status. They make an unusual statement for a report that is dedicated to co-operation with the army to emphasise that it was now a fully established part of the British defence establishment:

> It is most essential that sufficient attention should be devoted to purely RAF training. Requests from the army for demonstrations or co-operation with formations smaller than a brigade should be carefully reviewed.[57]

The rationale of close air support lies in reinforcing formations smaller than brigade size and the RAF intended to restrict the army's access to both training and demonstrations of air support in this area. As a result, lower formations within the army were denied the practical experience of the capabilities of air support, and army co-operation squadrons of working with ground forces. This also meant that ground formations would not be aware of the limitations of air support.

The most fundamental issue with regard to the planning and delivery of air support, however, was a recurring issue in the army co-operation exercises. The 1930 report again highlighted that air and ground headquarters were not co-located, despite the recommendations that came out of the 1927 report. It was a lesson that was not to be put into practice in active operations until the middle of the Second World War.[58] The report stated that 'it should be an established principle that where possible, corps and, possibly, divisional commanders should site their headquarters in close proximity to land suitable for the squadron aerodrome'.[59] That this had to be repeated several times during the interwar period alone, and then when introduced was seen as a new and important innovation during the Second World War, calls into question how far and widely these reports were read and assimilated into learned doctrine. This is particularly the case in terms of the army, who had as much of an interest in the efficient application of air support as the RAF.

Despite the co-location of headquarters being seen as an established principle, it had to be reiterated and further expanded upon in the 1931 army co-operation report:

> The following notes with regard to the use and nature of advanced landing grounds are issued for guidance:
> (i) Squadron aerodromes should usually be located near corps' headquarters and should move with it.
> (ii) The ideal situation for such an advanced landing ground is within one mile or so of divisional headquarters.[60]

That more explanation was required, particularly further guidance as to the distances air and land headquarters should be apart, adds further weight to the idea that these concepts were either fundamentally misunderstood or possibly ignored. It would be surprising that something as relatively simple as co-locating headquarters could be misunderstood, especially given that it was a concern in the late 1920s that was not deemed worthy of further note until 1930. At issue may have been the high turnover of army co-operation staff and newcomers not being familiar with the procedures involved in the planning of air support with the army. There may also have been an issue with regard to the co-operation of the two services at lower tactical formations. This would have been unusual as generally very little interservice rivalry was encountered at these levels and co-operation between them was relatively good during the First World War, even after the creation of the RAF as an independent service.

The difficulties of conducting close air support were still posing problems for the RAF as late as 1934, when the last army co-operation exercises at brigade and division levels were conducted, caused in no small part by increased demands from the army. The RAF were also now required to act as targets as part of the army's small-arms anti-aircraft training to counter enemy close support attacks. The RAF's response to these increased demands was the same as in 1929—heavy restrictions were placed upon when and how squadrons would be able to conduct this style of attack. They would only be undertaken to train regular troops; requests for close support training should be kept to a minimum; and the aircraft would only conduct straight dives upon the ground forces.[61] They would not conduct missions such as trench strafing. These restrictions on training with the army, as well as the overall development of army co-operation during the interwar period, can be explained through an appreciation of the dangers posed in conducting missions such as close support even when during exercises. However, a far more deep-rooted explanation lies at the heart of the RAF's doctrinal development and its bid to remain an independent force. By becoming over proficient in conducting support of land and naval forces at the expense of the application of air power at the strategic level, there would be more pressure on the RAF to scale back its strategic ambitions and concentrate on applying air power at the tactical level.

It was not just in Britain that developments were being made in tactical air power. The RAF was expanding its role to provide support for the army in policing some of the more unstable parts of the Empire, where commanders were, on the whole, far removed from the bitter interservice politics and rivalries in Britain and real co-operation between the army and RAF flourished. However, difficulties and arguments between the services were still experienced to a degree in India.[62] Co-operation overseas was driven by the fact that there were real consequences for failure, a situation that did not exist under the training conditions present in Britain.

The Empire also provided the ideal testing ground for new ideas. In the aftermath of the First World War, the territorial extent of the British Empire was the greatest it had been in its entire history. However, due to the financially stringent economic policies adopted by interwar governments, there was little extra money available to fund policing around the globe.[63] The CID was at pains to point out the difficulties that the increased size of the Empire presented to Britain when expenditure had to be reduced:

> The financial exhaustion consequent with the war renders it essential that expenditure be reduced without delay to minimum consistent with national security. At the same time, our responsibilities have been greatly increased; and we are faced with the necessity of paying all our fighting personnel on a much higher scale than was the case before the war.[64]

The RAF were able to exploit this economic situation by reducing costs through substituting expensive army garrisons with relatively cheap squadrons of aircraft to support a reduced land force, at the same time reinforcing the importance of an independent air force.[65] The cost of this policing work increased dramatically as the newly acquired imperial territories, or League of Nations mandated territories, proved to be more troublesome.[66] This was not a policy of substituting air power for land power, but an increase in the use of aircraft in conjunction with a smaller land force. The use of the RAF reduced the overall cost of policing the Empire and provided the political expediency for governments of the interwar period to continue to rule over the Empire.[67] The work of the RAF is historically important as it demonstrates the reach of tactical air power in a co-operative environment and there was a significant (although unfulfilled) potential for cross-fertilisation of these ideas between Britain and her Empire.

There were many areas where air power was used in conjunction with land forces to police the Empire and this chapter will highlight the techniques that emerged from operations in Somaliland, Mesopotamia and India.[68] Far greater development and more sophisticated techniques emerged from the RAF's work across the Empire than the training exercises in Britain during the interwar period, but they were not seen as applicable to European warfare as they had been conducted against 'non- or semi-civilised' people, who reacted differently under aerial bombardment to those people from a 'civilised' nation. With the safety of the British homeland being of paramount importance to governments of the day, the priority for spending the little money that was available was the defence of Britain over the Empire.[69]

The first example of aircraft co-operating with land forces, and indeed an excellent example of the developments in communications between the two services whilst on operations, was in Somaliland. In 1919, a decision was taken to restore stability to the region following a rebellion that had broken out during the middle of the First World War, led by the 'Mad Mullah', Said Mohammed Bin Abdulla Hussan. This required close co-operation between the RAF and army and the efficient transfer of intelligence based upon ideas gleaned from the First World War.[70] Aircraft would locate troops loyal to the 'Mad Mullah' and advise the Commanding Officer of their location through message drops and 'conveying despatches between the commanders of the two forces and the headquarters of the Somaliland Field Force'.[71] The air power historian

James Corum has argued that Trenchard and the Air Staff exaggerated the role played by air power in subduing the Mad Mullah's rebellion in order for the RAF to gain a greater role in imperial policing and to allow it to retain its independence in Britain.[72] An Air Staff looking to make the most out of any minor success may well have exaggerated it.

The success of military action in Somaliland was quickly built upon with operations conducted in the newly established, but troublesome, territory of Mesopotamia. Even as a newly created state, Mesopotamia was of great strategic importance—control of this area guaranteed the security of imperial trade routes and the safety of the Empire's most important possession, India, would be enhanced greatly.[73] The threat to trade routes was caused by a rise in nationalistic fervour mainly due to the collapse of the Ottoman Empire at the end of the First World War.[74] Whilst in Somaliland the RAF had been able to showcase the increased efficiency that air power could bring to intelligence gathering and communications—in Mesopotamia they were able to demonstrate its speed and power.

The traditional method of imperial policing had been to station large garrisons of troops who might be required to march to inhospitable regions, a slow, costly and time-consuming practice. For instance, when troops had been sent to put down a full-scale revolt in 1920, they had had very little impact and it was clear that a new method was required.[75] Preparations for land campaigns were slow and cumbersome and took time to reach the rebellious region, with many troops required to protect lines of communication. Aircraft could be deployed with much greater speed and efficiency to remote regions in Mesopotamia and they also had a far more immediate effect than a column of troops. Trenchard was quick to capitalise on the costs and failings of land forces in putting down rebellions in the country when another insurrection broke out in 1922 and he used it to consolidate the RAF's foundering independent status.[76] This move by Trenchard caused a great deal of friction between the War Office and the Air Ministry in Britain and was never fully resolved.[77]

Mesopotamia was the first region of the Empire to experience relatively large-scale aerial bombardment, and it was here that the RAF began to learn the operational implications and difficulties that an independent force would face in putting strategic operational theories into practice.[78] There have been many critics, both present and past, of the use of air power for imperial policing. One of the most outspoken was the army itself who argued that the use of bombs to put down rebellions was an inhumane way of keeping the peace. It is testament not only to the abilities of air power in this area but also the army's concerns over the effectiveness of an independent air force subjugating a traditional army role that they made these claims, as they could hardly take the moral high ground. The methods used by the army included the burning of crops and food stocks and the destruction of livestock.[79] The attitude of the army, at least on the ground in the Empire, is demonstrated in an event recounted by Slessor after his retirement as CAS in a memoir published in 1956. As a mid-ranking officer in Waziristan, Slessor was planning an attack on a rebellious native village—an army officer suggested that he attack it from the air without warning. Slessor pointed out to the officer that to launch such an attack without first warning the inhabitants was against government policy for air attack. The officer replied, 'Oh come on, that will be alright, we'll say we shelled it!'[80]

It was in Mesopotamia that the use of air power in a semi-independent role came of age and acted as a force multiplier for the ground troops they were supporting. The RAF were able to engage hostile forces outside the range of troops far more quickly and effectively, but were also able to co operate not only with land forces but also with the political officers in overall command of the region to great effect.[81] The RAF's most impressive feat in Mesopotamia was the ease with which aircraft could be deployed over several days and inflict a heavy cost on those who transgressed and rebelled against the British government. The RAF was able to do this with very little risk to their own aircrews, and after a time a simple flypast was enough to bring the government's message to the people of the remote regions of the country.[82] The use of aircraft in Mesopotamia, it has been argued, had a greater effect than just restoring peace and stability to a far-flung part of the Empire. The action was crucial for the survival of the RAF as an independent force. As they were pursuing this role, the Salisbury Committee in England was receiving evidence about the functions of the army, navy and air force and deemed imperial policing to be the 'most significant defence task for all three services'.[83] This did not provide the RAF with a focus in terms of the development of tactical air power for use in a European war as that was seen as being a radically different theatre in which to operate compared with the Empire.

It was the combination of physical and moral effects that led the RAF to continue to employ air power in the very, and still to this day, difficult and hostile terrain of the North-West Frontier of India.[84] The work conducted by the RAF in this region was of a more co-operational nature, and was largely confined to close air support of land forces rather than an independent or semi-independent role.[85] Despite aircraft being used in the North-West Frontier from 1919, it was not until the 1930s that efforts were made to codify the experience gained into learned doctrine and exercises employed to test the ideas that had emerged. A training exercise involving No. 3 (Indian) Wing of the RAF was held in Khaisora in 1936 to develop tactical and operational procedures for the application of close air support in what was difficult terrain to conduct such operations. The report concluded that due to topographical hazards, the use of close air support from above an altitude of 3000 feet against troops that were not in contact with friendly forces was not possible. The report recommended that the only time this should be employed for this situation was if the area had already been 'proscribed as hostile'. If friendly troops were engaged with hostile forces, then bombing would have to take place at much lower heights to prevent any friendly fire casualties. The use of low flying close support attacks was not advised due to the potential for casualties amongst pilots conducting this sort of attack.[86]

The training exercises also explored different ways of communicating between air and ground, taking advantage of the increasingly sophisticated developments in wireless communications technology. Developments were made also in more traditional non-wireless communications systems, but this was always limited by the amount of information that could be conveyed to pilots in the air, and required good visibility to be at all effective. The most used non-wireless communication system was the Panel and Strip Code, or 'Popham Panels'. In order to enhance the effectiveness of the 'Popham Panels', it was recommended that pilots should be fully briefed prior to take-off. This system lent itself to the application of pre-planned and not impromptu close air support. If intelligence and air support plans for pilots were not clear, or even non-existent, when pilots were ordered to take-off, then it was preferable that they should be supplied with the information when airborne via radio telegraphy (R/T) or wireless telegraphy (W/T). Squadrons that were on standby to provide this support were to be in the air twenty minutes after the request for impromptu support, combined with a brief situation report, was received. The full order should then be passed on to the pilots whilst in the air by W/T. If a system such as this could be incorporated into the army's communications network, a fully functioning impromptu air support system could be used to request air support as and when required. This could only enhance the RAF's ability to provide air support for the army in any theatre. Even though the benefits were clear to those involved in planning and conducting air support operations, the focus was still on pre-planned air support and the opportunity to develop a system that could act as a real force multiplier for close air support was missed. It must also be questioned how far the Air Staff in Britain would have taken note of the developments being made in far flung corners of the Empire against non- or semi-civilised peoples.

Where air support operations were pre-planned, a full written order was to be sent to the squadron to allow them to plan adequately how this support would be conducted. This communications system was similar to the one employed during the Battle of France, and would be overhauled in its aftermath under Army Co-operation Command auspices. The tactics that aircraft should employ when conducting close support were also subject to codification in the North-West Frontier.

This was happening around the same time that the *Luftwaffe* were developing their tactical procedures for close air support in the Spanish Civil War. The RAF and *Luftwaffe* reached almost polar opposite conclusions on this matter. The RAF felt that formation bombing should not be used for air support operations—aircraft were to attack the target singularly and to reform once the attack had been completed.[87] The *Luftwaffe*, on the other hand, found that in a more urban environment, formations of massed aircraft attacking at the same time placed the enemy under constant attack. They described this technique as the 'shuttle attack'.[88] As a result of their experiences in Spain, the *Luftwaffe* hit upon the key element to provide air support for land forces—the co-ordination of air action with the operations planned by the ground commander. To allow this to happen, liaison and communications teams from the *Luftwaffe* were placed within ground formations to allow this to occur effectively. They had also realised that the co-location of headquarters was essential for good co-operation. The difference between the RAF and *Luftwaffe* on this was not in recognising the requirement, but in its implementation in active operations.[89] The *Luftwaffe*'s experience in Spain, alongside its central European geo-political position meant it would prioritise air power at the tactical level over the strategic level, provided it with the experience to develop 'a comprehensive military doctrine that made joint operations the focus of the operational planning and training'.[90] This difference in the tactics developed can be explained by the different terrain that the RAF and *Luftwaffe* were operating in, and the standard of the enemy they were facing.

The RAF believed that any potential lessons or overall direction over the use of air power would not apply to a major European war as the

Spanish Civil War was a proxy war fought internally by a second-rate power and only with the assistance of first-rate powers.[91] The lack of overall interest in the Spanish Civil War is further demonstrated by the fact that very few articles on the conflict appeared in the RAF's flagship journal *RAF Quarterly*.[92] The conflict in Spain did, however, allow the RAF to substantiate some of its pre-existing doctrinal ideas. The most important confirmation was the need to gain air superiority over the battlefield before any support of land forces could be attempted. This had allowed the rebel forces 'the freedom of action in the employment of their military forces and enabled them to combine air attacks with artillery action'.[93] One factor that was missing, and which would have a far-reaching impact on any land support mission in a major European war, was a lack of hostile anti-aircraft capability to target the aircraft conducting those missions. There was also a relative lack of artillery, which meant that aircraft were more readily used in their place to support ground troops.[94] Despite their institutional propensity against ground attack, there was a certain amount of RAF praise for how the war was conducted and also the effects that it had in Spain, as the targets of such attacks would be similar to those targeted by the RAF in a major European war. The Air Staff noted that '[air] attacks have been carried out with fair accuracy and have been directed against aerodromes and factories'. The Air Staff did not look to the Spanish Civil War to provide a barometer by which to alter its own doctrine. It was, however, cited where it confirmed what they were already thinking, highlighting a degree of conformational thinking bias, something that should be avoided to prevent doctrine becoming dogmatic and of little use.[95]

The RAF undertook a degree of analysis of the use of ground attack during the Spanish Civil War but it combined the effects of air superiority and ground attack. The moral effect of this, it was claimed, was out of all proportion to the force that had been deployed to conduct it.[96] Trenchard had once claimed that the moral effect of air power was to the physical as ten to one, which was expanded from Napoleon Bonaparte's dictum of three to one. On one occasion Trenchard expanded on this to make the moral to physical effect to be twenty to one, something that was based on no evidence whatsoever. This has led Peter Gray to highlight the fact that Trenchard has been described as the master of the unfounded statistic.[97]

A serving RAF officer, Brian Armstrong, has questioned the validity of the orthodox argument that senior RAF officers in the 1930s were ignorant of the Spanish Civil War and its implications.[98] It is further argued that these experiences should have called into question the RAF's thinking about tactical air power. The RAF's thinking had, by this point however, become somewhat institutionalised and it is difficult to see any event except defeat in operations on the European continent that could have altered this, despite an expert on the use of tactical air power (Slessor, at the time a Group Captain) being well placed to influence a change in policy.[99]

The ground on which the fighting in Spain took place influenced how the RAF interpreted the effect of tactical air power in the conflict. The lack of industrial targets made conducting attacks on enemy land forces the only viable target for aircraft if they were going to have an operational and strategic level influence on the campaign. It was also believed that the relative inferiority of the Spanish troops made them more vulnerable to this type of attack than troops of the major European nations, who would be able to withstand attack from the air to a greater extent.[100]

Whilst the *Luftwaffe* was developing its air support system in Spain, the operations undertaken in India led to moves to codify the lessons emerging. A report based on the army co-operation training that took place in 1936 between No. 2 (Rawalpindi) Infantry Brigade and No. 3 (Indian) Wing RAF, highlights the developments being made in India. The training was to allow the formations to 'gain practical experience in … and to evolve tactical methods for close air support in mountain warfare'. The report highlighted the fundamental issue in the delivery of close air support: good communications. In order to enhance the development of these communications procedures, the report divided them into two distinct and separate areas and these were 'between [the] column HQ and the [squadron] advanced landing ground', and 'Between Column HQ and aircraft in the air'.

The report also detailed methods that could be employed to improve the efficiency of communications between air and ground, namely that RAF commanders should locate their advanced landing grounds as close as possible to where the operations were being conducted. This was required for two reasons. Firstly, due to the topography of the areas of operations, there were still limits on the range of R/T and W/T communications and this affected the ability of land forces to request impromptu air support. Secondly, the speed at which air support could be conducted once it had been requested was fundamentally dependent upon the distance that the aircraft had to travel from their advanced landing ground to the zone of operations. Anything that could be done to reduce the lead time from the request for support to the actual delivery of support would enhance the RAF's close air support capability in this theatre. It would further enhance the connection between reconnaissance missions spotting potential targets and operations being conducted against them if wireless and landline communications were more fully integrated. There was also an emphasis on the use of landline telephone communications over wireless communications, due to the often limited range of transmitters and receivers in the North-West Frontier. This would require a substantial upgrade of wired communications technology:

> These resources are admittedly not available normally in Bde [Brigade] or even Divisional Signals [networks]. But we think it hardly an exaggeration to say that a land line is essential if full value is to be gained from close support or reconnaissance in this form of warfare.[101]

W/T had been used as a reserve means of communication and was seen as a secondary method between troops on the ground and aircraft prior to the training exercise. The primary method of communication was the Popham Panel. This was easily understood by pilots in the air and relatively quick and simple to deploy. The experience of the training exercise was that whilst the Popham Panel was both reliable and useful, it was too slow to be of practicable use in operations. Due to this, two recommendations were made. The first was that the Popham Panel should be kept as a reserve method of communication as its speed and reliability would still be of use in operations if the primary methods of communications failed. The second was that a reliable wireless communications set that utilised W/T and R/T be made available to land forces, advanced landing grounds and aircraft as a priority.[102]

The report also dealt with C2 methods and how to enhance operational capabilities in this area. Similar ideas that had emerged from the training exercises conducted in Britain were also coming out of operations and training in the North-West Frontier. This again raises issues as to how far lessons had been learned, not only from training exercises, but also from active operations. That the operations were being conducted against what were seen at the time to be less civilised people than would have to be faced in a conflict against a first-class European enemy may have influenced those who were planning the operations. The theoretical developments made in Britain were reinforced through the experience gained in the Empire, but the fact that little changed at home in terms of practice lends weight to the argument that doctrinal publications were not read or assimilated. It does not, however, alter the fact that active operations and training exercises had highlighted some of the most effective ways of ensuring how air support could be delivered. The report into the 1936 training exercise in the North-West Frontier stressed the importance of headquarters location with direct reference to that theatre. The report noted that the most efficient way to gain full value out of army co-operation squadrons in mountain warfare was to have an 'Air Force Commander at [the] Column HQ'.[103] It was also recommended that an air force commander should accompany the column commander at all times as, due to the nature of close air support, it would 'usually be required quickly'.[104] Through employing operational principles such as this, the lead time in the delivery of close air support would be dramatically reduced.

Further attempts to increase the effectiveness of air support operations were made after active operations were conducted between November 1936 and January 1937, and attempts were made to learn lessons from them. One of the major aspects that was highlighted as a result of these operations was combining the roles of reconnaissance and air support. It was argued in the report that looked to codify the experiences gained during these operations that aircraft would be better employed in not only discovering potential targets but attacking them as well. This idea was fully adopted in January 1937. The report also confirmed that the tactics laid down in the new operations manual were sound but required refining in the light of further operational experience. It had been realised that the use of continual bombardment of a target was not necessary and that a simple flypast was often just as effective after an initial aerial bombardment had taken place, as 'once the enemy had felt the effect of air action—the mere presence of aircraft overhead has an equivalent effect'. The use of multiple aircraft conducting close support operations was seen to be impracticable, if not impossible, given the difficulty of the terrain that aircraft were expected to operate over. These operations also confirmed that close air support was more effectively managed when land and air headquarters were co-located.[105]

The document that drove the air support operations throughout the empire was the 'Grey Book', which was the war manual for operations across the Empire. One of the fundamental tenets of this doctrinal publication was the emphasis placed on making the British government appear fair-minded and just in their actions against rebellious tribes. In order to ensure this, aircraft could only respond to threats on the ground if those who were responsible for them could be clearly discerned. Even in the Empire, the RAF was still drawing a large distinction between close air support and low flying attacks. The Grey Book defined close air support as being more akin to a battlefield air interdiction role, that could, and should, be pre-planned in line with the operations of the army. Low flying attack, according to the Grey Book however, was to be avoided unless a grave emergency presented itself. Pilots were advised that, as low flying attacks were only to be conducted in an emergency, orders would be passed to them whilst in the air either through Popham Panels or via R/T. Pilots were also required to use their own initiative if, during reconnaissance or close air support operations, they spotted a situation that might leave ground forces in grave danger. This would require far more in-depth training, not only in what might constitute a grave danger for ground forces, but also the best tactical method to employ in support of them. As a result, the Grey Book instructed pilots to pass the information on to the nearest body of friendly troops.[106] This further demonstrates that the attitudes of the RAF in Britain were having a direct effect on air support operations in the Empire. Many of the officers, such as Slessor, would have risen through the ranks in Britain and been greatly influenced by the doctrinal thinking that was developing in Britain prior to being assigned to an imperial command role.

The use of specialist air power terminology also caused a great deal of confusion. Air Commodore R. H. Peck received a letter from the Headquarters of No. 2 (Indian) Wing, Cheklala, which stated that after experience of conducting support operations with land forces the terms close air support and low flying attack led to confusion between land and air force commanders over what they were expecting these different forms of tactical air power to provide. The letter suggested that this confusion was due to the term close air support not being the best expression to be used as it was 'too all embracing'.[107] This confusion about the precise meaning of air power terms would hamper the continuing development of tactical air power, particularly in Britain, for the majority of the Second World War.[108] The one thing that neither these operations nor the training exercises achieved, whether conducted in Britain or overseas, was to change the fundamental view of the army that it was best served by an air force under its direct operational control and focused solely on supporting ground forces in the field.

The problems faced by all three of the British armed services during the interwar period has been subject to detailed and wide-ranging historical study and analysis, and it is not the intention of this book to look into the topic in detail. It is, however, necessary to give a brief overview to provide the necessary context to explain how and why air power developed as it did in Britain in this period, and why tactical air power was somewhat neglected prior to the Second World War.

Throughout the interwar period, the RAF continued to press upon the government, army and Royal Navy, the importance of an independent air force that could project air power at a strategic level. By the mid-1930s this was a fundamental pillar of British defence policy against the backdrop of an increasingly unstable and dangerous Europe and Far East. The potential threats of Germany, Italy and Japan stretched all three services in Britain as each threat required a different strategic answer. Given the precarious economic situation of Britain after the Great Depression funds were not available for each of the services to implement their preferred strategic responses—the focus of rearmament was on the RAF as this provided the best combination of attacking threat and, after the development of an aerial early warning system and fighters that could match bombers in the sky, defensive protection. This rearmament could also be carried at out at a lower cost than would be involved in rearming the army or Royal Navy.[109] It also called for a dramatic expansion of Britain's burgeoning aviation industry.

A mass reduction in demand for aircraft followed from the end of the First World War, caused due to the relatively peaceful European strategic situation and the economic policies followed by successive British governments that prioritised public spending on social policies rather than on defence.[110] This resulted in a natural reduction in the size of the British aircraft industry as it had expanded greatly due to the overwhelming demand for aircraft on the Western Front.[111] With the reduction in the Air Ministry budget, the RAF cancelled future orders for aircraft across the board and relied on stocks of aircraft and spares that had built up during the First World War to keep it supplied.[112] In order to allow a framework of the aviation industry to survive, and more importantly to keep experienced design teams in employment during what the industry referred to as the 'lean years', the Air Ministry 'adopted a policy of rationing design contracts between fourteen different airframe firms, eleven of which were wholly or predominantly dependent on the Air Ministry for their survival'.[113] Peter Fearon has argued that for the whole of the 1920s 'no government felt politically strong enough, or had sufficient control of the economic situation, to keep Britain as the premier air power of the world. David Edgerton, however, has claimed that, 'The idea that the Air Ministry was short of money for the purchase of aircraft, and that somehow the amount of money fell in the interwar years, bears little relationship to reality.'[114]

The biggest issue the aircraft industry faced, however, was not a lack of money or production orders to allow them to survive, but how to adapt their manufacturing processes and increase their labour force to cope with the revolution in aircraft design which accompanied the move away from the wood, string and canvas biplanes of the First World War to the all-metal, stressed skin monoplanes that had been competing in the many international speed races of the late 1920s and early 1930s.[115] This revolution also dramatically increased both the costs of individual aircraft and delivery lead times.[116] Issues were experienced in the rearmament of the RAF, but they were no longer financial. Neville Chamberlain's government was unwilling to adopt wartime controls over industry, which meant that the defence industries were competing with civilian industries for raw materials, tools, jigs and labour.[117] The focus of the Chamberlain government during this period of rearmament prior to the Second World War was on fighter and bomber squadrons—there was very little, if any, capacity for an increase in the number of army co-operation squadrons. The RAF had also experienced further political pressures on rearmament issues during the interwar period through government policies of unilateral disarmament.

The most important international attempt to pursue unilateral disarmament was through the Geneva Disarmament Conference of 1932–4, although other attempts such as the Kellogg-Briand Pact were made in this period.[118] The attempts to limit the armaments of the major European nations came from a general revulsion, particularly amongst the political classes of Europe, at the cost of the First World War in blood, let alone treasure. The Geneva Disarmament Conference provides vital context on two issues. Firstly, how the RAF saw the development of air power and the potential impact it could have on the British homeland and secondly, the extent to which the RAF was responsible for the extreme fear amongst the political leaders of Britain over what effect such an attack could have on the structural fabric of British society.[119] The British delegation at the conference set out to restrict the European nations' ability to conduct aerial warfare.[120] This restriction was only to apply between the nations of Europe, however, as the use of aerial warfare against imperial possessions was still to be permitted.

There are two possible explanations for the British government's policy at Geneva. Firstly, the warnings of the RAF over the destruction a hostile strategic air campaign could wreak on Britain had had such an effect that the politicians genuinely wanted to outlaw aerial warfare between major European nations. (If this motivation was genuine and had been accepted at the conference, it would almost certainly have led to the destruction of the RAF as an independent force, its *raison d'être* having been eliminated.)[121] The other, more likely, explanation is that given the pacifist feelings amongst the British people as a whole, politicians did not want to incur their wrath if it could be shown that through their unwillingness to compromise to gain greater disarmament as a whole, they would be blamed for the failure of the Conference and the disarmament movement in its entirety. By suggesting policies that they knew were unacceptable to the other nations, and playing realpolitik at the Conference, Britain could avoid the charge that it was fundamentally to blame.[122] The Conference fell apart after Germany withdrew in 1933 under the direction of the new Chancellor, Adolf Hitler. Concerted attempts were made to bring Germany back to the Conference, but the country's foreign policy goals were now totally at odds with any kind of European-wide disarmament and the Conference ended in 1934 in embarrassing failure.

Air power in Britain was at a fundamental crossroads at the end of the First World War, and the RAF was faced with hard choices as to how it would be developed further and applied in any future conflict. The choice was one of the traditional roles of army and naval support as conducted by the RFC and RNAS respectively or the application of air power at the strategic level of war. The interwar period saw many ideas being debated and indeed trialled in theory.[123] Despite the emphasis on the development of strategic air power in the interwar period, many sound theoretical developments were made in Britain in the realm of tactical air power, contrary to the arguments that have been put forward in the literature currently available. The relations between the RAF and army, the disarmament policies followed by several interwar governments, the economic problems of the time resulting in a contraction of the aviation industry and the institutionalised thinking on tactical and strategic air power, all hampered any radical developments. By 1939, the thinking of the RAF and the army had radically diverged. This was due to fundamental differences in how the two services interpreted the application of tactical air power, the almost constant wrangling and an inability to see the issue from the other side—none of these was ever fully resolved prior to the Second World War.[124]

The army still clung to the idea that the best way for aircraft to support ground forces was in a close air support, or low flying attack role, and that the forces allocated to this role should come under the operational control of the army, thereby breaking one of the fundamental principles of air power codified by the RAF. In a document drawn up by the War Office shortly after the declaration of war in 1939, the army explained in more detail what they would expect from being assigned their own army air arm. It would be dedicated to providing support for land forces by conducting attacks in what the RAF had termed the close support zone.[125] The RAF continued to emphasise the ability of aircraft to act in an interdiction role to seal off the battlefield from enemy reinforcements and *matériel*.[126] The army's plans for its own air arm also included the provision that aircraft within it would be designed specifically for a close support role. This demonstrated a fundamental misunderstanding of the time required to design and build such an aircraft and how the British aircraft industry, already operating at full capacity producing bombers and fighters, could produce such an aircraft in significant numbers.[127] The development of tactical air power on the RAF's side was further hampered by the lack of political direction given to the army over its size, composition and role.[128] In fact, the decision for the army to join French forces in France was not made until September 1938. This meant that there was little time for the army to work out the operational procedures that would be best suited to a continental campaign against the Germany army, and no time for the RAF to consider or trial the implications of this in terms of providing air support.[129] The developments that had been made throughout the Empire in tactical air support were sound in and of themselves but the 'lessons regarding C2, integrated planning and efficient communications proved remarkably difficult to transfer between theatres'.[130] This was partly due to the theatres in which the RAF was conducting operations, the mind of the contemporary senior RAF officer and the nature of the peoples that were targeted by them.

By the time of the outbreak of war in September 1939, the RAF had confidence in the air support doctrine that had been developed in the interwar period. This was despite there being no joint doctrinal foundation on which it was based, a lack of understanding on the part of the RAF as to how the army was planning on conducting its operations once hostilities began and an almost deliberate misunderstanding of what the army expected from co-operation missions.[131] There is much in this comment that can be disputed and coming as it does from a recently retired Major General, highlights the fact that the interservice rivalry that was so prevalent in the period between the wars is still strong today. But the author of this study is convinced that the RAF was clear in its communications, both in its doctrine and in in-depth discussions with the army; understood the application of air power at the tactical level; and in no way misunderstood or misled the army on this.

Of course more could, and always could, have been done, but the RAF's position was made perfectly clear many times. There is very little, if any, evidence to suggest that there was any malicious intent on either side to mislead the other. The problems encountered during the early operations in France were down to a failure in communications between the two parties and resolute defiance on the army's part to accept the fact that they had to work closely with the RAF in developing tactical air power and abandon plans for their own operational army air arm. That said, when the British armed forces crossed the Channel there was a degree of agreement both about the conduct of air support and where there was further room for improvement, particularly in the communications system established to direct it. Both the RAF and army identified that the communications system might not stand up to the stresses of war as it '[will be] dependent on several liaison links, some of which have to communicate over great distances'. The War Office were, however, happy to accept this communications system as for them it was 'the best expedient under [the] present system of control of bomber aircraft'.[132] Priority targets for air support missions were also detailed by the War Office and represented classic interdiction targets along the lines that the RAF had argued should be the focus of air support.[133] Any future complaints over the failure of air support should be read with these points clearly in mind. The following chapter will analyse how well the RAF fared in the application of army support during the Battle of France as well as the reaction of the both the Air Ministry and War Office to the events in France.

NOTES

1. See Arthur Marwick, *The Deluge: British Society and the First World War* (2nd edition) (Macmillan: Basingstoke, 1991) for further details on the social transformation of Britain in the First World War.
2. Royal Air Force Museum (RAFM) Hendon, Trenchard Papers, MFC 76/1/357—Lecture VIII Air Strategy. Hall, *Strategy for Victory* p. 14.
3. Coningham, 'The Battle of Amiens', pp. 221–2.
4. Ibid., pp. 222–3.
5. Richard R. Muller, 'Close air support: German, British and American experiences, 1918–1941', in Williamson Murray and Alan R. Millett (eds), *Military Innovation in the Interwar Period* (Cambridge University Press: New York, 1996), p. 152.

6. Dean, *The Royal Air Force*, pp. 3–4.
 7. David Edgerton, *England and the Aeroplane: Militarism, Modernity and Machines* (Penguin Books: London, 2013 [Macmillan: Manchester, 1991]), pp. 34–5. David Edgerton, *Warfare State: Britain 1920–1970* (Cambridge University Press: Cambridge, 2006), pp. 43–7, 58. David Edgerton, *Britain's War Machine: Weapons, Resources and Experts in the Second World War* (Penguin Books: London, 2012 [Allen Lane: London, 2011]), pp. 30–7.
 8. Cmd. 467, Permanent Organisation of the Air Force. Note by the Secretary of State for Air on a Scheme Outlined by the Chief of the Air Staff. R. A. Mason, *Air Power: A Centennial Appraisal* (revised edition) (Brassey's: London, 2002 [Brassey's: London, 1994]), p. 43.
 9. Jordan, 'The Royal Air Force', p. 15.
10. Alistair McCluskey, 'The Battle of Amiens and the Development of British Air-Land Battle, 1918–45', in Gary Sheffield and Peter Gray (eds), *Changing War: The British Army, The Hundred Days Campaign and the Birth of the Royal Air Force, 1918* (Bloomsbury: London and New York, 2013), pp. 231, 238.
11. Charles Carrington, *Soldier at Bomber Command* (Leo Cooper: London, 1987), p. viii.
12. Dean, *The Royal Air Force* p. 39. Bond, *Military Policy* p. 25.
13. N.H. Gibbs, *Grand Strategy Vol. I: Rearmament Policy* (HMSO: London, 1976), p. 44.
14. John Ferris, *The Evolution of British Strategic Policy, 1919–1926* (Macmillan Press: London, 1989). John Ferris, 'Treasury Control, the Ten Year Rule and British Service Policies, 1919–1924', *The Historical Journal*, 30: 4 (December 1987), pp. 859–83. K. Booth, 'The Ten Year Rule: An Unfinished Debate', *JRUSI*, 116, (March, 1971), pp. 58–62.
15. Hyde, *British Military Policy*, p. 59.
16. Booth, 'The Ten Year Rule', pp. 58–62. Brian Bond and Williamson Murray, 'The British Armed Forces, 1918–1939', in Allan R. Millett and Williamson Murray (eds), *Military Effectiveness Vol II: The Interwar Period* (new edition) (Cambridge University Press: New York, 2010 [Unwin Hyman: 1988]), p. 98.
17. Peter Fearon, 'The British Airframe Industry and the State, 1918–1935', *The Economic History Review*, 27: 2 (May, 1974), p. 244. Keith Hayward, *The British Aircraft Industry* (Manchester University Press: Manchester and New York, 1989), p. 11. Ritchie, *Industry and Air Power*, p. 7.
18. Peter Fearon, 'The Formative Years of the British Aircraft Industry, 1913–1924', *The Business History Review*, 43: 4 (Winter, 1969), p. 495.
19. TNA CAB 24/131, 24/132, Interim Report of the Committee on National Expenditure, December 1921.

20. TNA CAB 5/4, CID Paper 141-C, May 1921.
21. TNA CAB 24/131, 24/132, Interim Report of the Committee of National Expenditure, December 1921. Powers, *Strategy Without Slide-Rule*, p. 43.
22. TNA CAB 2/3, CID and Standing Defence Sub-committees meetings, Minutes of the 137th meeting of the CID, 6 May 1921. TNA CAB 2/3, Appendix by the Chief of the Air Staff to the statement made at the 137th meeting, May 1921. Mason, *Air Power*, p. 43.
23. TNA AIR 9/5, The Air Force in relation to the Army and Navy, A Note by the Chief of the Imperial General Staff on Mr Balfour's Memorandum CID 149-C, 16 September 1921. Balfour's memorandum can be found at AIR 9/5, 26 July 1921.
24. Brian Bond, *British Military Policy between the Two World Wars* (Clarendon Press: Oxford, 1980), p. 377.
25. TNA AIR 9/5, Comments by the Air Staff on General Staff Paper Nos. 40, 49, 50 and 52, II ND 40, undated, *c.*September 1921.
26. TNA AIR 5/280, Army Requirements for Peace Training, January 1923.
27. TNA AIR 5/280, Agenda for a Conference of CIGS and CAS on the Combined Training of the Two Services, January 1923.
28. Ross Mahoney, *The Forgotten Career of Air Marshal Sir Trafford Leigh-Mallory. 1892–1937: A Social and Cultural History of Leadership Development in the Inter-War Royal Air Force* (PhD Thesis, University of Birmingham, 2015), pp. 226, 215–33.
29. TNA AIR 5/280, Draft notes for Agenda for the Conference between CIGS and CAS, January 1923.
30. Hyde, *British Air Policy*, p. 75. Barry D. Powers, *Strategy Without Slide-Rule: British Air Strategy, 1914–1939* (Croom Helm: London, 1976), p. 186.
31. Hyde, *British Air Policy*, pp. 134–5. Phillip S. Meilinger, 'Trenchard and "Morale Bombing": The Evolution of Royal Air Force Doctrine Before World War II', *Journal of Military History*, 60: 2 (April, 1996), p. 254. Also see TNA AIR 14/2/38 Air Policy and Strategy: A Lecture by Air Vice-Marshal A.S. Barratt, 14 February 1938.
32. Colin Sinnott, *RAF Operational Requirements, 1923–39* (PhD Thesis, King's College London, 1998), p. 37. Also see Colin Sinnott. *The RAF and Aircraft Design: Air Staff Operational Requirements* (Frank Cass: London and Portland, Oregon, 2001). John Ferris, *The Evolution of British Strategic Policy, 1919–1926* (Macmillan Press: London, 1989). John Ferris, '"Far Too Dangerous a Gamble?" British Intelligence and policy during the Chanak crisis, September–October 1922', *Diplomacy and Statecraft*, 14: 2 (2003), pp. 139–84. Malcolm Cooper, 'The Royal

Air Force, Air Power and British Foreign Policy, 1932–37', *Journal of Contemporary History*, 12: 1 (January, 1977), pp. 153–77. 21 John Ferris, 'The Theory of the French Air Menace: Anglo-French Relations and the British Home Defence Air Force Programmes of 1921–1925', *The Journal of Strategic Studies* 10: 1 (March 1987), pp. 64–8.
33. TNA AIR 5/280, Draft Conclusions of a Conference between CIGS and CAS, 5 February 1923.
34. TNA AIR 5/280, Minutes and Conclusions of a Conference between the War Office and Air Ministry, 13 February 1923.
35. Hall, *Strategy for Victory*.
36. TNA AIR 10/1910 AIR 10/1911 (AP 1300) RAF War Manual Part I. TNA AIR 10/5547, AHB Narrative Close Support.
37. TNA AIR 5/280, Minutes and Conclusions of a Conference between the War Office and Air Ministry, 12 February 1923.
38. Hall, *Strategy for Victory*, p. 28.
39. TNA AIR 10/1206, Manual of Combined Naval, Military and Air Operations, Chapter X, Air Co-operation with the Navy and Army, General Remarks, 1925. J. C. Slessor, *Air Power and Armies* (University of Alabama Press: Tuscaloosa, Alabama, 2009 [Oxford University Press: London, 1936]), p. 10.
40. TNA AIR 10/1206, Manual of Combined Naval, Military and Air Operations.
41. TNA AIR 10/1910, Royal Air Force War Manual Part I (Air Publication 1300)—Operations, Chapter XII, 1928.
42. TNA AIR 10 /1911, Royal Air Force Manual Part I, 1935.
43. TNA AIR 10/1889, Royal Air Force Manual of Army Co-operation (2nd Edition), The Royal Air Force Component with the Army in the Field, Strength and Composition, 1937. An excellent overview of the origins of the Second World War can be found in P. M. H. Bell's *The Origins of the Second World War in Europe* (2nd edition) (Pearson Education: Harlow, 1986). The political and military difficulties of how best to use the army prior to the Second World War is in Michael Howard's *The Continental Commitment: The Dilemma of British Defence Policy in the Era of Two World Wars* (Pelican Books: Harmondsworth, Middlesex, 1974 [Temple Smith: London, 1972]). Brian Bond, *British Military Policy between the Wars* (Clarendon Press: Oxford, 1980), p. 210.
44. Dean, *The Royal Air Force*, p. 75. Edgerton, *England and the Aeroplane*, p. 68. N. H. Gibbs, *Grand Strategy Vol. I: Rearmament Policy* (HMSO: London, 1976), p. 313. Hyde, *British Air Policy*, p. 421. M. M. Postan, *British War Production* (HMSO: London, 1952), pp. 18–19. Sebastian Ritchie, *Industry and Air Power: The Expansion of British Aircraft Production, 1935–1941* (Frank Cass: London and Portland, Oregon, 1997), p. 35.

45. TNA AIR 10/1889, RAF Manual of Army Co-operation, Chapter VIII, 1937.
46. Derek J. P. Waldie, *Relations between the Army and Royal Air Force, 1918–1939* (PhD Thesis, King's College London, 1980), p. 108.
47. Ibid., p. 124.
48. For more details on the development of British thinking on strategic air power, see W. Scot Robertson, *The Development of British Strategic Bombing Doctrine, 1919–1939* (Praeger: Westport, Connecticut and London, 1995) and Biddle, *Rhetoric and Reality*. For details of the interwar developments that led to the creation of Fighter Command see John Ferris, 'Fighter Defence before Fighter Command: The Rise of Strategic Air Defence in Great Britain, 1917–1934', *Journal of Military History*, 63: 4 (October 1999), pp. 845–84.
49. TNA AIR 10/1708, Army Co-operation Report 1927.
50. Ibid.
51. Hugh Trenchard, 'Aspects of Service Aviation', *The Army Quarterly*, 2: 1 (April, 1921), pp. 10–21. Hall, *Strategy for Victory*, p. 13.
52. Ibid., pp. 154–5.
53. TNA AIR 10/1708, Army Co-operation Report 1927.
54. TNA AIR 10/1759, Army Co-operation Report 1928, Part II—The Year's Work.
55. TNA AIR 10/1777, Army Co-operation Report 1929, Part II.
56. TNA AIR 10/1759, Army Co-operation Report 1928, Part II—The Year's Work. TNA AIR 10/1777, Army Co-operation Report 1929, Part II. Parton, *The Evolution and Impact of Royal Air Force Doctrine*, pp. 98–9.
57. Hall, *Strategy for Victory*, p. 70.
58. TNA AIR 10/1794, Army Co-operation Report 1930, Part I.
59. TNA AIR 10/1827, Army Co-operation Report 1931, Part II.
60. TNA AIR 10/1914, Army Co-operation Report 1934, Part I.
61. Peter W. Gray, 'The Myths of Air Control and the Realities of Imperial Policing', *Air Power Review*, 4: 2 (Summer, 2000), pp. 37–52.
62. Howard, *The Continental Commitment*, p. 72.
63. David Ian Hall, 'Ruling the Empire out of the Central Blue: The Royal Air Force and Counter-Insurgency (COIN) Operations in the Inter-War Period, *Air Power Review*, 10: 2 (Summer, 2007), p. 69.
64. David Killingray, '"A Swift Agent of Government": Air Power in Colonial Africa', *Journal of African History*, 25: 4 (1984), p. 431.
65. Hall, *Strategy for Victory*, p. 21.
66. TNA CAB 5/4, Committee of Imperial Defence: Colonial Defence Memoranda (C Series), The Part of the Air Force in Imperial Defence, March 1921.

67. W. Michael Ryan, 'The Influence of the Imperial Frontier on British Doctrines of Mechanized Warfare', *Albion: A Journal Concerned with British Studies*, 15: 2 (Summer, 1983), p. 135. The RAF was also deployed in Ireland during the inter-war period and more information on its role and impact can be found in Michael O'Malley, *Military Aviation in Ireland, 1921–45* (University College of Dublin Press: Dublin, 2010) and William Sheehan, *A Hard Local War: The British Army and the Guerrilla War in Cork, 1919–1921* (The History Press: Stroud, 2011). Sebastian Ritchie, *The RAF, Small Wars and Insurgencies in the Middle East, 1919–1939* (Air Historical Branch: London, 2011).
68. TNA AIR 10/1911, Royal Air Force War Manual Part I. G.C. Peden, 'The Burden of Imperial Defence and the Continental Commitment Reconsidered', *The Historical Journal*, 27: 2 (1984), p. 406. Also see Williamson Murray, 'The Collapse of Empire: British Strategy, 1919–1945', in Williamson Murray, MacGregor Knox and Alvin Bernstein (eds), *The Making of Strategy: Rulers, States and War* (Cambridge University Press, Cambridge, New York and Melbourne, 1994). John Darwin, 'Imperialism in Decline? Tendencies in British Imperial Policy between the Wars', *The Historical Journal*, 23: 3 (September, 1980, pp. 657–79.
69. Ritchie, *The RAF*, pp. 4–5.
70. TNA AIR 5/846, RAF Operations Somaliland: Reports and Despatches, Extract from the Second Supplement to the London Gazette, 8 November 1920.
71. James S. Corum, 'The Myths of Air Control: Reassessing the History', *Aerospace Power Journal*, (Winter, 2000), http://www.airpower.au.af.mil/airchronciles/apj/apj00/win00/corum.pdf. Accessed 17 February 2011.
72. TNA AIR 8/6, Memorandum by the Chief of the Air Staff on Air Power Requirements of the Empire, Air Ministry, 9 December 1918. David Omissi, 'The Mediterranean and the Middle East in British Global Strategy 1935–1939', in Michael J. Cohen and Martin Kolinsky (eds), *Britain and the Middle East in the 1930s: Security Problems* (St. Martin's Press: New York, 1992), p. 3.
73. Gray, 'The Myths of Air Control', p. 42.
74. David Omissi, *Air Power and Colonial Control: The Royal Air Force 1919–1939* (Manchester University Press: Manchester and New York, 1990), p. 37. Paul Horne, 'The RAF in Command: The Policing of Mesopotamia from the Air', *Air Power Review*, 13: 2 (Summer 2010), p. 34.
75. Horne, 'The RAF in Command', p. 34.
76. TNA AIR 10/1367, Air Staff Memorandum No. 48—Notes on the History of the Employment of Air Power, September 1922.

77. Priya Satia, 'The Defense of Inhumanity: Air Control and the British Idea of Arabia', *The American Historical Review*, 111: 1 (February, 2006), p. 16.
78. Corum, 'The Myths of Air Control'.
79. John Slessor, *The Central Blue* (Cassell: London, 1956), pp. 66, 132.
80. TNA AIR 23/542, Letter from Air Headquarters British Forces in Baghdad, Iraq to the Air Ministry, 3 April 1924. Horne, 'The RAF in Command', p. 35.
81. Horne, 'The RAF in Command', p. 36.
82. Gray, 'The Myth of Air Control', pp. 44–5.
83. Andrew Roe, 'Friends in High Places: Air Power on the North-West Frontier of India', *Air Power Review*, 11: 2 (Summer, 2008), p. 32. See also Pardeep Bardua, 'Strategies and Doctrines of Imperial Defence: Britain and India, 1919–45', *The Journal of Imperial and Commonwealth History*, 25: 2 (May, 1997), pp. 240–66.
84. Omissi, *Air Power*, p. 12.
85. TNA AIR 75/31, Official Papers of Marshal of the Royal Air Force, Sir John Slessor, Folder V, North-West Frontier per-1939, Tactics and Training in Air Support, Khaisora, 1936.
86. Ibid.
87. James S. Corum, 'The Luftwaffe's Army Support Doctrine, 1918–1941', *Journal of Military History*, 59: 1 (January, 1997), p. 67.
88. James S. Corum, 'The *Luftwaffe* and Lessons Learned in the Spanish Civil War', in Sebastian Cox and Peter Gray (eds), *Air Power History: Turning Points from Kitty Hawk to Kosovo* (Frank Cass: London and Portland, Oregon, 2002), pp. 75–7.
89. James S. Corum, 'The Luftwaffe and the Coalition Air War in Spain, 1936–1939', in John Gooch (ed.), *Airpower: Theory and Practice* (Frank Cass: London, 1995), p. 83. For further information on how the geopolitical positions of Britain and Germany affected their attitudes to, and the subsequent development of air power, see Williamson Murray, 'British and German Air Doctrine between the Wars', *Air University Review*, XXX: III, (March/April, 1980), pp. 39–85, http://www.airpower.au.af.mil/airchronicles/aureview/1980/mar-apr/murray.html. Accessed 18 May 2009.
90. TNA AIR 75/31, Combined Report on Air Co-operation Training between 2 (Rawlpindi) Infantry Brigade and 3 (Indian) Wing, RAF Khanpur Area, 17–25 November 1936.
91. Ibid.
92. TNA AIR 9/137, Air Attack in Direct Support of Field Forces, 1939. The report does discuss in depth how aircraft were utilised during the Spanish Civil War but reaches the conclusion that was in line with the

doctrinal thinking of the RAF that had determined the direction of the interwar army co-operation exercises.
93. James S. Corum, 'The Spanish Civil War: Lessons Learned and Not Learned by the Great Powers', *Journal of Military History*, 62: 2 (April, 1998), pp. 315–18.
94. TNA AIR 9/137, Army Co-operation—Air Attack in Direct Support of the Field Force: The Attack of Land Forces—Close Support, 1939. TNA AIR 40/219, Notes on Air Employment in the Spanish Civil War, 1 October 1936.
95. TNA AIR 193/685, Aircraft for the Field Force: RAF provision for army requirements—support by low flying attack, June 1938.
96. Richard Overy, 'Doctrine Not Dogma: Lessons from the Past', *Air Power Review*, 3: 1 (Spring, 2000), p. 33.
97. TNA CAB 53/33, Joint Intelligence Committee, 624, 29 September 1937.
98. Peter W. Gray, *The Strategic Leadership and Direction of the Royal Air Force's Strategic Air Offensive Against Germany from Inception to 1945* (PhD Thesis, University of Birmingham, 2009), pp. 73–4.
99. Brian Armstrong, 'Through a Glass Darkly: The Royal Air Force and the Lessons of the Spanish Civil War 1936–1939', *Air Power Review*, 12: 1 (Spring, 2009), p. 47.
100. Armstrong, 'Through a Glass', p. 47. TNA AIR 2/2190, CID JIC Sub-Committee: Report on Air Warfare in Spain, 8 December 1938. Slessor, *Air Power and Armies*.
101. TNA AIR 9/137, Air Attack in Direct Support of Field Forces, 28 June 1939.
102. TNA AIR 75/31, Operations in Waziristan, 24 November 1936 to 15 January 1937.
103. Ibid.
104. Ibid.
105. TNA AIR 75/29, Official Papers of Marshal of the Royal Air Force, Sir John Slessor, folder V (b), India and Pakistan Frontier Operations, pre 1939, Draft of the Grey Book directing Direct Air Support with Land Forces.
106. James Pugh has noted that a lack of precise definitions of air power terms still exists within the academic air power literature today. *The Conceptual Origins of the Control of the Air*, pp. 20–6.
107. TNA AIR 75/29, Letter from Headquarters No. 2 (Indian) Wing, RAF Cheklala to Air Commodore R. H. Peck, Headquarters RAF India, New Delhi, 10 April 1936.
108. Booth, 'The Ten Year Rule', pp. 58–62. Brian Bond and Williamson Murray, 'The British Armed Forces, 1918–1939', in Allan R. Millett and

Williamson Murray (eds), *Military Effectiveness Vol II: The Interwar Period* (New Edition) (Cambridge University Press: New York, 2010 [Unwin Hyman: 1988]), p. 98.
109. G. C. Peden, *British Rearmament and the Treasury, 1932–1939* (Scottish Academic Press: Edinburgh, 1979), p. 134. Denis Richards, *The Royal Air Force 1939–1945 Vol. I: The Fight At Odds* (HMSO, 1953), pp. 21–6. Malcolm Smith, *British Air Policy between the Wars* (Clarendon Press: Oxford, 1984), p. 240.
110. This economic policy was one the interwar governments could afford to employ given the European strategic outlook. G. R. Simonson, 'The Demand for Aircraft and the Aircraft Industry, 1907–1958', *The Journal of Economic History*, 20: 3 (September, 1960), pp. 361–82.
111. Peter G. Dancey, *British Aircraft Manufacturers since 1909* (Fonthill: London, 2014), p. 12. Hayward, *The British Aircraft Industry*, p. 11.
112. Robin Higham, 'Government, Companies and National Defense: British Aeronautical Experience, 1918–1945 as the Basis for a Broad Hypothesis', *The Business History Review*, 39: 3 (Autumn, 1965), p. 325. G. C. Peden, *Arms, Economics and British Strategy: From Dreadnoughts to Hydrogen Bombs* (Cambridge University Press: New York, 2007), p. 98. Fearon, 'The Formative Years', pp. 479–80. Further information on the British aircraft industry and Treasury policy can be found in Peden, *British Rearmament* and Robert Shay Jr., *British Rearmament in the Thirties: Politics and Profits* (Princeton University Press: Princeton, New Jersey, 1977). David Edgerton has looked to revise orthodox historical opinion about Britain and its attitudes to disarmament and rearmament arguing that in terms of the aviation industry at least, Britain was well placed to rearm the RAF when this became necessary in the mid-1930s. *Warfare State*, pp. 18, 42–5. *England and the Aeroplane*, pp. 34–59.
113. Peter Fearon, 'Aircraft Manufacturing', in Neil K. Buxton and Derek H. Aldcroft (eds), *British Industry between the Wars: Instability and Industrial Development, 1919–1939* (Scholar Press: London, 1979), p. 222. Ritchie, *Industry and Air Power*, p. 7. Postan, *British War Production*, p. 5.
114. Peter Fearon, 'The British Airframe Industry and the State, 1918–1935', *The Economic History Review*, 27: 2 (May, 1974), p. 236. Robin Higham, 'Quantity vs. Quality: The Impact of Changing Demand on the British Aircraft Industry, 1900–1960', *The Business History Review*, 42: 4 (Winter, 1968), p. 450. Edgerton, *England and the Aeroplane*, pp. 34–5.
115. William Hornby, *Factories and Plant* (HMSO: London, 1958), pp. 15, 18. Sinnott, *RAF Operational Requirements*, pp. 84–5.
116. Ritchie, *Industry and Air Power*, p. 33.

117. Ritchie, *Industry and Air Power*, pp. 76, 79. For more details of the defence industries problems of recruiting enough labour to meet government demands see P. Inman, *Labour in the Munitions Industries* (HMSO: London, 1957), pp. 14–35.
118. For more information on interwar disarmament policy in Britain, see Dick Richardson, *The Evolution of British Disarmament Policy in the 1920s* (Pinter: London, 1989).
119. Further details of the RAF's thinking during the period of attempted disarmament can be found at TNA AIR 20/32, Review of Air Defence Policy: The Armaments Truce and Disarmament Conference, undated. The review covers the years 1924–1935.
120. Phillip S. Meilinger, 'Clipping the Bomber's Wings: The Geneva Disarmament Conference and the Royal Air Force, 1932–1934', *War In History*, 6: 3 (July, 1999), pp. 317–18.
121. Phillip S. Meilinger, 'Trenchard and Morale Bombing', pp. 261–2; 'Clipping the Bomber's Wings', p. 308. Peter W. Gray, 'The Gloves Will Have to Come Off: A Reappraisal of the Legitimacy of the RAF Bomber Offensive Against Germany', *Air Power Review*, 13: 3 (Autumn/Winter, 2010), p. 20. Barry R. Posen, *The Sources of Military Doctrine: France, Britain and Germany between the World Wars* (Cornell University Press: Ithaca, New York and London, 1984), p. 168.1
122. Dick Richardson and Carolyn Kitching, 'Britain and the World Disarmament Conference', in Peter Catterall and C. J. Morris (eds), *Britain and the Threat to Stability in Europe, 1918–1945* (Leicester University Press: London, 1993), p. 44.
123. For more details of the ideas and the nature of the debate surrounding the application of air power at the strategic level, see M. Everett, 'Fire Support from the Air', *JRUSI*, 83 (February/November, 1938) pp. 587–91. W. F. MacNeece Foster, 'Air Power and its Application', *JRUSI*, 73 (February/November, 1928), pp. 247–261. E. L Gossage, 'Air Co-operation with the Army', *JRUSI*, 72 (February/November, 1927), pp. 561–79. T. L Leigh-Mallory, 'Air Co-operation with Mechanized Forces', *JRUSI*, 75 (February/November, 1930), pp. 565–77. F. A. Pile, 'The Army's Air Needs', *JRUSI*, 71 (February/November, 1926), pp. 725–27. C. R. Samson, 'Aeroplanes and Armies', *JRUSI*, 75 (February/November, 1930), pp. 676–80. Stewart Oliver, 'Air Forces and the Great War: Some Strategical Lessons', *JRUSI*, 79 (February/November, 1934), pp. 289–93.
124. David Syrett, 'The Tunisian Campaign', in Benjamin Franklin Cooling (ed.), *Case Studies in the Development of Close Air Support* (Office of Air Force History, United States Air Force: Washington D.C., 1990), pp. 158–60.

125. TNA WO 193/678, Air Requirements of the Army—Memorandum of the Deputy Chief of the Imperial General Staff. 22 September 1939.
126. TNA AIR 9/137, Army Co-operation: Air Attack in Direct Support of the Field Force, 1939.
127. TNA WO 193/678, Statement [on air requirements for the army], unsigned and undated, c.December 1939. Peden, *Arms, Economics*, p. 137.
128. Bond, *British Military Policy*, p. 312. W. A. Jacobs, 'Air Support for the British Army, 1939–1943', *Military Affairs*, 46: 4 (December, 1982), p. 174.
129. TNA CAB 66/3/12, Air Requirements of the Army, Memorandum by the Secretary of State for Air, 3 November 1939. Shay, *British Rearmament*, p. 235.
130. Sebastian Cox, 'The Air/Land Relationship', p. 4.
131. Mungo Melvin, The Land/Air Interface: An Historical Perspective', in Peter W. Gray (ed.), *Air Power 21: Challenges for the New Century* (The Stationery Office: Norwich, 2000), p. 159.
132. TNA WO 106/1597, Air Component of the British Expeditionary Force, France: Composition—Notes by the Chief of the Imperial General Staff on CAS's Memorandum on Arrangements for Bomber Support for the Allied Army in France, November 1939.
133. These targets included the delay of armoured columns and the interference of mobilisation arrangements among others. TNA WO 190/435, Military Air Targets of an Army Nature, 18 May 1936. TNA AIR 9/137, Memorandum on Air Attack in Direct Support of the Field Force, unsigned and undated, c.July 1939.

CHAPTER 2

Tactical Air Power and the Battle of France, 1940

The RAF was relatively unprepared for the role it was expected to conduct when it moved to France in 1939. This was despite the good work that had been done during the interwar period on developing a theoretical basis from which to conduct tactical air power operations. The RAF was a force that had been designed to apply air power at the strategic level, targeting the industrial and transport infrastructure of the enemy homeland, although how far it was able to do this at the start of the Second World War is subject to fierce debate. With its move to France, the RAF was now expected to act as a component in the larger military machine of the BEF away from its home base.[1] The late 1930s had seen a major shift in production and procurement policy for the RAF, with an increase in the number of fighter aircraft being manufactured and a reduction in the relative number of bomber aircraft.[2]

No military operations were conducted in Western Europe until May 1940 and this gave the RAF ample breathing space to alter the fundamental organisation of its forces and to review the role that it would look to conduct. Part of the reason for this reorganisation was the realisation that its aircraft were unable to conduct the long-range strategic bombing operations expected of them, even from the advanced airfields at which they were based in France. This had a particular relevance for the aircraft of the Advanced Air Striking Force (AASF), which was the part of the RAF expected to conduct this role. When the German invasion of France, Belgium and the Netherlands began, the Allied forces found that their expectations regarding the pace of operations, on which their plans were heavily based, was deeply flawed. They were quickly thrown off balance by the speed of the German break in and their subsequent break out around Sedan.[3] As the *Wehrmacht* advanced across France towards the Channel coast at a pace that would have been unthinkable during the First World War, the Allied forces that had advanced into Belgium were cut off and forced to retreat to the Channel ports. This retreat ended in the 'miracle' of Operation Dynamo, where almost all the BEF and many French troops were evacuated from the beaches of Dunkirk.[4]

This chapter will argue that the campaign in France had a profound impact on relations between the RAF and the army and ultimately how Army Co-operation Command was created. It would also provide guiding principles for the future development of tactical air power, particularly the C2 system that would have influence overseas. Part of the reason for the deterioration of relations between the RAF and the army was due to the latter's interpretation of the fighting in France—the army did not believe that it had received sufficient air support to defend against the German advance. This was combined with a fundamental misreading of the *Luftwaffe*'s ability to conduct impromptu close support missions and how the *Luftwaffe* fitted into the overall C2 system of the *Wehrmacht*. The underestimation of German capabilities would have to be countered by Army Co-operation Command but they did provide the necessary drive to develop an air support system that was ultimately superior to that of the *Luftwaffe*. To support these arguments, this chapter will examine the issues in depth through a detailed analysis of the RAF's organisational structure and how it was modified. It will also consider the fighting in France, with a particular emphasis on air sorties. These will include decisive operations conducted by the *Luftwaffe* in order to provide the necessary context of how the army interpreted air support operations during the Battle of France and how this interpretation affected its perceptions of the work of Army Co-operation Command.

There are certain myths, particularly in Britain, about the fighting in the Battle of France, one in particular that relates directly to the influence of air power on the outcome of the campaign. The role of the Ju-87 'Stuka' has been vastly exaggerated, particularly its impact on the *Wehrmacht*'s ability to cross the Meuse River opposite Sedan.[5] How this came about will be investigated in greater depth in the next chapter. The current historiography, and indeed wider public opinion, is that the Stuka had a decisive role in the initial German attacks and the outcome of the battle as a whole.[6] There have been attempts to revise the accepted historical opinion that the blitzkrieg method employed by the Germans in 1939 and 1940 was truly revolutionary or simply the development of ideas that had first emerged from the German storm troop tactics at the end of the First World War.[7] Recent historiography has begun to reverse the argument that the Allies were outnumbered by the Germans both quantitatively and qualitatively in armour, infantry and air power.[8] Ernest R. May has argued that

> Overall, France and its allies turn out to have been better equipped for war than Germany, with more trained men, more guns, more and better tanks, more bombers and fighters. On the whole they did not even lag in thinking about the use of tanks and airplanes.[9]

May is correct in the assertion that the Allies were at least a match for the Germans in terms of the number and quality of troops and equipment used, but not in the claim that the doctrinal thinking of the two forces was at similar levels.[10] It was only the *Wehrmacht* that was thinking about how armoured and mechanised formations might transform the battlefield and return fast-flowing mobile operations to it. The British and French were, on the whole, preparing for operations that unfolded at a similar pace to those of the First World War, including the operations of the Hundred Days of 1918. The thinking on tanks was to use them distributed in penny packets, acting as an infantry support weapon and not spearheading attacks or acting in a semi-independent role.

There is also still much debate between historians about the effectiveness of the RAF in conducting air support operations, although the argument has advanced to take into account the unexpected increase in operational tempo and mobility faced by the service. In terms of the *Luftwaffe*, it is fair to argue that it was not as effective or decisive as has been argued previously. Greater factors led to the Allied defeat in France in 1940. These included the increased operational tempo mentioned previously and a slow and cumbersome command, control and communications (C3) system combined with a defensive strategic plan. The battle highlighted the divergence in thinking on tactical air power that still existed between the RAF and army despite the agreements that had been reached between the two services prior to their embarkation to France. When faced with the dire emergency caused by the German break out at Sedan, 'the RAF attempted to intervene and influence the campaign as best it could in the only way it knew how'.[11]

In support of the land battle, the RAF regarded the interdiction of enemy reserves as the principal contribution of bomber aircraft, and further, generally, to create disorganisation and confusion behind the enemy front while the ground forces achieved their objectives.[12]

The RAF of 1940 was a force that had been designed to conduct single-role campaigns and not multi-role joint operations due to its mono-role command structure that organised its forces based on aircraft type and not the tasks they might be expected to perform:

> This created a framework that was ideal for managing single-role campaigns fought from well-found, permanent bases in the metropolitan homeland, where inter-command cooperation was required ... the single role command model did not provide the structure that could be readily used to deploy and support an expeditionary air component in the field.[13]

Such a command structure was of great benefit to the RAF during the rearmament push of the late 1930s, allowing it to expand with relative ease.[14] With the coming of war, however, this command structure would be difficult to apply to a foreign campaign that required the support of land forces. This role had had little consideration during the majority of the interwar period and the bulk of the RAF's planning had taken place after the rearmament drive had begun. Further to this, the strategic thinking was based around applying a policy of limited liability that would not require an expeditionary force to be sent to the continent.[15] The RAF originally divided its force into two separate formations, both of which had polar opposite tasks. These were the AASF and the RAF Component of the field forces.[16] The command of these formations fell to RAF officers, much to the consternation of the army, who were still pushing for their own army air force under their operational command.[17] One month after the declaration of war, the Secretary of State for War, Leslie Hore-Belisha, argued that the

> Spasmodic allocation [of aircraft] on request will not work. These aircraft must be permanently at the disposal of the Army.[18]

The AASF headquarters opened on 1 September 1939 at Reims, chosen because it was felt that it would be easier for the aircraft of this formation to attack strategic targets deep within Germany from there (the bombers did not have the range to conduct these missions from Britain) and it was a clear indication of how the RAF originally saw this force being deployed.[19] It would also be under the command of the Air Staff in Britain at this time. Air Chief Marshal (ACM) Sir Cyril Newall, who was CAS at this time, argued in the War Cabinet that provided the French undertook the burden of the fighting on land, he was happy for the AASF to conduct interdiction missions as the Germans had done against Poland in 1939.[20]

There is evidence to suggest that as early as September 1939 plans were in place to utilise the AASF as an interdiction force to support a French offensive in the Saar region. Newall was being pressed by the French General Mouchard, commander of the South Eastern Air Army, to deploy the AASF in this role.[21] Newall was in favour of this in principle, but not unless the French *Armée de l'Air* were also conducting offensive operations. The plan eventually drawn up for the support of this offensive was to utilise ten Fairey Battle squadrons to conduct interdiction support missions despite these squadrons being at sixty per cent efficiency. The Battles would attack fuel and weapons dumps, aerodromes, troop columns and transport traffic in the Saarlauten–Neunkirchen–Zeibruchen–Pirmassens area.[22] The plan was agreed at a meeting between Mouchard and the commanders of Nos. 1 and 2 Missions, Air Officer Commanding-in-Chief (AOC-in-C) AASF, Group Captain Collier and Wing Commander Baker.[23] The Chiefs of Staff (COS) also argued that the bombers comprising the AASF, classified as medium but in reality light, would be

> suitable for undertaking operations against the enemy's Army including communications and installations in its immediate rear. This part of the Striking Force [is] suitable therefore, for undertaking that direct action against the advancing German Army which is advocated by General Gamelin.[24]

The role of the AASF if it was tasked to act in a support role would be interdiction—it would not take on a close support role as the army had argued for during the interwar period.[25] Despite there not being an agreed definition of close air support, and the persisting lack of enthusiasm for tactical air power within the RAF as a whole, the AASF's focus was not simply on its strategic role.

The ongoing 'phoney war' allowed the RAF to continue to counter the War Office's demands for an army air arm by altering the make-up and role of the AASF. The Air Ministry proposed that the aircraft of the AASF would be allotted to the army 'in such proportions as may be necessary', but did not specify how they defined necessary or how they were to be allotted. The Secretary of State for Air, Sir Kingsley Wood, also confirmed that the 'Air Ministry are arranging for a proportion of the bomber force [AASF] to receive special training with the Army'.[26] This training was hampered by the unsuitability of some airfields and the bad weather during the winter of 1940 rendering others unserviceable.[27] The army's renewed push for its own air arm was founded on German actions during the invasion of Poland in September 1939.[28] In fact the War Office did not create a specialist department to develop its own thinking on tactical air power until January 1940 under Lieutenant Colonel F. W. Festing. The conclusions that this department (MO 7) reached have been described 'as [neither] enlightening or even a surprise', as they simply reiterated the army's previous arguments about the nature of the air support they felt they required.[29]

The War Office further claimed that the 'Allocation of aircraft for support of specific land operations [was] NOT (repeat NOT) good enough'.[30] It is clear that despite the agreements reached between the Air Ministry and War Office at the outbreak of war, there was still a great deal of tension and ill feeling between the two over tactical air support. In an attempt to resolve these tensions, and potentially form its own army air arm, the War Office put forward proposals for an aircraft designed to fulfil a close support role. This aircraft was to be of simple construction that could be mass-produced quickly by utilising the spare production capacity that was available to the Air Ministry.[31] In the army's eyes such an aircraft would be operationally available by the spring of 1940 and due to the speed at which it was produced would come as a complete surprise to the enemy.[32] How the Air Ministry was to design such an aircraft and have it in production in enough time for meaningful numbers in an aircraft industry that was already running at full capacity producing fighter and bomber aircraft, demonstrates a lack of understanding on the part of the War Office about production lead times and the difficulties this would pose.[33] There was, at the very least, a degree of wishful thinking on the part of the War Office. At the very worst, they were already looking for a scapegoat in the event of a defeat and ejection from the continent. The Air Ministry responded by highlighting the fact that current production demands prevented the design or building of a new aircraft for at least eighteen months.

To resolve the growing tensions between the Air Ministry and War Office over air support in the field, the War Cabinet proposed that 'The General Staff and the Air Ministry should reach an agreement on the proportion of the Advanced Air Striking Force ... allocated to army work and the training required'. As a result of this decision, it was agreed that ten Battle squadrons that were a part of the AASF and six Blenheim squadrons based in England were to be given training with the army to provide the air support required.[34] The Battle squadrons were also reorganised into five wings whilst they were in France.[35] The AASF found its role in France modified to such an extent that its aircraft were unable to conduct strategic level operations against the German homeland:

> During the first months of the war ... it became apparent that the slow and obsolescent aircraft of the AASF could not penetrate over enemy territory by day, and from this time onwards there was very little doubt that their main employment could be tactical.'[36]

The French armed forces and government were also fearful that conducting such attacks against Germany would lead to retaliatory attacks from the *Luftwaffe* on their own population and industrial centres. As the senior partner in the alliance they were reluctant to sanction such raids whilst there was no fighting on the ground.[37]

The other formation of the RAF stationed in France was the RAF Component attached to the BEF. This was the force originally designed and tasked to provide air support that the BEF would require. The arguments that occurred between the Air Ministry and the War Office highlight to a great extent the faith the War Office had in the RAF Component to conduct this role and also speaks volumes of the War Office's concept of air support—they felt that all air resources in a given theatre should be focused on providing what they saw as the correct form of support for their troops. The RAF Component established itself in France with great speed, advanced parties of the force moving as early as mid-September 1939,[38] and final transfers complete by mid-October.[39]

The RAF Component was originally placed under the operational command of the General Officer Commanding-in-Chief (GOC-in-C), BEF, Lord Gort. In his position as CIGS prior to his appointment as GOC-in-C, Gort had been heavily involved in arguments with the Air Ministry over the conduct of air support operations, and so must have been content with being given the initial operational control of this force. In order to support Gort with the planning and understanding of the RAF's air support operations, Air Vice-Marshal (AVM) C. H. R. Blount was the Air Officer Commanding (AOC) of the RAF Component.[40] The Air Historical Branch (AHB) monograph that investigated the history of air support and photographic interpretation states that the force was to be commanded according to accepted doctrine. It is, however, lacking in detail as to whether this was the doctrinal thinking favoured by the RAF or the army. Given the work done by the RAF in this area, combined with the agreements reached by the Air Ministry and War Office at the outbreak of war, it is right to assume that it would be the doctrinal principles favoured by the RAF that were used to guide air support operations.[41]

The RAF Component consisted of four Lysander squadrons for short-range reconnaissance and four Blenheim squadrons for long-range reconnaissance—escort protection was provided by four squadrons of Hurricanes. Carrington has commented that the RAF Component was 'no better equipped than any other limb of our military effort'.[42] When the make-up of the RAF Component is understood and the lack of confidence that the War Office had in it, their attempts to transform the AASF into a tactical strike force become clearer. The component was a force designed to conduct reconnaissance for the army, but with the aircraft it had it would be capable of very little else. Whilst both the Lysander and Blenheim could, in theory, conduct bombing sorties in support of land operations, their relative obsolescence meant that without almost complete air superiority, they would find this task difficult to accomplish. Attaining and maintaining such a dominance in the air against a *Luftwaffe* force that would be contesting it keenly would prove to be difficult.

The theory behind the RAF Component was that it would be able to provide all the support the BEF could need in the field. A contingency had, however, been developed if further support was required and the AASF would then be tasked with meeting the extra demand, but the communications system developed to allow this meant that in practice it would prove next to impossible to accomplish. To request this extra support, the BEF had to make a request to the War Office, although at what level this request was to be made is unclear, meaning that small and medium sized formations might have to send an original request to higher level formations prior to it being sent to the War Office, increasing the length of an already cumbersome communications change. Upon receiving a request for additional support, the War Office would pass it to the Air Ministry who, potentially unaware of the tactical situation on the ground, would either approve or deny the request. If the request was approved, it then fell to the Air Ministry to pass this on to the independently commanded bomber force in France that formed a part of the AASF.[43]

There is no evidence to confirm if a reverse communications system existed to inform the formation that had originally made the request whether it had been approved or denied. Given the work done after the Battle of France to develop such a system it must be assumed that the originating formation would have had no confirmation of the success or otherwise of their request for support. This again adds to our understanding of why the War Office had little confidence in the ability of the RAF to provide any real form of effective air support and why it felt that the latter was 'dangerously inadequate both in resources and organization'.[44] The War Office again voiced their concern about which service had operational control of the air support force, arguing that 'no part of our bomber force [is] permanently under the command of the commander fighting the battle on land'.[45]

The RAF Component was also able to request the loan of two squadrons of bombers from the AASF to attack 'fleeting opportunity' targets.[46] To resolve the issues that had been raised by the War Office over the organisation of air support forces, a full and frank discussion took place between the two services and agreement was reached on a new organisation to conduct this role as the Air Ministry could also see the potential issues. The RAF did not, however, agree to break one of their fundamental principles—that air forces should remain under their operational control. How such a system was to function effectively given the complex communications in place for the BEF to request additional support from the AASF, the administrative friction that would be caused during active operations, and the need to attack time sensitive targets effectively, is not mentioned.[47] One squadron was to be on standby at all times but, given the lengthy communications chain, it is doubtful if enough information could have reached the squadron in time to ensure they could attack a target effectively. This was an issue that was raised by the RAF Component in a memorandum to the AASF that discussed the channels of control in such circumstances. The memorandum stated that AASF squadrons 'will probably be called up to bomb fleeting opportunity targets and it will be extremely difficult to get information as to targets through sufficiently quickly if the aircraft are right outside our area'.[48]

The discussions between the Air Ministry and War Office, combined with the thinking about the abilities of the AASF to conduct the strategic role it had originally been given, eventually led to a radical change in both policy and the command structure of the RAF in France.[49] The War

Office continued their push for outright control of the air support force during these discussions.[50] However, there was a desire for change within the RAF in Britain as well as in France. The weaknesses of the current air support organisation were clear to one of the leading authorities on air support, Barratt, who was AOC-in-C No. 1 Mission, RAF.[51] It was suggested by ACM E. R. Ludlow-Hewitt, AOC-in-C Bomber Command, that in order to resolve the current problems that plagued the RAF's air support force in France, a new headquarters should be established that would 'button up the divergent or convergent requirements of the French and British forces, the Air Component, the AASF and Bomber Command'.[52] The result of the discussions between the Air Ministry and the War Office was the establishment of a new RAF formation that would be responsible for all the air support conducted by the RAF in France, including that of the AASF. The responsibility of this new command was also extended to include all parts of the Allied front and not just the British sector.[53] The AASF, which had been under the nominal operational control of Bomber Command, was transferred to this new formation, British Air Forces in France (BAFF), when it came into official existence on 15 January 1940.[54] These discussions demonstrate that there must have been a degree of goodwill between the two services to reach an agreement on the make-up of this new command. This goodwill, however, would not last longer than the end of the campaign itself.

The position of the new commander of BAFF, Barratt, had to be clarified. It was stated as being a similar position to that of Gort, except that Barratt would not be under any French authority in the chain of command, despite now being responsible for potentially supporting both French and British ground offensives. The Air Ministry and War Office took the command relationship that existed between the Royal Navy and Coastal Command as the basis for how they saw the new AOC-in-C's role. There was still, however, a great deal of confusion regarding the role of the AASF despite its transfer to BAFF. If it were required to support Bomber Command in strategic operations, then its command would pass back to the AOC-in-C Bomber Command. Orders would be issued to the AASF in this scenario by the COS Committee after having the operation sanctioned by the War Cabinet.[55] This was still a highly complex way of controlling a force overseas, despite one link in the communication chain being removed. With this system Barratt was unable to prevent the AASF from conducting strategic raids against the German homeland when they may have been better employed conducting operations at the tactical level.[56]

Barratt was further charged with ensuring that Gort had 'full assurances regarding the provision of air support'.[57] Barratt's appointment to BAFF was confirmed at the end of December 1939.[58] Stuart Peach has described Barratt's major role as the AOC-in-C of BAFF as attempting to 'bring a semblance of coherence to his command' that had been missing when the AASF and RAF Component had existed as two separate formations and under different operational commands.[59]

To the RAF at least, the creation of BAFF was the end of the two-decade struggle with the War Office over the operational control of tactical air forces in Britain, with the RAF emerging victorious.[60] The War Office were, for the time being at least, happy to accept this settlement over operational control but still voiced concerns about the timing of air support on the battlefield and the resources that the RAF dedicated to this role.[61] Barratt's position as AOC-in-C BAFF was an unusual and difficult one. The expanded role allowed him to co-ordinate the RAF's air support plans and intentions with the French armed forces to a greater extent, but he had no control over the administration of his force except at the highest level possible. The RAF explained this anomaly by stating that 'a working system of administration, under the AASF and the Air Component, was already in existence' and that they wished to 'avoid swamping an operational commander with administrative detail'.[62]

Discussions took place between BAFF, the AASF and Bomber Command for a contingency communications system to be utilised if communications between the AASF and Bomber Command were interrupted during operations owing to the complexity of the primary system. In this scenario, BAFF was to assume overall command of the AASF, and they were to advise how many squadrons were to be kept in reserve for 'Special Opportunity Targets' (fleeting opportunity targets). The nature of the orders was also subject to discussion and it was decided that at certain times it would be 'more appropriate for Advanced Headquarters BAFF, to allot *tasks* rather than *targets* and AASF and Bomber Command will best be judges in the light of results which they were obtaining, as to the exact targets to be attacked [emphasis added]'.[63] This was a real sea change in the doctrinal thinking of the RAF, which previously had been as inflexible as the army with regard to orders. Previously, aircraft would be assigned a target and it was only this that they could attack—if this was not possible then the aircraft would have been sent on a wasted mission. Now, through an emphasis on tasks instead of targets, not only would the aircraft become more efficient in conducting this role, but the responsibility for conducting the mission in the best way possible and attacking the best possible target available passed from the squadron or wing commander and down to the pilot himself. This was a similar system employed by the *Heer* when conducting ground operations and will be looked at in more detail below when the fighting in France is the focus.

A further area of focus for BAFF was the ability of its new squadrons to conduct an air support role both by day and night. As the original plan for the Battle squadrons in particular had been strategic day bombing raids against Germany, they had little knowledge of conducting air support operations, particularly at night. This carried with it an increased risk. In order to reduce this risk extensive training would be required before they could be sent on active operations. The space to conduct this training was simply not available in northern France and the restrictions laid down by the French High Command with regard to Allied aircraft crossing the border with Germany meant that any potential space could not be exploited. The AASF conducted its training in air support by day and night from an aerodrome far away from the French border in Perpignan.[64]

The creation of BAFF also saw a limited reorganisation of personnel within it. After it had been created, a conference was held to discuss the issues the new command faced:

> It was pointed out the any decision as to the strength of allocation of bombing effort was, in essence, a military problem. Only a limited amount of bombing effort was available, and if 'the demand exceeded supply' it would ultimately be for General Georges to decide where this effort was to be expended. It was therefore suggested that to meet any difficulties that might arise, a Staff Officer from General George's Headquarters should be at the Headquarters of the AOC-in-C in order to represent or obtain General George's decision when necessary.[65]

Whilst Barratt was not officially under General Georges command, such discussions could only have made clear who the senior partner in the Alliance was and who was driving both the strategy and priorities when any fighting began.

BAFF's thinking with regard to what was then termed the 'close support role' was in real terms no different to that of the RAF during the interwar period and lends weight to the argument made above that the doctrine used in France and highlighted by the monograph on air support and photographic interpretation was indeed based on the Air Ministry's and not the War Office's thinking on the subject:

operational instructions issued by BAFF and Bomber Command ... stated that 'Bomber aircraft had proved extremely useful *in support* of an advancing army, especially against weak anti-aircraft resistance, but it is not clear that a bomber force used *against* an advancing army, well supported by all forms of anti-aircraft defence and a large force of fighter aircraft will be economically effective. For this reason it is intended that the scale of our bomber effort shall depend on the gravity of the situation [emphasis in original]'.[66]

Hall has gone as far, and correctly, to argue that 'BAFF was what three years later would be called a Tactical Air Force, affiliated with an Army Group in a designated theatre of operations'.[67] It was also a force similar in make-up to BAFF that the army agreed to create in mid-1942 in preparation for invading the continent.

The area in which BAFF had its biggest impact, and laid the foundations for Army Co-operation Command when it was created in the wake of the Battle of France, was close air support communication techniques. The breakthrough made by the Allied Central Air Bureau (ACAB), set up in November 1939 at Chauny, allowed the development of a system that could provide impromptu air support in the field. The ACAB was based upon some of the ideas that had emerged from the First World War and interwar army co-operation reports. It also demonstrated that the interservice friction over air support was felt more at the higher levels of command within the two services as the ACAB functioned with efficiency in its role. The ACAB had a joint air/army staff with an army officer representing Gort. This officer, Lieutenant Colonel J. D. Woodall, was crucial to the further development of air support communications in Britain.[68]

The ACAB began as a signals organisation 'built on a series of landlines with ciphered Wireless [Telegraphy] backup'.[69] A centralised communications hub could only serve to improve the RAF's response time when being tasked to attack time sensitive targets. Its functions fell into three distinct areas: the first was to sort information received from the various reconnaissance missions that were flown. The ACAB would then be able to request further reconnaissance to monitor potentially dangerous developments and allot bombing tasks where necessary based on the reports.[70] The efficiency of reconnaissance and mission selection would improve vastly in the hands of a centralised body such as this, one that was capable of handling a complex task and that was also aware of the tactical and operational plans of both services. Secondly, the ACAB played a further role in improving the communications between the British and French forces. They were entrusted with the task not only of maintaining close liaison with General d'Astier on all points which concerned the two Air Forces in his Zone, but also of studying the whole problem of air action in the event of operations in Belgium and Holland; the plans for which were being prepared by the French High Command.[71]

Thirdly, the ACAB was also perfectly placed to take advantage of another joint service development that had taken place while the RAF was in France. This was the creation of 'a specialised ground reconnaissance unit, composed of a joint army/air' unit called 'Phantom'.[72]

There was little initial enthusiasm for the ACAB, or the plans for the conduct of air support in general from Gort and he wrote a vociferous letter to the CIGS General Sir Edmund Ironside, stating that

> On paper this Bureau makes the best of a somewhat confused air situation. I am doubtful if it will work in war, if only because of its reliance on long communications.[73]

That Gort wrote a letter to his superior arguing against a communications system that was under joint service command and an air support force under the operational command of the RAF should not come as a surprise. That does not mean that everything that Gort said about the air support system prior to the German invasion of France in May 1940 should, however, be dismissed. After observing an exercise of the communications system, Gort identified that the lead time between an aircraft conducting reconnaissance and the target being engaged was still too long, and would be an issue if time was of the essence during operations:

> Last week the board carried out a two-day practice scheme which worked pretty well, but it brought out the delays which now occur between a reconnaissance aircraft sighting a suitable target and the bombers leaving the ground to engage it, delays which must be overcome.[74]

The resolution of this issue was the key to providing timely air support to land forces in the field.

The ACAB continued in existence despite initial hesitations and looked to develop solutions to the problems that an air force supporting ground troops would face. The primary concern was improving the speed of communications from reconnaissance aircraft in the air to the bomber squadrons on standby at forward aerodromes. The ACAB's operation room expanded its communications network allowing it to have 'continuous contact with [the] Air Ministry, Bomber Command, the BEF and the Advanced Air Striking Force'.[75] In his despatch written after BAFF had been evacuated from the continent, Barratt highlighted the work undertaken by ACAB to improve the RAF's ability to provide air support to the BEF: 'Full scale exercises were held to test out the organization of the AAB in relation to the probable task of knitting together air reconnaissance and information generally with the selection of objectives for air bombardment.'[76] The importance of Phantom and the ACAB should not be underestimated—they provided the intellectual framework that would transform the RAF's ability to conduct air support in future campaigns:

> It became clear from signals exercise that special provision was required for getting back directly to ACAB at Chauny up-to-the-minute information about the ground situation and requirements for air action. For this purpose a special ground reconnaissance unit comprising a joint army/air mission but best known by its code name of 'Phantom', was set up under command of [an] RAF officer with an army officer borrowed from the GHQ as his second in command and head of the army element. The task of 'Phantom' was to get rapid information back to BAFF at all costs and for the purpose it was provided with mobile wireless stations or 'tentacles' to be sent out to forward positions from which the course of the battle could be observed and reported. This unit—a measure of whose value can be gained by the fact that when the battle began BAFF usually had the information thirty-hours sooner than the French Army and was in fact the origin on the one hand of the Air Support Signals Unit (ASSU) ....[77]

Their importance is demonstrated further through Gort's despatch at the end of the fighting in which his opinion of the communications had changed dramatically and for the good. He was also clear in his thinking about the potential future implications of its further development. To have changed the thoughts of a man who was so ingrained in his own service's thinking was no mean feat and demonstrates just how important the two formations were for the future development of tactical air power in Britain:

> The development of the ACAB and of its communications to the headquarters of higher formations in France and to the Royal Air Force at home, was likewise to prove its worth in the days to come as an organisation for co-ordinating information and requests for air action.[78]

The ACAB has rightly been described as 'one of the very few positive developments to come out of the fighting against the Germans the following spring'.[79]

Artillery co-operation was one of the most important and successful roles conducted by the RFC/RAF during the First World War, and its development continued under the direction of the army in the late 1930s—the ideas that emerged were due to be trialled in operations in France. It is, however, necessary at this point to give a brief overview of the system that was pioneered in the First World War and the developments that emerged in the interwar period to provide the necessary context to understand progression in the field of artillery reconnaissance and observation. As a former artillery officer before transferring to the RFC in the First World War, Barratt was able to apply the specialist knowledge he had gained in this area to assist in much needed improvements.

During the First World War aircraft were employed to spot for artillery batteries, correcting the fall of shot by employing the 'clock code' system that was pioneered by Donald Lewis and Baron James. The fall of shot was corrected by an artillery co-operation pilot via R/T, indicating to the battery commander how far away and in what direction the shells had fallen. The target was placed in the middle of an imaginary clock face and used as a guide for both the pilot and artillery commander. A shot to the east of the target, for example, would be indicated by the number three; the number six indicated a shot that had fallen short. The distance from the target was then given in multiples of one hundred yards.[80] The War Office felt that whilst the clock code system had functioned efficiently enough during the static trench warfare phase of the First World War, its efficiency had fallen away when semi-mobile warfare was restored to the battlefield and the department pushed for trials of a new system. As may be expected, given the difficulties that existed between the two services during the interwar period, the Air Ministry and War Office interpreted the results of these trials in opposite ways and despite further experiments with aircraft more suited to this role, little further development was undertaken prior to the outbreak of the Second World War.[81] These further trials

> Showed reasonably conclusively that effective fire [control] could be reached considerably quicker than the existing [artillery control] procedure, and that this fire could be observed [from] up to some 8,000 yards. A trial [using] Spitfires ... showed that a light aeroplane, even without previous warnings, had quite a good chance of dodging the fire of a modern fast fighter.[82]

Despite the issues that existed between the two services, the development of artillery reconnaissance was not retarded with the coming of war and the first Air OP was established in Britain in February 1940. The original term for this formation was a Flying Observation Post (Flying OP), not Air OP, and consisted of Taylorcraft Plus and Stinson Voyager aircraft. The Flying OP moved to France on 19 April 1940 and trials were conducted in order to gain greater experience in active operations, to settle flight handling issues and to decide what organisation was best suited to this developing role.[83]

The trials were to be conducted in three stages–one was to be a test 'in the French Army area including shoots ... against actual German targets'. The final phase of training was to be active operations trialling the results of the previous tests in the Saar sector.[84] The course of history, however, would prevent these trials being conducted as they were planned to begin the day after the German invasion. Two figures, Majors A. G. Matthews and H. C. Bazeley of A/E Battery Royal Horse Artillery (RHA), who were the pioneers of the Air OP concept in the interwar period, were based in the Saar sector in preparation to conduct the trials. The artillery batteries assembled in this sector were ordered to join their formations to support the BEF in response to the German invasion. The RAF flight that had been selected to conduct trials (D Flight) moved to Mailly 'in the hope that the campaign would stabilize enough for them to continue the last vital phase of the tests'.[85] When it was clear that this would not happen, D Flight was removed from France to continue the Air OP tests in Britain. Despite showing some promise of improving the efficiency of artillery observation, the trials had been planned too late to have any real impact on the fighting in France. The idea of the Air OP, however, was not to be forgotten and its development would occur at pace under Army Co-operation Command. This episode confirms that British forces were not expecting the German attack and probably also believed that any operations that did occur would unfold at a similar pace to those of the First World War.

Whilst preparations were being made for the trial of the Air OP concept, a great deal of planning had been done by the RAF prior to the German attack on how they would support the BEF in the field, utilising the approximately three hundred aircraft available in twenty-five squadrons.[86] Four squadrons of Lysanders were to conduct tactical reconnaissance, four squadrons of Blenheims would conduct strategic and special reconnaissance of bombing objectives, and six squadrons of fighters (four Hurricanes and two Gladiators) would provide the escort for the reconnaissance aircraft and provide 'general security of the BEF Area and Lines of Communication'.[87] It had been agreed that the French *Armée de l'Air* would limit their operations to night bombing and would only conduct bombing by day in an emergency.[88] It must be questioned why, as the senior partner in the alliance, the *Armée de l'Air* was restricted in the role that it would play in the operation. There is no evidence to suggest that the night bombing training conducted by the RAF at Perpignan was not successful and the conclusion must be reached that the commanders of the *Armée de l'Air* felt that their forces were incapable of conducting daylight bombing missions in support of their own land forces.[89]

The RAF Component fighters were assigned the task of 'maintain[ing] air superiority, defend[ing] important points, such as Headquarters, aerodromes and lines of communication, protect[ing] the BEF in its advance to the Dyle, and to protect reconnaissance aircraft operating in the British tactical reconnaissance area'.[90] In keeping with the doctrinal thinking of the RAF in the interwar period, 'Aircraft were to be placed in direct support of the army when they are directed against targets whose destruction will immediately contribute to the success of the land battle.' The support provided would be interdiction and not close support, in order

> to isolate the battlefield from reinforcements and supply; to block and delay the movement of reserves; to create disorganisation and confusion behind the enemy concerned by bombing his communications, headquarters and supply services; in attack—by holding off enemy reserves to prevent hostile counter-attack and eventually turn the 'break-in' into a 'break-through'; in defence—to stop the enemy reinforcing his first attacking wave and to prevent the continuation of the attack and the possibility of his exploiting any partial success.[91]

The German invasion began with a surprise attack through Belgium and Luxembourg. The Belgian military attaché based in Berlin had already warned his government of the date of the attack but, due to the many invasion scares that had occurred since the Germans had successfully defeated Poland, little notice of this warning was taken by the Allies.[92] The *Armée de l'Air* did attempt to conduct operations against the *Wehrmacht*, but quickly found itself outnumbered in terms of operational aircraft availability.[93] This in turn placed greater pressure on the RAF to undertake an increased number of air support operations and, as a result, affected their ability to provide general support across the front. The Germans did not, however, have a material superiority in terms of operational availability in any other area.[94] The *Wehrmacht* utilised an operational concept to create a decisive advantage against the enemy. This concept is the *schwerpunkt*, the centre of gravity and point of maximum effort of the attack, and was crucial to the success of the blitzkrieg, where decisive numbers and material superiority were focused at what the attacker wished to be the decisive point of the operation.[95]

As soon as the attack had been confirmed, the Allies put their strategic plan into action and advanced to the Dyle River in Belgium to defend against the expected German attack through Belgium and into northern France in a similar way to the attack in 1914. The first operations conducted by the RAF were reconnaissance sorties around the Dyle sector where the BEF planned to operate.[96] The Allied forces faced little opposition when conducting the manoeuvres.[97] Part of the reason for this was that at the start of operations, the *Luftwaffe* had very little interest in providing close support for the *Heer* (army) whilst it was moving up to its starting positions. Instead, they acted as an interdiction force, concentrating on attacking airfields and aircraft that were on the ground. Through these attacks the *Luftwaffe* were attempting to gain localised air superiority and to seal off the battlefield.[98] The *Luftwaffe* continued their interdiction role on 11 May by attacking Allied communication centres. This resulted in a paralysis of operations in a 'vital area; and on Allied troops advancing or deployed for battle'.[99] The flexibility of command given to junior German army officers in the field was also given to the pilots of the *Luftwaffe*:'Wehrmacht High Command Directives ordering air support for the Army did not specify whether this should take the form of attacks to seal off the battle area or direct support over the battlefield, or a combination of both.'[100] This is a classic example of the German military concept of *Auftragstaktik* or mission command. This concept simply specified to the junior commander what the objective for the mission was and is closely tied to the *schwerpunkt*. It was left to the junior commander to plan and decide how best the mission could be accomplished. The missions conducted by the *Luftwaffe* prior to the German attack at Sedan are a clear demonstration that it was more than simply a tactical level close support force tied organisationally to the army.

Whilst the *Luftwaffe* were conducting their interdiction missions, the *Wehrmacht* were advancing their spearhead Panzer formations through the Ardennes Forest.[101] This part of the Allied sector was poorly defended and was not subjected to the same detailed reconnaissance as the Dyle sector. Part of the reason for this was that the French believed that the

Ardennes was impassable to a modern armoured and mechanised force given the poor road network available:

> Even allowing for the distortions of hindsight, after one has actually explored the terrain, it is hard to comprehend how anyone (except perhaps a *Deuxieme Bureau* officer who had never set foot outside the *Crillon Bar*) could possibly have deemed the Ardennes 'impenetrable' for a modern army. It becomes still more extraordinary when one learns that, in 1938, manoeuvres were actually conducted under General Pretélat (then commander designate of the Second Army) which *exactly* paralleled the German attack of May 1940 [emphasis in original].[102]

Taking Alistair Horne's analysis of pre-war French manoeuvres into account, it is extremely difficult to understand how the idea of the impenetrable Ardennes persisted. One must conclude that, as with the RAF's investigations into the Spanish Civil War, there was a degree of conformational thinking bias within the French High Command.

It was at Sedan and across the Meuse River that close air support had it greatest effects in the Battle of France, but it was an isolated example and should not be taken as indicative of the battle as a whole. The *Wehrmacht* planned to utilise their *schwerpunkt*—Lieutenant Colonel Heinz Guderian amassed his Panzer forces at Sedan squeezing them 'into a combat sector barely ten kilometres wide'.[103] The build-up of German forces around Sedan and stretching back through the Ardennes provided the ideal target for a force specialising in interdiction operations, but the focus for BAFF was in supporting the movement of the BEF to the Dyle.[104] A degree of reconnaissance was conducted around the Ardennes but the results were dismissed as they did not fit into official French thinking—German presence was deemed to be a feint to draw French forces away what was expected to be the main German thrust into northern France through Belgium: 'The French High Command was still clinging to its refusal to consider the passage of the Ardennes as practical despite warnings from French airmen who had seen signs of massive troop concentrations.'[105] Barratt, as head of BAFF, was keen to attack the massive troop build-up, but was denied permission to divert his resources to this sector. The German tailback stretched into Germany itself and the French High Command were still fearful of the potential reprisals that could be inflicted upon the French population if the interdiction missions missed the military targets and instead hit civilians.[106]

The attack on the defences at the Meuse opposite Sedan began on 12 May and the *Luftwaffe* were able to exploit the local air superiority their interdiction missions had given them to the fullest extent.[107] The Germans had also launched an offensive feint when Army Group B advanced towards the Dyle River, confirming the Allies thinking about German strategic intentions. The *Luftwaffe* began its assault across the Meuse aiding Guderian's ground forces. Guderian had also taken the tactical decision that the *Luftwaffe* would provide air support continuously and not group their forces together for 'a massive short attack'.[108] The importance of air superiority has been noted by Byford who also provides some explanation as to why the British army of the interwar period did not grasp just how fundamentally important it was, not only attaining but also retaining it during the course of an operation:

> What had achieved success for the Germans was primarily indirect air support—isolating the battlefield and cutting communications—following the achievement of air superiority, but both of these effects were invisible to the soldier on the battlefield and consequently, not well understood.[109]

The basic tactical and communications doctrine of the RAF mirrored that of the *Luftwaffe*. Both emphasised the importance of the co-location of air and ground headquarters, but only one force put that into practice.[110] The French were faced with grave and potentially fatal problems at Sedan. The forces manning the sector were third-rate, poorly trained conscripts posted there as it was expected to be a quiet part of the line. These forces were older, unused to combat and ill-disciplined. The defensive position from which they were to suppress any potential attack was incomplete as the focus for the French had been on the building of the Maginot Line. Their artillery support was also somewhat diminished as it was felt that if an attack was unlikely, these formations could have a more decisive role to play in other sectors.[111] In any event, the artillery in the sector was quickly neutralised by attack from the air on the evening of 12 May.[112]

The attacks of 12 May were, however, only a preliminary as the full weight of the *Luftwaffe* was brought to bear upon the defenders around Sedan the following day. It appeared to the Allies that these attacks were building upon a surprise success for the Germans, and the air attacks especially were unplanned. In fact, they had been fully planned the previous evening and incorporated into the wider *Wehrmacht* plan for the crossing of the Meuse that day. One interesting aspect of the air support attacks conducted by the *Luftwaffe* is the lack of physical damage they caused the defenders and the defences. Where it had its greatest success, however, was the psychological impact upon the third-rate conscripts. This prevented the French troops from mounting any form of coherent defence and proved to be decisive in what could have been a very hazardous crossing of the Meuse for the Germans:

> These ungainly craft [Ju-87 Stukas] hurtling out of the sky in near vertical dives with their screeching sirens, dropping their bombs with pinpoint precision, systematically destroyed the French defences, wrecking artillery batteries and reducing the French reservists to a state of numb resignation.[113]

As the Allies still believed the offensive around Sedan to be a feint, little was done to counter it, particularly in the immediate aftermath when the Germans had been unable to gain a secure bridgehead over the river.[114] If the opportunity that presented itself to the Allies had been taken in the

> hours after the German crossing of the Meuse they would have found a force of infantry with very little in the way of tank and artillery support and could have contained the attack on the banks of the Meuse. By the end of the 13th May, each Panzer Corps had been able to establish a bridgehead on the far bank of the Meuse.[115]

This was the only offensive action conducted by the *Wehrmacht* where air support played a decisive role.[116] Every other crossing of the Meuse was successfully achieved without the intervention of the *Luftwaffe*.[117]

> Every available plane was being committed to support Guderian that day [13 May], the tactical air strikes on Major General Erwin Rommel's front had been strictly limited, and they could at most have been partly responsible for the chaos which was to exert so disastrous an influence in the mounting of French counter-attacks.[118]

It was through the support of tanks and artillery rather than air power that the other crossings of the Meuse were achieved successfully.

The crossings themselves were not a certainty. The danger of the attack lay in having to cross a vast swathe of open ground when conducting the crossing itself and many German troops were reluctant to do this in inflatable dinghies. In an attempt to spur his troops on, Guderian took a huge personal risk and led the first wave of the attack personally. By the evening of 13 May this potential problem had been neutralised as German engineers had successfully built a series of pontoon bridges across the Meuse allowing armoured formations to cross and prepare to defend against the expected counter-attack.

A planned French reorganisation in the Sedan sector added to the already confused situation, preventing any real organisation of resistance. The 1st Cavalry Division were in the process of withdrawing from Sedan to be replaced by the 18th Infantry Division. The latter had only just taken up their defensive positions and were without anti-tank guns or artillery support.[119]

As has been demonstrated, whilst air support was important to Guderian's crossing of the Meuse at Sedan, it was not a prerequisite for German success. The image of Stuka aircraft conducting raids on troops became burned, to a certain degree, on the collective conscience of the British army at the time and subsequently the public. The possible reasons why this myth has continued to endure will form part of the next chapter. After their success supporting Guderian, the *Luftwaffe* would not have a mass of troops contained within a relatively small area against which to conduct similar attacks.[120] The French cavalry which was engaged with the German feint on the Belgian Plain suddenly found themselves without any form of air support. This was because the majority of the aircraft supplying cover were transferred to conduct attacks around the Sedan region in an attempt to stem the flow of German armour and *matériel*.[121]

The *Wehrmacht* tried to exploit their success around Sedan as quickly as possible to gain maximum advantage from the fact that the Allied forces were off balance and attempting to put their own plans into action.[122] The intention was to sweep across France as soon as possible to reach the Channel coast and pin the Allied forces against the Franco-Belgian border. If successful, such a manoeuvre would cause tensions within the Allied relationship as there was the very real danger of their being cut off from the Channel ports and any means of escape.

However, the offensive also presented problems for the *Wehrmacht*—such a drive would involve an extended and exposed right flank susceptible to counter-attack. This fear was based on the experience of the opening phase of the First World War when the German advance was attacked from the flank by French forces coming from Paris and which resulted in a German defeat at the First Battle of the Marne. Such anxiety permeated the German High Command over this issue (going all the way to Hitler) that in order to prevent a potential disaster after such astounding initial success, several stop orders were sent to Guderian who, realising the opportunity that presented itself, proceeded to ignore them, and at one point offered his resignation if he was prevented from continuing the advance.[123]

The *Luftwaffe*'s task now turned back to interdiction and observation as they acted as flank cover for the advancing German formations.[124] The RAF was forced to watch as the *Luftwaffe* demonstrated what could be achieved by an air force that was able to successfully provide aerial support for land forces. As had been planned, the break out from Sedan caused massive disruption in the French rear, disruption from which they would never recover: 'A chaos of guns, tanks, military vehicles of all kinds, inextricably entangled with horse-drawn refugee carts, covered the roads and verges.'[125] The *Heer* was also assisted in its speedy advance by the Henschel 126 observation aircraft acting in a forward reconnaissance role reporting the movements of Allied troops.[126]

Prior to the German assault at Sedan, the RAF had been ably supporting the BEF in its advance to the Dyle, encountering little resistance and facing very little competition for air superiority around that sector.[127] The reason for this was that the Germans 'were too astute and polite enough to hinder the enemy when he was making a fatal mistake'.[128] BAFF set up their headquarters in line with the thinking in the *Manual of Combined Naval, Military and Air Operations*. Its forward headquarters was located close to the French Commander of *Zone d'Opérations Aériennes Nord* (ZOAN) at Chauny. This was, however, some distance away from the BEF's headquarters which was located at Arras, ignoring the interwar idea of co-location of headquarters.[129]

The first actions of BAFF was, surprisingly, 'low flying bombing raids against enemy columns in Luxembourg'.[130] These attacks were a total failure and added even greater pressure on BAFF to improve its air support capabilities in a short space of time if they were to provide meaningful support to the BEF. BAFF received reports of the German invasion of Belgium and Luxembourg through the Ardennes as early as 09.10 hours on 10 May. Being the junior partner in the alliance, however, meant that in order to initiate any sort of aerial response to this relied upon the permission of the French High Command. This permission was denied to BAFF, and after several hours of deliberating over the unfolding situation, Barratt ordered attacks on the troop build-up on his own initiative and against the wishes of the French.[131]

Even at this stage of the battle, RAF pilots were reporting severe problems flying offensive operations. Despite BAFF conducting as many missions as possible, multiple requests for support were not met due to a lack of resources.[132] There are several possible explanations for why the requests for support could not be met: BAFF may have simply been under-resourced for the tasks they were expected to perform; the BEF may have been making requests for support when it was not necessary, instead of relying on artillery support; the BEF may also have been originally somewhat hoodwinked by the French with regard to how far the French would be able to provide support from the air. Given the attitude of the BEF as a whole to air support, combined with the fact that the French had dedicated few resources to that function, it is fair to conclude that BAFF's failure was due to a combination of these two factors. That is not to say the BAFF had not been under-resourced, but these two issues are of greater importance.

One of the major problems faced was that due to increasing number of refugees on the roads fleeing the advancing German armed forces, picking out military targets and avoiding civilian casualties was extremely difficult.[133] Another difficulty was one that had been raised by Gort prior to the German invasion: 'Even at this early stage of operations, the difficulties of operating against fleeting targets became evident.' The columns against which raids had been despatched proved to have disappeared or to have moved elsewhere by the time the raid reached the area of operation.[134] Reconnaissance had been restricted to the BEF's area of operations until 12 May when it was conducted on enemy troop movements.[135] This reconnaissance revealed to the Allies the true nature and direction of the German offensive. In response to this, Blenheims of the AASF launched attacks around the Maastricht region, taking severe losses. Only two of the nine aircraft that were sent on this mission returned.[136] A section of Battles was sent to attack the pontoon bridges that crossed the Meuse. During this raid, advancing German columns also came under attack.[137]

Full-scale attacks against the German bridges spanning the Meuse did not take place until 14 May, two full days after the Germans had originally begun their assault and with a full day to establish anti-aircraft defences. The Germans had also deployed 'a protective umbrella of Messerschmitts' around the battle area.[138] Generals Gamelin and Georges had agreed late on 13 May that there would be a full air attack on the German positions at Sedan and the Meuse. The responsibility for the attack would be divided with BAFF conducting the morning raids and the French attacking in the afternoon.[139] It would consist of four waves of bombers at approximately three-hour intervals with a fighter escort. Its objective was to be the destruction of the bridges spanning the Meuse, thereby cutting the advancing German forces from their means of supply.[140] Four bridges crossing the Meuse and one crossing the Cheirs River were selected as targets. The result of the morning raid by BAFF was disappointing to say the least. Only one aircraft was able to confirm hitting any of the selected targets.[141] The RAF had investigated the attacking of bridges as early as November 1939 as it was believed that more disruption could be caused to an advancing enemy through their destruction. The problems associated with conducting attacks on these targets were made abundantly clear: 'The penetration [to destroy them] must be obtained by high or medium altitude bombing' as the targets' small size and the anti-aircraft defences that would surround them required greater accuracy.[142]

The attacks of the afternoon, again conducted by BAFF as the *Armée de l'Air* did not have sufficient resources, have been described as a 'modern day charge into the valley of death for the bomber crews'.[143] The forces tasked with defending the bridges were on full alert after the attacks of the morning.[144] The bomber forces detailed to carry out this raid had no real chance of success, but had little option but to try, given the graveness of the situation if the bridges were not destroyed. Barratt was fully aware of the suicidal nature of the mission and asked only for volunteers to conduct it.[145] All of the crews on duty that afternoon volunteered:

> Even if not said in so many words, the sacrifices were made to prevent any further invasion and to save Allied forces. Barratt knew it when he committed his BAFF forces, but he had little option. It has been said it almost broke him.[146]

When the volunteer forces reached Sedan,

> they were set upon by hordes of Messerchmitts and many were destroyed. Others fell to flak and many more were shot out of the sky on the way home; only thirty-one [of seventy-one that conducted the attack] returned. Five days of daylight operations had cost about half the RAF's bomber strength in France, and some squadrons had been taken out of the line.[147]

The losses sustained in the afternoon attack at Sedan, whilst heavy, were not unusual as the AASF had been suffering similar loss rates in the previous days. Barratt had been told by the Air Staff that the losses being incurred could not continue if BAFF was to be an effective force in France.[148] What was becoming clear to all those in BAFF was the obsolescence of the aircraft being used to conduct the attacks. One of the issues that Barratt and

BAFF faced in France was that there were simply not enough escort aircraft to protect the pilots when they were conducting air support missions and this left them vulnerable to the superior *Luftwaffe* fighters.[149] Shortly after Barratt had received his order from the Air Staff, the French government appealed to the new Prime Minister in Britain, Winston Churchill, for more RAF fighter squadrons to be sent to France to aid them in their attempts at defending their homeland. This request was refused as it was believed that those fighter squadrons would be required to defend Britain and would simply be wasted in a hopeless cause if sent to France.[150] The AOC-in-C Fighter Command, Air Marshal Sir Hugh Dowding, felt that the squadrons were vital to the security of Britain and put this view to the War Cabinet on 15 May and furthered his opinion in a letter written the following day. Vincent Orange has described this letter as 'the most famous written by any airman at any time'.[151]

Even though the fighting in France continued for several weeks, the result was never in doubt after the German success at Sedan and the surrounding area. The Allied forces were never able to recover sufficiently to be little more than a thorn in the side of the *Wehrmacht*. One of the major causes of the fall of France in 1940 was a communications system that, already slow and cumbersome, was made even more so because the commanders were 'security conscious [and this] limited their use of radios and forced them to depend on couriers, who were slower'.[152] Whilst the fighting continued, BAFF attacked the extending German lines of communication and supply but caused little disruption to the German advance,[153] which eventually cut the Allied forces' communications and ground troops were no longer able to keep in touch with BAFF or Phantom.[154] BAFF was forced to communicate with the BEF through RAF Hawkinge to provide the support it still required.[155] The almost continual withdrawal of the BEF meant that BAFF lost its aerodromes and forward airfields that had been utilised by the RAF Component. It abandoned Poix and moved to Abbeville, whilst the AASF moved from Rheims to central France.[156] The Air Component withdrew from France between 19 and 21 May.[157] On the same day medium bombers were also withdrawn from active operations due to the heavy losses they had sustained.[158]

After BAFF's withdrawal from France, it found air support far easier to conduct. Utilising the French trunk cable and its own W/T system they were able to maintain 'almost continuous contact with airfields, the French High Command, army formations [who had not been] cut off by the German dash to the coast and the Air Ministry'.[159] The fact the BAFF found air support operations easier to conduct from Britain than they were from

France highlights to a great extent the validity of the army's misgivings over the communications system in France prior to the start of the German invasion. It also confirms that this factor was the key to improving the RAF's capabilities in this area of operations.

The defeat in France was a huge shock to all involved. This was hard enough to take for the protagonists, but was made worse by the speed, manner and completeness of the defeat. Both Gort and Barratt wrote detailed despatches on the performance of their forces in France and these were very different in their tone and analysis of the operations conducted. Both of these despatches have formed part of the analysis of the fighting in France, and it is clear where the lines had previously been drawn, and where they would continue to be drawn as the search for responsibility continued over the summer of 1940.

Barratt's despatch is a large document detailing the operations of BAFF and its subordinate formations.[160] The tone of the report differs greatly from that of Gort's, and is not that of a recently defeated commander who had lost faith in the formations or systems for which he was responsible. The despatch offered suggestions on how the air support system could be improved but did not believe that it required a radical overhaul as, in the opinion of Barratt, it was theoretically sound.[161] He also reiterated one of the fundamental principles of air power codified by the RAF just after the First World War: one air commander having supreme operational and administrative control over all air forces in a given theatre. This had not been the case in France as Gort had operational control of the Air Component.[162] In Barratt's opinion there was scope for the delegation of command where formations were to co-operate with land forces but an air force officer should remain in overall operational command.[163]

The ACAB and its work came in for special commendation. It had allowed all information and requests for support from French, Belgian and British commanders to be 'collected and assessed, and the necessary bomber and fighter operations ordered'. It also prevented the launching of attacks against friendly targets.[164] The co-location of headquarters of ZOAN and North BAFF Operations Room allowed resources to be pooled, and operations where British fighters escorted French bombers and vice-versa to be planned with relative ease. This again highlights the work done in Britain during the interwar period. Barratt could also see that the centralised control that BAAF gave allowed him to see the broader strategic picture and select targets that were worthwhile whilst not wasting his scarce resources. Whilst he acknowledged that such a centralised command system had its flaws, he noted that some of these could be overcome by not relying on landline communications as the French High Command had done. Given the increased tempo of operations Barratt was of the opinion that a centralised operations room was the only 'organisation, particularly on the defensive [that] can cope with the speed and range of modern warfare or permit the economical and efficient use of all available forces'.[165]

The despatch written by Gort, however, fully reflected the army's attitude towards air support that had developed during the interwar period. The blame for the BEF's failure was laid squarely at the door of BAFF and the RAF. When faced with both reports on the fighting in France, the Air Staff, almost understandably, felt that Barratt's report was the correct interpretation of BAFF's role in France. They argued, and indeed would continue to argue, that the army 'had failed to recognise the new approach being taken [with regard to war] on land' and that this was the fundamental reason behind the completeness of the defeat suffered.[166]

Gort believed, as he had done prior to the start of German operations in France, that there had been a lack of aircraft detailed for army support and that what aircraft had been assigned this task did not provide the 'correct' form of air support for the BEF. In Gort's view, this took the form of a protective umbrella of fighters patrolling the BEF's area of operations to prevent enemy air forces attacking. Gort's overall solution to improving air support capabilities was simply to reorganise the RAF's capabilities based upon his reading of the German model that had been employed in France. As will be demonstrated, both Gort's and the War Office's reading of the German model to provide air support were fundamentally flawed.[167]

The Battle of France had demonstrated serious shortcomings in the RAF's overall thinking about the application of air power at the tactical level in modern warfare. There were, however, certain basic concepts that had survived the battle. The communications system that had been employed would be overhauled but kept to the same basic concepts, and the ASSU would be subject to further trials in order to develop its efficiency in providing air support against time sensitive targets. These developments would take place against the backdrop of the War Office continuing to push demands for its own separate army air arm, as they had done since the end of the First World War. The Battle of France provided the catalyst for the RAF to look again at its air support capabilities in Britain. The major result of this change was the creation of Army Co-operation Command. It was, however, to be created in an atmosphere of mistrust and by an RAF that found itself in a difficult position within the interservice political sphere.

Notes

1. Byford, 'False Start', p. 122.
2. Vincent Orange, *Dowding of Fighter Command: Victor of the Battle of Britain* (Grub Street: London, 2008), pp. 110–21.
3. The major problem of the First World War was not breaking into the enemy defensive system but how to maintain the momentum of operations to break out of the defensive system. This was not investigated by the British army until the 1930s and reflects how the British perceived operations would be conducted during the next major European war. TNA WO 33/1297, Report of the Committee on the Lessons of the Great War (The Kirke Report), October 1932. John Ellis, *Brute Force: Allied Strategy and Tactics in the Second War* (Andre Deutsch: London, 1990), p. 6.
4. More information on Operation Dynamo can be found in John Masefield, *The Nine Days Wonder: Operation Dynamo* (Heinemann: London, 1941). Patrick Oddone, *Dunkirk 1940: French Ashes, British Deliverance: The Story of Operation Dynamo* (Tempus Publishing: Stroud, 2000). W. J. R. Gardner (ed.), *The Evacuation from Dunkirk: Operation Dynamo, 26 May–4 June 1940* (Cass: London, 2000).
5. Alfred Price has looked at the history of the Ju-87 as an aircraft in great detail, in 'The Rise and Demise of the Stuka', *Air Power Review*, 3: 4 (Winter, 2000), pp. 39–54. Also see Peter C. Smith, *Dive Bomber: Aircraft, Technology and Tactics in World War II* (Stackpole Books: Mechanicsburg, Pennsylvania, 2008).
6. John Buckley, 'The Air War in France', in Brian Bond and Michael D. Taylor (eds), *The Battle for France and Flanders 1940: Sixty Years On* (Leo Cooper: Barnsley, 2001), p. 111. This is clearly demonstrated in the television documentary *The World at War* (Thames Television, 1973) where in the episode *France Falls: May–June 1940* the emphasis is placed on the role of *Luftwaffe* in supporting the German crossing of the Meuse with no reference to any of the other successful crossings which were achieved without air support.
7. Further details on this debate can be found in the increasing historiography which is summarised here. James S. Corum, *The Roots of Blitzkrieg: Hans von Seeckt and German Military Reform* (University Press of Kansas: Kansas, 1992). Robert M. Citino, *Quest for Decisive Victory: From Stalemate to Blitzkrieg in Europe, 1899–1940* (University Press of Kansas: Kansas, 2002). Robert M. Citino, *The Path to Blitzkrieg: Doctrine and Training in the German Army, 1920–1939* (Lynne Reiner Publishers: Boulder, Colorado and London, 1999). John Mosier, *The Blitzkrieg Myth: How Hitler and the Allies Misread the Strategic Realities of World*

War II (HarperCollins: New York, 2003). J. P. Harris, 'The Myth of Blitzkrieg', *War In History*, 2: 3 (November, 1995), pp. 335–52. Shimon Naveh, *In Pursuit of Military Excellence: The Evolution of Operational Theory* (Frank Cass: London and Portland, Oregon, 1997). Azar Gat, 'British Influence and the Evolution of the Panzer Arm: Myth or Reality? Part I', *War In History*, 4:2 (April, 1997), pp. 150–73. Azar Gat, 'British Influence and the Evolution of the Panzer Arm: Myth or Reality? Part II', *War In History*, 4: 3 (July, 1997), pp. 316–38. Hew Strachan, *European Armies and the Conduct of War* (Routledge: London and New York, 1983). G. D. Sheffield, '*Blitzkrieg* and Attrition: Land Operations in Europe 1914–1945', in Colin McInnes and G. D. Sheffield (eds), *Warfare in the Twentieth Century: Theory and Practice* (Unwin and Hyman: London, 1988).
8. John Buckley, *Air Power*, p. 128.
9. Ernest R. May, Strange Victory: Hitler's Conquest of France (I.B. Tauris: London and New York, 2000), pp. 5–6.
10. Faris R. Kirkland, 'The French Air Force in 1940: Was it Defeated by the Luftwaffe or by Politics?', *Air University Review*, XXXVI: 6 (September–October, 1985), http://www.airpower.au.af.mil/airchronicles/aureview/1985/sep-oct/kirkland.html. Accessed 2 December 2011. Robert J. Young, 'The Strategic Dream: French Air Doctrine in the Inter-War Period, 1919–39', *Journal of Contemporary History*, 9: 4 (October, 1974), p. 67.
11. Buckley, 'The Air War', pp. 111, 117.
12. Melvin, 'The Land/Air Interface', p. 161.
13. Byford, 'False Start', pp. 122.
14. Byford, 'Fair Stood', p. 41.
15. Byford, 'False Start', pp. 122–3.
16. The aircraft that formed the AASF came from No. 1 Group TNA AIR 24/6/9, Order of Battle for the Advanced Air Striking Force, undated *c.*March 1940.
17. TNA CAB 66/3/10, Air Requirements for the Army, Memorandum by the Lord Privy Seal, 2 November 1939.
18. TNA CAB 92/111, Air Requirements for the Army, Memorandum by the Secretary of State for War, 21 October 1939. Alistair Byford, 'The Battle of France, May 1940: enduring, combined and joint lessons', *Air Power Review*, 11: 2 (Summer, 2008), p. 64.
19. TNA CAB 66/3/18, War Cabinet Air Policy, Report by the Chiefs of Staff Committee, 11 November 1939. Kate Caffrey, *Combat Report: The RAF and the Fall of France* (The Crowood Press: Swindon, 1990), p. 17. Brian Bond, *Britain, France and Belgium 1939–1940* (2nd edition) (Brassey's: London, 1990), pp. 14–15. George Forty and John Duncan,

The Fall of France: Disaster in the West 1939–1940 (Guild Publishing: London, 1990), p. 85. Buckley, 'The Air War', p. 121.
20. TNA CAB 66/3, War Cabinet WM (39) Conclusion, 14 September 1939.
21. TNA AIR 14/170, Note on the Employment of the AASF in Support of a Limited Offensive by the French Army in the Saar Area, 7 September 1939.
22. TNA CAB 65/1/2, Conclusions of a Meeting of the War Cabinet, 4 September 1939. The importance of good intelligence for conducting air support operations is covered in Brad William Gladman, *Intelligence and Anglo-American Air Support in World War Two: The Western Desert and Tunisia, 1940–43* (Palgrave Macmillan: Basingstoke and New York, 2009).
23. TNA CAB 65/1/2, Conclusions of a Meeting between General Mouchard and Group Captain Collier and Wing Commander Baker, 1 September 1939.
24. TNA CAB 66/3/18, paragraph 9, 1 November 1939.
25. Hall, *Strategy for Victory*, pp. 43–8.
26. TNA CAB 66/3/12, Air Requirements for the Army, Memorandum by the Secretary of State for Air, 3 November 1939.
27. Hall, *Strategy for Victory*, p. 50.
28. TNA CAB 66/1/33, The Possible Future Course of the War, an Appreciation by the Chiefs of Staff, 18 September 1939. Jordan and Sheffield, 'The British Army and Air Power', p. 76.
29. Hall, *Strategy for Victory* p. 53.
30. TNA WO 106/1597, Memorandum from the War Office to Brassard, 17 October 1939 (emphasis in original was capital letters).
31. The specifications of such an aircraft were not made clear at the time the army made this suggestion but it is possible to gain an understanding of what they may have been by looking at the specifications put forward after the Battle of France for such an aircraft. TNA AIR 39/139, Draft Air Staff Requirements for a Light Bomber for Close Support Duties with the Army, 19 August 1940. Operational Requirements Committee, Minutes of a Meeting to Discuss Operational Requirements for an Aircraft for Close Support Bombing and Tactical Reconnaissance Duties, 9 September 1940. Army Air Requirements (COS (41) 39 (0)), Appendix I Technical Considerations Affecting Army Air Requirements—Specifications, 8 June 1940.
32. TNA CAB 66/3/10, Air Requirements for the Army, Memorandum by the Lord Privy Seal, 2 November 1939. A. D. Harvey, *Collision of Empires: Britain and Three World Wars 1793–1945* (Phoenix: London, 1994 [Hambledon Press: London, 1992), p. 645.

33. TNA CAB 92/11 (LF 39), Air Requirements for the Army, Comments by the Secretary of State for Air on the Memorandum by the Secretary of State for War, 24 October 1939. TNA AIR 10/5547, AHB Narrative, Air Support, 1955.
34. TNA CAB 65/2, War Cabinet 75 (39), 8 November 1939. The War Cabinet postponed making a decision as to who should have operational control of the AASF at this time.
35. TNA AIR 41/21, The Campaign in France and the Low Countries September 1939–June 1940, I The Move to France.
36. TNA WO 277/34, Historical Monograph Army Air Support and Photographic Interpretation, 1939–1945, Chapter II Air Support in the Battle of France, 1939–1940: The BEF and its Air Support, undated.
37. May, *Strange Victory*, p. 311.
38. TNA CAB 66/1/35, Air Operations and Intelligence Second Weekly Report by the Secretary of State for Air, 18 September 1939.
39. TNA CAB 66/2/38, Weekly Resume No. 6 of the Naval, Military and Air Situation, 12 Noon 5 October to 12 Noon 12 October 1939.
40. Dean, *The Royal Air Force*, pp. 119–20.
41. TNA WO 277/34, Historical Monograph Chapter II.
42. C. E. Carrington, 'Army Air Co-operation, 1939–1943', *JRUSI*, 115 (December, 1970), pp. 37–8.
43. Hall, *Strategy for Victory*, pp. 48–9. Jacobs, 'Air Support', p. 174. Victor Bingham, *Blitzed: The Battle of France May-June 1940* (Air Research Publications: New Malden, Surrey, 1990), p. 25.
44. TNA WO 193/678, Note by the CIGS, 27 September 1939. Jacobs, 'Air Support', p. 174.
45. TNA WO 106/1597, Note by the CIGS on the CAS' Memorandum on Arrangements for Bomber Support for the Allied Army in France, November 1939.
46. TNA AIR 14/170, Letter from Headquarters AASF to Headquarters RAF Component Field Force, 9 November 1939.
47. Ibid.
48. TNA AIR 14/170, Memorandum from Headquarters RAF Component to Headquarters AASF, Channels of Control of the Advanced Air Striking Force and Relations between the Field Force, the Air Component of the Field Force and the Advanced Air Striking Force, 1 November 1939.
49. John Terraine, *The Right of the Line: The Royal Air Force in the European War 1939–1945* (Sceptre: London, 1985), p. 122.
50. Jordan and Sheffield, 'The British Army and Air Power', p. 76.
51. TNA AIR 41/21, The Campaign in France and the Low Countries, September 1939–June 1940, The Formation of the British Air Forces in France. J. R. M. Butler, *Grand Strategy Vol. II: September 1939–June 1941* (HMSO: London, 1957), pp. 153–4.

52. TNA AIR 41/21, The Campaign in France and the Low Countries, The Formation of British Air Forces in France.
53. TNA AIR 24/681, Minutes of Conference held at General Headquarters, 17 January 1940 to discuss certain aspects in connection with the reorganisation of the Royal Air Force in France and the Appointment of an Air Officer Commanding-in-Chief, British Air Forces in France. Dean, *The Royal Air Force*, p. 120.
54. TNA AIR 41/21, The Campaign in France and the Low Countries, The Formation of the British Air Forces on France. TNA AIR 24/679, Order of Battle of the AASF, undated *c*.1939.
55. TNA CAB 66/3/27, Air Requirements for the Army in France, Memorandum by the Minister for the Co-ordination of Defence Part I, 2 December 1939.
56. TNA AIR 41/21, The Campaign in France and the Low Countries, The Formation of the British Air Forces in France.
57. TNA WO 106/1596, British Air Forces in France (Report), *c*.December 1939.
58. TNA WO 106/1596, Letter from A. W. Street, Air Ministry to Air Marshal Barratt, *c*.December 1939.
59. Stuart W. Peach, 'A Neglected Turning Point in Air Power History: Air Power and the Fall of France', in Sebastian Cox and Peter W. Gray (eds), *Air Power History: Turning Points from Kitty Hawk to Kosovo* (Frank Cass: London and Portland, Oregon, 2002), p. 150.
60. TNA WO 277/34, Historical Monograph on Army Air Support and Photographic Interpretation, 1949–1945, Chapter II British Air Forces in France.
61. TNA AIR 10/5547, AHB Narrative, Air Support.
62. TNA AIR 41/21, The Campaign in France and the Low Countries, The Formation of the British Air Forces in France.
63. TNA AIR 24/684, Methods of Controlling Air Bombardment from Advanced Headquarters, *c*.April 1940.
64. TNA AIR 24/681, Letter from Headquarters BAFF to Headquarters AASF, 22 January 1940.
65. TNA AIR 24/681, Minutes of a Conference held at GHQ to discuss certain aspects in connection with the reorganisation of the Royal Air Force in France and the Appointment of an Air Officer Commanding-in-Chief, British Air Forces in France, 17 January 1940.
66. TNA AIR 14/107, Operational Instruction No. 3, 11 November 1939. Richards, *Royal Air Force 1939–1945 Vol. I*, p. 110.
67. Hall, *Strategy for Victory*, p. 50.
68. TNA WO 106/1597, Letter from Gort to CIGS, 27 November 1939.
69. Hall, *Strategy for Victory*, p. 44.
70. TNA WO 106/1597, Letter from Gort to CIGS, 27 November 1939.

71. TNA AIR 35/354, BAFF Barratt's Despatch on Operations in France, The Establishment of the Allied Central Air Bureau, July 1940.
72. Hall, *Strategy for Victory*, p. 50.
73. TNA WO 106/1597, Letter from Gort to CIGS, 27 November 1939.
74. Gort would continue to argue for a separate army air force under the army's operational control in late November 1939 whilst discussions about BAFF were ongoing. TNA WO 193/678, Letter from Gort to CIGS, 27 November 1939.
75. TNA AIR 35/354, BAFF Barratt's Despatch, Establishment of the Allied Central Air Bureau, July 1940.
76. Ibid. A report on a Staff and Inter-Communication Exercise conducted in early April 1940 can be found at TNA AIR 24/681, ACAB (Northern Zone) Staff and Inter-Communication Exercise No. 3, conducted 5 April 1940. This is followed by a conference held on the Exercise on 10 April 1940.
77. TNA WO 277/34, Historical Monograph on Army Air Support and Photographic Interpretation, 1939–19454 Chapter II Air Support and the Battle of France, 1939–1940: The BEF and its Air Support.
78. TNA CAB 106/246, Despatches of the Operations of the British Expeditionary Force, 3 September 1939–19 June 1940. Written by GOC-in-C BEF, Lord Gort, 25 July 1940.
79. Hall, *Strategy for Victory*, p. 44. RAFM, Evill Papers AC 74/8, Operations in France, September 1939 to June 1940. WO 277/34, Historical Monograph on Army Air Support and Photographic Interpretation, 1939–1945, Chapter II Air Support and the Battle of France, 1939–1940: The BEF and its Air Support.
80. Barker, *A Brief History*, pp. 62–4.
81. H. J. Parham and E. M. G. Belfield, *Unarmed Into Battle: The Story of the Air Observation Post* (2nd Edition) (Picton Publishing: Chippenham, Wiltshire, 1986 [The Wykeham Press: London, 1953]), p. 14. Peter Mead, *The Eye in the Air: History of Air Observation and Reconnaissance for the Army 1785–1945* (HMSO: London, 1983), p. 154.
82. Parham and Belfield, *Unarmed Into Battle*, p. 14.
83. TNA AIR 35/113, Letter from Festing, MO 7 (War Office) to the Director of Military Co-operation (DMC) (Air Ministry), 20 January 1940. TNA AIR 35/111, Letter from Wing Commander J. Blackford to AOC Air Component Blount, 26 January 1940. Parham and Belfield, *Unarmed Into Battle*, pp. 15–16.
84. TNA AIR 35/111, Letter from Brigadier J. Swayne to Royal Artillery, 11 February 1940. TNA AIR 35/111, Letter from Blackford to Blount, 26 January 1940. Parham and Belfield, *Unarmed Into Battle*, p. 15.
85. TNA AIR 35/113, Instructions for Trials of the Flying Observation Post in France, February 1940, Letter from the Chief of the General Staff to

the French Military Mission at General Headquarters regarding D Flight, 22 March 1940. Parham and Belfield, *Unarmed Into Battle*, p. 16.
86. Dean, *The Royal Air Force*, p. 126.
87. TNA AIR 24/681, Employment of Bombers in the Event of an Enemy Attack on the Western Front, British Air Forces Available, Air Component, 6 March 1940.
88. TNA AIR 24/681, Employment of Bombers in the Event of an Enemy Attack on the Western Front, 6 March 1940. Martin S. Alexander, '"Fighting to the Last Frenchman?" Reflections on the BEF Deployment to France and the Strains in Franco-British Alliance', in Joel Blatt (ed.), *The French Defeat of 1940: Reassessments* (Berghahn Books: Providence, Rhode Island and Oxford, 1998), p. 298.
89. A. D. Harvey, 'The French Armée de l'Air in May–June 1940: A Failure of Conception', *Journal of Contemporary History*, 25: 4 (October, 1990), pp. 451, 460.
90. TNA AIR 41/21, The Campaign in France and the Low Countries September 1939–June 1940, Chapter XII Plans for the Battle: The Air Plan.
91. TNA AIR 20/323, Memorandum of the Employment of Air Forces in Direct Support of the Army, *c*.April 1940.
92. Richard K. Betts, 'Despite Warning: Why Sudden Attacks Succeed', *Political Science Quarterly*, 95: 4 (Winter, 1980–1981), p. 553.
93. Faris R. Kirkland, 'The French Air Force in 1940: Was it Defeated by the Luftwaffe or by Politics?', *Air University Review*, XXXVI: 6 (September/October, 1985), http://www.airpower.au.af.mil/airchronicles/aureview/1985/sep-oct/kirkland.html. Accessed 2 December 2011. Martin S. Alexander, 'The Fall of France', in John Gooch (ed.), *Decisive Campaigns of the Second World War* (Frank Cass: London and Portland, Oregon, 1990), p. 33.
94. Alexander, 'The Fall of France', p. 33.
95. Karl-Heinz Freiser, *The Blitzkrieg Legend: The 1940 Campaign in the West*, trans. John T. Greenwood (Naval Institute Press: Annapolis Maryland, 2005), pp. 156–7. Heinz Guderian, *Panzer Leader* (Penguin Books: London, 2000 [Michael Joseph: London, 1952]), pp. 18–46.
96. Brian Cull and Bruce Lander with Heinrich Weiss, *Twelve Days in May: The Air Battle for Northern France and the Low Countries*, 10–21 May, As Seen Through the Eyes of the Fighter Pilots Involved (Grub Street: London, 1995), p. 51. Gerhard L. Weinberg, *A World at Arms: A Global History of World War II* (2nd edition) (Cambridge University Press: New York, 2005 [1994]), pp. 123–4. Freiser has noted that 'ironically the French would become the victims of the Schlieffen Plan, not in 1914, but in 1940'. *The Blitzkrieg Legend*, p. 93.

97. Forty and Duncan, *The Fall of France*, p. 151.
98. Paul Deichmann, *Spearhead for Blitzkrieg: Luftwaffe Operations in Support of the Army, 1939–1945* (Greenhill Books: London, 1996), p. 106. Smith, *Dive Bomber*, pp. 185–6. Ellis, *Brute Force* p. 12.
99. TNA AIR 41/21, The Campaign in France and the Low Countries September 1939–June 1940, Military Summary, German Air Attack, 11 May 1940.
100. Deichmann, *Spearhead for Blitzkrieg*, p. 124.
101. William L. Shirer, *The Collapse of the Third Republic: An Inquiry into the Fall of France in 1940* (2nd edition) (The Literary Guild: London, 1970 [1969]), p. 610.
102. Alistair Horne, *To Lose a Battle: France 1940* (Macmillan: London, 1990 [1969]), pp. 243–4.
103. Ibid., p. 157.
104. Freiser, *The Blitzkrieg Legend* p. 142.
105. Caffrey, *Combat Report*, p. 39.
106. TNA 35/354, BAFF Barratt's Despatch Part II Work of BAFF Prior to the Land Battle, July 1940. Bingham, *Blitzed*, p. 49. Ronald E Powaski, *Lightning War: Blitzkrieg in the West, 1940* (Castle Books: Edison, New Jersey, 2006 [John Wiley & Sons: Hoboken, New Jersey, 2003), p. 87.
107. Nigel Cawthorne, *Steel Fist: Tank Warfare 1939–1945* (Arcturus Publishing: London, 2003), p. 69.
108. Williamson Murray, *Luftwaffe: Strategy for Defeat* (The Nautical and Aviation Publishing Company of America: Baltimore, Maryland, 1985), p. 41.
109. Byford, 'The Battle', p. 68.
110. James S. Corum, *The Luftwaffe: Creating the Operational Air War, 1918–1940* (University Press of Kansas: Kansas, 1997), pp. 276–7.
111. May, *Strange Victory*, p. 405. Powaski, *Lightning War*, pp. 109–10.
112. Guderian, *Panzer Leader*, p. 106. Freiser, *The Blitzkrieg Legend*, pp. 153–7.
113. Citino, *Quest for Decisive Victory*, p. 269.
114. Philip Warner, *The Battle of France, 1940* (Cassell Military Paperbacks: London, 1990), p. 62.
115. John Delany, *The Blitzkrieg Campaigns: Germany's 'Lightning War' Strategy in Action* (Caxton Editions: London, 2000 [1996]), p. 90.
116. Williamson Murray, 'The Luftwaffe Experience', in Benjamin Franklin Cooling (ed.) *Case Studies in the Development of Close Air Support* (Office of Air Force History, United States Air Force: Washington, D.C., 1990), pp. 92, 94. Murray, *Luftwaffe: Strategy for Defeat*.
117. Murray, 'The Luftwaffe Experience', p. 92.
118. Horne, *To Lose*, p. 330.

119. Williamson Murray and Allan R. Millett, *A War to be Won: Fighting the Second World War* (The Belknap Press: Cambridge, Massachusetts and London, 2000), p. 71.
120. Richard Hallion, *Strike from the Sky: The History of Battlefield Air Attack, 1911–1945* (Smithsonian Institution Press: Washington, D.C. and London, 1989), p. 145.
121. Jeffrey A. Gunsberg, 'The Battle of the Belgian Plain, 12–14 May 1940: The First Great Tank Battle', *Journal of Military History*, 56: 2 (April, 1992), p. 222.
122. Guderian, *Panzer Leader*, pp. 105–9.
123. Ibid., pp. 109–17. Charles Messenger, *The Art of Blitzkrieg* (Ian Allen: London, 1976), p. 148.
124. Guderian, *Panzer Leader*, pp. 112–13. Deichmann, *Spearhead for Blitzkrieg*, p. 143.
125. Murray and Millett, *A War to be Won*, p. 71. Terraine, *The Right of the Line*, p. 130.
126. Robert Jackson, *Air War over France 1939–1940* (Ian Allen: London, 1974), p. 112.
127. TNA AIR 10/5547, AHB Narrative Air Support: Chapter II The Campaign in France, 1940. TNA CAB 106/246, Despatches of the Operations of the British Expeditionary Force, 3 September 1939–19 June 1940.
128. Hall, *Strategy for Victory*, p. 51.
129. TNA AIR 35/354, BAFF Barratt's Despatch, Appendix N, Summary of Dispositions and Operations of BAFF during Various Phases of the Land Battle, First Phase 10–15 May 1940, Dispositions of BAFF, HQ BAFF, July 1940. TNA WO 106/1763, The Work of the Air Component during May 1940, Lessons, *c.*May 1940. Hall, *Strategy for Victory*, pp. 42–3.
130. TNA AIR 24/679, Advanced Air Striking Force, RAF Component and British Air Forces in France, *c.*July 1940.
131. TNA AIR 41/21, The Campaign in France and the Low Countries September 1939–June 1940, Military Summary 10 May. Bingham, *Blitzed*, p. 49.
132. Hall, *Strategy for Victory*, p. 51.
133. Hanna Diamond, *Fleeing Hitler: France 1940* (Oxford University Press: New York, 2007), p. 30.
134. TNA AIR 41/21, The Campaign in France and the Low Countries September 1939–June 1940, Military Summary, 10 May.
135. TNA AIR 41/21, Military Summary Reconnaissance, 12 May 1940.
136. TNA AIR 41/21, Military Summary, Bombing Operations near Maastricht, 12 May 1940. Kate Caffrey disputes the losses sustained in this attack claiming that only one Blenheim returned. *Combat Report*, p. 40.

137. TNA AIR 21/41, Bombing Operations in the Ardennes, 12 May 1940. J. E. Kaufmann and H. W. Kaufmann, *Hitler's Blitzkrieg Campaigns: The Invasion and Defeat of Western Europe, 1939–1940* (Combined Books: Pennsylvania, 1993), p. 211.
138. Bryan Perret, *A History of Blitzkrieg* (Stein and Day: New York, 1983), p. 94.
139. L. F. Ellis, *The War in France and Flanders* (The Naval and Military Press: Uckfield, East Sussex, 2004 [HMSO: London, 1953]), p. 55.
140. Cull and Larder with Weiss, *Twelve Days*, p. 121.
141. TNA AIR 41/21, The Campaign in France and the Low Countries September 1939–June 1940, Military Summary, Bombing Operations near Sedan, 14 May. Cull and Larder with Weiss, *Twelve Days*, pp. 122–3.
142. TNA AIR 14/107, Notes on the Attack of Armoured Fighting Vehicles (AFVs) and Mechanical Transport on Roads and the Attack of Railways, 1 November 1939.
143. Cull and Larder with Weiss, *Twelve Days*, p. 126.
144. Perrett, *A History*, p. 94.
145. Jackson, *Air War*, p. 54.
146. Bingham, *Blitzed*, p. 64.
147. J. E. Johnson, *Full Circle: The Story of Air Fighting* (Cassell Military Paperbacks: London, 2001 [Chatto & Windus: London, 1964]), p. 116.
148. Caffrey, *Combat Report*, pp. 44–5.
149. Richards, *Royal Air Force Vol. I*, p. 114.
150. TNA AIR 2/4474, Letter from Sholto Douglas to Bomber Command, 4 June 1940.
151. Orange, *Dowding*, p. 159.
152. May, *Strange Victory*, p. 449.
153. Warner, *The Battle*, p. 79.
154. TNA WO 277/34, Historical Monograph on Army Air Support and Photographic Interpretation, 1939–1945, Operations of the BEF and Air Component during the Battle of France. Hall, *Strategy for Victory*, p. 52.
155. TNA CAB 106/246, Despatches of the Operations of the British Expeditionary Force 3 September–19 June 1940. Hall, *Strategy for Victory*, p. 52.
156. TNA AIR 10/5547, AHB Narrative Air Support Chapter II The Campaign in France, 1940. Hall, *Strategy for Victory*, p. 52.
157. TNA AIR 35/354, BAFF Barratt's Despatch, July 1940, 2nd Period—15 to 22 May, 1940, Dispositions of BAFF.
158. TNA AIR 41/21, The Campaign in France and the Low Countries September 1939–June 1940, Bombing Operations near Arras, 16 May 1940.

159. Hall, *Strategy for Victory*, p. 52.
160. TNA AIR 35/354, BAFF Barratt's Despatch, July 1940.
161. Hall, *Strategy for Victory*, p. 53.
162. Ibid., pp. 42, 49.
163. TNA AIR 35/354, BAFF Barratt's Despatch, July 1940, Part V—Conclusions and Recommendations, Command.
164. Ibid.
165. Ibid.
166. Hall, *Strategy for Victory*, p. 53.
167. TNA CAB 106/246, Despatches of the Operations of the British Expeditionary Force, 3 September 1939–19 June 1940. Written by GOC-in-C BEF, Lord Gort.

CHAPTER 3

The Creation of Army Co-operation Command

The debate over the development of tactical air support in Britain, which the RAF at least thought had been settled with the agreements reached with the War Office when war was declared, continued with increased vigour. The army in Britain still clung to the idea first put forward by Gort that the BEF had failed due to the lack of a proper form of air support. Both services launched detailed investigations into the defeat in France. As may be expected given the wildly different opinions on air support, these inquiries reached very different conclusions on how best to ensure any future expeditionary force was fully supported from the air. The army's investigation focused mainly on the BEF but did also look at air support and its effects on the BEF's ability to fight effectively in France. Hall has argued that the fundamental issue that needed to be settled in the wake of the Battle of France, was 'who should control aircraft on the battlefield?'[1] As has been demonstrated in the previous chapter this was something that the RAF believed had been settled prior to the conflict. However, the army reopened the issue and continued to press claims for an army air arm under their operational control. It was an issue that would not be fully resolved in Britain until the invasion of the continent in 1944.[2] Army Co-operation Command was to play a vital role in this resolution.

Given its combat experience in France and perceiving the decisive nature of close air support, the army was convinced of the necessity of commanding their own air arm in a modern theatre of war.[3] With the evacuation of the BEF from France and the latter's occupation by a hostile power,

© The Author(s) 2016
M. Powell, *The Development of British Tactical Air Power, 1940–1943*,
DOI 10.1057/978-1-137-54417-9_3

83

the strategic, industrial and economic direction of the Second World War had changed dramatically. The RAF found itself in a very difficult position after the Battle of France, particularly in the political sphere of interservice relations. The investigations into the Battle of France, and this political pressure meant that the RAF had to at least appear to be prioritising the development of tactical air power in Britain—this would placate the army and prevent the creation of an army air arm, an issue that went against the fundamental principles of air power identified after the First World War.[4] The Battle of France led to a deterioration in relations between the Air Ministry and War Office. Despite this, both services realised, after the shock of defeat in France, that they would have to work more closely to fully resolve the problems. The idea of the creation of an Army Co-Operation Command within the RAF was, in fact, a War Office and not Air Ministry idea. This potential new command would, in the mind of the War Office, be an expert command solely responsible for the development of army co-operation in Britain both in theory and in practice.

Although devised by the War Office, the Air Ministry was responsible for the creation and structure of the new command. Under huge interservice political pressure the RAF were forced to create an organisation whose sole aim was the development of tactical air power, with a special focus on the development of a communications system that would allow any future expeditionary force to call for air support on an impromptu basis. The RAF hurriedly created Army Co-operation Command to demonstrate to the War Office how seriously it took air support and its development. Army Co-operation Command was also, however, created to be a toothless tiger. Despite this, its existence would foster an atmosphere that allowed better relations to develop and, more importantly, allow the army to see first-hand the operational level impact tactical air power could have. The Air Ministry were concerned that such a command could easily become an army air arm and its operational abilities were deliberately restricted to prevent this from becoming a viable option. To support these arguments, this chapter will analyse discussions that took place between the Air Ministry and War Office regarding the creation of the Army Co-operation Command reports from the RAF and army, and the joint experiments that were conducted to develop an impromptu close support ability.

The new command was deliberately created as a non-operational command whose responsibility for the development of tactical air power was in the realm of experimentation only. It would have no input in further developments after this basic experimental stage. Carrington has claimed that 'From the beginning there was an air of unreality in the role of Army Co-operation Command.'[5] It is arguable that the RAF created Army Co-operation Command in such a way that it would develop procedures and strategies devised from exercises with ground forces without having to conduct active operations. It was also not expected that the RAF would have to conduct such support operations for several years given the bleak strategic outlook. With the Germans dominating the Channel and Atlantic coasts, and the army having been forced to leave most of its equipment in France, the focus was on preventing any possible invasion attempt and not preparing for continental operations. The RAF looked to limit the role Army Co-operation Command played with the army to keep its resources centralised within its own framework. Carrington has further argued that the 'RAF's solution to [to army co-operation] was to tuck the matter away … with the cordial support of … the army'.[6] Despite these restrictions, Army Co-operation Command was able to play a vital role in the development of tactical air power.

There is no doubt that the War Office was keen to see the creation of an organisation whose sole focus would be on air support. How far they were aware of the very real and severe limitations that were placed on Army Co-operation Command is open to question. As will be demonstrated in subsequent chapters, the War Office were not happy with the way in which the Air Ministry created Army Co-operation Command and pushed for it to be given a wider role and for it to become an operational command. The War Office's initial enthusiasm for Army Co-operation Command as well as the RAF's intentions to placate the War Office, can be seen clearly in the discussions that took place within the Air Ministry on how the new command was to be organised.[7] The fear of potential invasion, combined with the catastrophic defeat suffered in France, led to a renewed impetus to establish a system that could provide the required support on an impromptu basis to forward formations in the field. As Brad Gladman has stated, 'The events in France in 1940 provided the impetus for army/air co-operation that had not existed in Britain throughout the interwar period.'[8] That this impetus existed during the interwar period has been demonstrated in Chapter 2, but there can be no doubt that the events of 1940 sharpened the focus of both the Air Ministry and the War Office.

Gort was invited to give his account of the Battle of France prior to the army setting up its own internal investigation.[9] This provided Gort with the opportunity to develop the line of argument he had put forward in his despatch from the field.[10] He spoke little of air support—this omission spoke volumes to the War Cabinet and led to the setting up of an internal investigation under the chairmanship of General Sir William Bartholomew. This investigation was the army's major search for responsibility for their defeat in France.[11] The fact that the War Cabinet did not request Barratt, as commander of BAFF to speak with them demonstrates that they were satisfied with the evidence given by Gort as to why the BEF had been so roundly defeated. The remit of the committee was to investigate why the BEF had suffered such a catastrophic defeat. This would also include examining the actions of the RAF in France. It was the findings of the Bartholomew Committee that placed the RAF in such a difficult position and increased the interservice political pressure on them to be seen to be doing more to develop tactical air power in Britain.

The Committee and its chairman, however, launched their work with one major blunder—the investigations pre-judged the doctrine, training and organisation of the BEF, assumed that it was sound and concluded that it did not require major modification. All that was needed was 'new and better equipment'.[12] The reality was that the defeat in France had been due to a 'variety of reasons ... such as the paucity of its troops, equipment and air support, and a poor allied plan'.[13] The Committee also took the War Office's ideas and interpretations of what air support should consist of to be the correct ones. The blame for the defeat in France, in the War Office's eyes was the lack of an army-controlled and administered air arm, with aircraft that had been designed specifically to conduct this role—dive-bombers.[14] W. A Jacobs has commented that the defeat in 1940 had a two-fold and contradictory effect: 'It greatly strengthened the Army's moral case; after all they had fought and lost without adequate air support even if that difficulty did not explain the whole of their failure.'[15] This was especially the case for the Committee's chair, Bartholomew.

Unless the War Office deliberately selected Bartholomew to 'do a job for them' in chairing the investigation into the fighting in France, his selection is open to justified criticism: 'General Bartholomew [was] an officer who had been renowned in the interwar period for his undisguised hatred of the RAF'.[16] Whilst he was serving as the Commandant of the Imperial Defence College, from 1929 until 1931, he had been posted overseas due to his negative attitude towards the RAF and joint service solutions and what air support any potential expeditionary force would require.[17] The Committee's evidence was gathered almost exclusively from army officers. The only senior airman to go before it was Blount and there is little evidence from the report that the evidence he gave was considered in the final findings and conclusions of the inquiry. Despite it being a Committee established to investigate the fighting of the BEF, air support was one of the dominant themes to be found within its pages.[18]

Despite the many failings and flawed conclusions of the Bartholomew Report, which will be subject to analysis below, it did put forward certain ideas that reflected the soldiers' experience on the ground. The report argued that the focus of the *Luftwaffe* was on shattering the morale of the enemy rather than on the physical destruction of troops or their defences.[19] The report also argued, basing its opinion upon despatches received from formations in France, that air support had been the single most important factor in the breakthrough of the *Wehrmacht* across the Meuse.[20] This conclusion must be questioned, based on the analysis of the attack in the previous chapter and on available research by other historians. The Committee took the isolated example of the support provided by the *Luftwaffe* for Guderian's forces at Sedan and extrapolated this to apply to all the breakthroughs across the Meuse. The Committee's focus on the potential psychological effects of tactical air power on ground forces (strongly slanted in the BEF's favour), meant the RAF were faced with a very difficult defence of their policy not to provide an almost continual protective fighter umbrella over the zone of operations:

> The magnificent work done by the RAF in the face of German numerical superiority is appreciated by all. The committee would, however, like to point out that by the nature of things, *neither the actual bombing carried out by the RAF in support of the BEF nor its effects was seen by the man in the field. All day he saw swarms of enemy bombers escorted by fighters and suffered from their attack. Unlike the German soldier, he had never seen aircraft closely co-operating with him to defeat his own particular enemy opposite him. All this had a very definite effect on morale and gave the impression that the enemy superiority was complete and that our own air force hardly existed* [emphasis added].[21]

Whilst it must be acknowledged that the soldier on the ground felt isolated due to attack from the air as the RAF did not have the will or the resources necessary to protect the infantry, there is no mention of how the *Luftwaffe* were able to gain aerial superiority. BEF infantry felt that they alone were facing the brunt of the German onslaught as they did not and could not be aware of the interdiction missions being conducted many miles away by the RAF.[22] The focus of the report was simply on the results of this dominance, not how it came about, and demonstrates what is one, among many, fundamental misinterpretations of how air power functions at the tactical and operational levels. Also, the idea contained within the report that the BEF suffered the onslaught of the *Luftwaffe* alone through almost continual attacks is simply untrue, as the focus for the German air force after the breakthrough at Sedan was on reconnaissance and flank protection. The report did, however, provide the committee with a useful example with which to strike at the ideas of the RAF. In a report written by the RAF that examined air support operations, it is highlighted that

> Most of the bomber attacks both by day and by night, were directed against German formations which were passing through the areas originally defended by the French 9th Army. In consequence, their actions would be completely unknown to the troops of the BEF who would see nothing of them.[23]

The vulnerability that must have been felt by the soldiers of the BEF is understandable, especially given the rumours that must have been spreading like wildfire through the lower formations. In order to prevent this occurring again, the report put forward a recommendation that again demonstrates a fundamental misunderstanding of air power's inherent flexibility and the difficulties for an air force operating against an enemy who controls the skies. It recommended that in future operations 'the RAF must "show the flag" to the troops in forward areas—even at the expense of other tasks—by carrying out some bombing with existing machines in sight of our lines'.[24] As Byford succinctly noted, 'What delivered success for the Germans was primarily indirect air support—isolating the battlefield and cutting communications—following the achievement of air superiority, but both of these effects were invisible to the soldier on the battlefield and consequently, not well understood.'[25] By focusing on the performance of the RAF rather than on that of its own forces, the report may have been attempting to divert attention away from the fragility of morale that had existed in the British army prior to their embarkation to France. This morale was even weaker after the months of inactivity of the phoney war and the completeness of the defeat suffered at the hands of the Germans.[26] A focus on the failings of the RAF and its ability to provide the BEF with air support provided a quick and convenient scapegoat for the War Office.

The conclusions reached in the report itself were based on a substantial misreading of the basic concepts of how the Germans conducted operations. The first section of the report compared British and German operations, including tactics, organisation and material management.[27] It has been described as 'particularly instructive … for historians because of its failure to distinguish the seminal features of the Wehrmacht's new Blitzkrieg tactics'.[28] The report stated that, 'In spite of the enemy's superiority in materials, on no occasion were we forced to relinquish the main position by a frontal attack against the BEF.'[29] The committee regarded German operations through the filter of their own operational and tactical ideas and failed to grasp an understanding of German tactics that sought to bypass enemy points of resistance and look for gaps in the defensive system through which they would pour the majority of their forces in order to attack the enemy's C3 system. Although the German tactic of probing enemy defensive lines for weak spots is discussed, all that is revealed is the committee's misunderstanding of the situation:

> The German method of preparing for attack consists of rapid reconnaissance, which taps along the front line until a weak spot or gap is found. As soon as such a spot is located, the crossing of the obstacle is affected and a small bridgehead made ... Once such a crossing is made the bridgehead is widened to allow the passage of more troops.[30]

Whilst this analysis is correct it does not mention the armoured and mechanised forces that lead the attack and cause such disruption in the enemy rear areas. By ignoring this aspect of the German tactical method, the committee were able to pronounce that British tactical and operational thinking was sound.[31] This overarching false conclusion allowed the report to reach further conclusions on British tactics—it even stated that if the British were to fight the Germans on their own terms they would emerge victorious.[32] That such an obvious statement could pass without further inquiry calls into question the thinking of those on the committee and many of their conclusions. Any armed force fighting an enemy on their own terms should be able to gain victory in the field.

The report fundamentally misunderstood the concept and definition of air superiority and the effects it had on a force battling in the skies against a superior enemy.[33] To those on the committee, and indeed the army as a whole, air superiority was a defensive umbrella of fighters patrolling over friendly forces on the ground.[34] Even if BAFF had the resources to achieve this, it would have been costly in terms of men, machines and fuel. This had been demonstrated during the First World War as the way to gain and maintain air superiority was through offensive action. The report also highlighted several shortcomings in the BEF. It recommended that the army improve its capabilities in motorised transport, wireless communications and mobility. Despite not understanding the specific terminology, the need to gain air superiority to allow an air force to operate effectively was understood. What the committee failed to comprehend was that gaining air superiority was a prerequisite for the *Luftwaffe* to provide ground support:

> There is little doubt that the policy of equipment, organization and training of the enemy has been directed to this end [close support]. Even in the case of 'impromptu' attack it was seldom more than 25 minutes before the call was answered. This indicated not only good organization and communications for the purpose, but the siting of their landing grounds close up behind their own troops. Efforts should be made to simplify and improve our own intercommunications between ground and air for similar purposes … It is imperative to ensure forthwith that a system comparable to that of the Germans should be introduced into our Army and Air Force.[35]

The committee, and the army as a whole, were under the impression that the *Luftwaffe* was simply a close support force that was effectively, although not officially, under the *Heer*'s control. The report made little mention of the interdiction missions conducted prior to the German assault across the Meuse; the focus was simply on the use of aircraft in a close support role. Nor was there an analysis of where the *Luftwaffe* had sited their landing grounds and there was no attempt to link this with what the army co-operation exercises had revealed in the interwar period. The claims made by the report on German actions were most likely based on their performance in Spain rather than in France. The focus of the *Luftwaffe*'s operations in France was in attacking enemy airfields and isolating the battlefield.[36] The focus of the evidence received by the committee was on the supposed impact of close support and not interdiction. The status of the *Luftwaffe* with regard to the *Heer* was poorly interpreted.[37] The idea that the *Luftwaffe* was fully subordinate to the *Heer* allowed the War Office to continue to push their claims for an army air arm under their control.[38]

When looking at the effects of close support, the committee again misinterpreted its impact. The conclusion stated that close support was to be given 'as supporting fire to cover the assault of armoured and, at times, infantry formations'.[39] The committee effectively saw the *Luftwaffe*'s close support work as a flying artillery force, which is what the War Office had been arguing for throughout the interwar period. The supposed impact of the dive-bomber, and the subsequent myth that has grown up and surrounded it, can be seen to begin with the conclusions of the Bartholomew Report.[40] The BEF itself had suffered little in the way of dive-bomber attack while it was in France and their impact overall was greatly over-exaggerated. This led to the War Office continuing its demand for the development of a dive-bomber capability for a close support force for several years.[41] The differences of opinion that existed between the Air Ministry and War Office over the dive-bomber were outlined by Festing:

> the relative failure of our bombers to contribute effectively to the military operations for stopping the advance of German armoured columns was not entirely due to Allied lack of air superiority and lack of adequate numbers of bombers, it was largely due to the inability of our bombers to perform effective bombing tactics which would achieve destruction and demoralisation. Many of our bombers, incapable of diving with their bombs, were destroyed by machine-gun fire from the columns they were attacking … The Air Ministry holds that given air superiority over the battlefield the needs of the Army can be provided by bombers not necessarily expressly designed for a battlefield role.[42]

The army believed that by having an air arm under its control they would be able to develop a dive-bomber capability that could mirror what the *Luftwaffe* had done in France. This would be a balanced force that comprised army co-operation (reconnaissance and observation aircraft), fighter and bomber squadrons.[43] This force composition would continue to be at the heart of tactical air power developments, and the source of bitter fighting between the Air and General Staffs in 1942–3. There were, however, several issues that needed to be overcome if such a formation was to be created and these were discussed by the Air Ministry and War Office.

The first major problem was the lack of fighter aircraft available to form an army air arm, as these aircraft were required for an anti-invasion role and defeating the *Luftwaffe* in the skies over south-east England in the Battle of Britain.[44] The army proposed that a solution to this problem could be found if an army air arm was raised by the army itself, 'starting from scratch, using its own factories, training its own officers, crews and ground personnel, thus making no inroads on RAF resources'.[45] Part of this force would consist of dive-bombers as the War Office believed this was the panacea to any future expeditionary force's close support problems. The Secretary of State for War, Anthony Eden, claimed the development of a potential new dive-bomber, in the form of the American Vultee, 'should go some way to meeting the Army requirements in tactical support'.[46]

That the RAF's focus was well away from the development of army co-operation in the wake of the Battle of France should come as no surprise.

The War Office had little to plan for as the majority of its equipment had been left in France and the prospects of a return to the continent were bleak. In a bizarre turn of events, the only role that the army could prepare for was in defeating a potential German invasion force, but only if the *Luftwaffe* were able to defeat the RAF.[47] With little else to occupy them, the War Office was able to concentrate its attention on the causes of their defeat in France and to advocate how best to ensure that they were not repeated.

The War Office's thinking on this issue, however, was not consistent. One of those whose opinion differed wildly from others was the new CIGS Field Marshal Sir John Dill. Dill wrote to Group Captain H. Fraser at the Directorate of Military Co-operation (DMC), stating that with regard to the close support work conducted by BAFF and the evidence given to the Bartholomew Committee,

> Many officers and men have arrived back from France with a strong feeling that had they only received a greater measure of close support from the RAF they could have achieved more and suffered less. This feeling in the circumstances is probably inevitable, but it would be grossly unfair to the RAF if it were translated into statements that the RAF had in any way failed the Army during recent operations. The RAF had gone all out, and what their fighters have achieved has been limited only by distance and the numbers of aircraft available.
>
> Important lessons have been learnt about the co-operations which the Army needs from aircraft and we shall profit from these lessons.[48]

In the letter, Dill also criticised the evidence given to, and as a result the conclusions reached by, the Bartholomew Committee:

> criticisms of the RAF, in many cases based only on local knowledge is not only unjust but also prejudicial to the interests of the Army. It is important that this criticism should be checked and you and all other officers should do all you can to check it.[49]

In a letter to Fraser, Festing showed a perception that was missing from the Bartholomew Report, highlighting the fundamental problem that had affected close support operations in France, which the RAF had found difficult to explain or deny in the aftermath of the fighting: 'the time lag between the call for support and the arrival of aircraft'.[50] A concluding memorandum identified the cause of this problem:

> Although the control of the British Air Forces in France has been designed as a result of a great deal of thought and controversy it did not provide an answer to the problem. This was in no doubt primarily due to its supreme

dependence on a complex system of communications and to the general disorganisation caused by the rapid advance of the enemy.[51]

The German air support control system was also considered within this memorandum, and the lack of understanding of their methods is clear, along with the implications this lack of understanding had for the army's demands for a separate air arm.[52]

> The primary role of the German Air Force is to get the Army forward. Exact details are not known of the system of communications but the organisation is certainly fluid. Air strength can be quickly concentrated as and where required. On occasions it is probable that armies and possibly corps have direct command. The results are certainly immediate and effective and several wireless intercepts showed that demands for support were answered in as short a space of time as half an hour.[53]

The AHB study on air support in the Second World War highlights just how difficult it would be for the army to create and develop its own air arm in 1940: 'A specialised Army Support Force could only be provided at great expense to the growing power of the Royal Air Force for strategic action, and there seemed little prospect of defeating the enemy except by the development of a superior bombing force.'[54] This was the strategic outlook of 1940 and is reinforced by a memorandum prepared by Churchill that was given to the War Cabinet and Chiefs of Staff:

> The Navy can lose us the war but only the Air Force can win it. Therefore our supreme effort must be to gain overwhelming mastery in the air. The Fighters are our salvation, but the Bombers alone provide the means of victory.[55]

Investigations into the fighting in France conducted by the RAF, unsurprisingly, reached radically different conclusions to those found in the Bartholomew Report. The RAF and Air Ministry were willing to acknowledge that there had been a lack of aircraft in France and they identified that this was the major issue in why air support had failed to the degree that it had, but not necessarily how the aircraft had been used to conduct that support.[56]

The experiences gained through BAFF's work went further than a basic confirmation that the air support system was structurally sound. There was now a mixed staff of airmen and soldiers who had had recent experience of attempting to conduct air support in active operations against a first-class enemy. These experienced men were now fully available for the RAF to exploit as it looked to further develop air support in Britain.[57] This would be achieved under the auspices of Army Co-operation Command with its joint staff preventing the views of any one service becoming dominant. The reports put forward by the airmen in the wake of France, and after having had time to digest the Bartholomew Report, stated that the fundamental concept of a unified air force was once again under attack from the army. They also believed that the creation of an army air arm would in no way improve the chances of success of a future expeditionary force without first gaining control of the air.[58] The RAF's investigations added further evidence to the fact that the War Office fundamentally misunderstood what was meant by air superiority:

> Experience during the first years of the war confirmed that success in a ground battle depended largely upon air superiority. No carefully balanced force of reconnaissance, bomber and fighter squadrons forming an integral part of each Corps and Army could ensure the success of the land campaign.[59]

One of the greatest successes that came out of BAFF's experiences in France was in signals capability and this will be explored in more detail below through an analysis of the Wann–Woodall experiments. At this time, however, the main focus of the RAF with regard to air support was in relieving the pressure that had been placed upon the service by the scathing criticisms of the Bartholomew Report. In order to achieve this, the Air Ministry placated the War Office by issuing a specification for a new light bomber to conduct close support. The BAFF's Fairey Battles and Lysanders had proved inadequate in conducting such a daylight role to provide support for the BEF. This new close support aircraft was

> to be capable of operating in all parts of the world, to undertake the duties of short range operations in close support of the Army. These duties will include low level bombing and dive bombing; also machine gun fire from heights below 15,000 feet.[60]

However, pressure on the Air Ministry to take a more active role in the development of air support was coming from additional sources. Eden used his role as Secretary of State for War to continue to demand that the RAF become more proactive in this area and to develop a dive-bomber capable of supporting the army, through letters sent to the Sinclair.[61] But there was simply no capacity within the British aircraft industry for any development of this kind, suggesting that any new design might have to be manufactured in the United States (US).

In a conference held in early June at the Air Ministry, the RAF tried to settle the issue of the *Luftwaffe–Wehrmacht* command structure and notes of the conference confirm that the Air Ministry were fully aware of how it operated. It was pointed out that the only air units attached to the *Heer* were reconnaissance formations. Other air formations such as fighter and dive-bomber squadrons could be temporarily allotted to ground formations and it was this system that allowed them to answer the few impromptu requests for air support so quickly.[62] The analysis of the German command system, however, failed to appreciate that it was the communications system itself that allowed the *Luftwaffe* to answer calls for air support so quickly, regardless of the state of attachment of the aerial formations. This was arguably, however, the area where BAFF had its greatest achievement through the establishment of the Phantom signals network combined with the ACAB. This communications network provided Barratt with information from the front line twelve hours ahead of the BEF's GHQ, and up to twenty-four hours ahead of the French Grand Quartier Général.[63] The fighting in France had overwhelmingly shown

> The advantage of having a single authority for the command and administration of all Royal Air Force formations in a theatre of war was clearly demonstrated and indicated the need for one supreme commander of all the air forces in one theatre with a fully representative headquarters.[64]

Due to the huge interservice political pressure as a result of the War Office's investigations into the fighting in France, and despite tactical air power development being low on the list of its priorities, the Air Ministry felt forced to at least appear to be doing something as quickly as possible. It was agreed between the Air and General Staffs as early as 2 August that experimental training with No. 22 (Army Co-operation) Group would take place in Northern Ireland, not only demonstrating how much pressure the Air Ministry was under, but also the desire of the War Office to create a functioning tactical air power capability without delay. At this time both sides still approached the problems this entailed from their own viewpoints, with little or no unified strategy.[65] These discussions also took place against the backdrop of Fighter Command battling the *Luftwaffe* in the skies above south-east England.

Prior to discussions on how structural changes for the development of tactical air power development were to be achieved, experiments were conducted to develop a communications network that would allow forward land formations of a future expeditionary force to request impromptu air support.[66] With the very real threat of invasion focusing the minds of both services, 'the first steps were taken to reorganise the means of providing and co-ordinating air support'.[67] This was despite the army needing an extended period of time to re-equip and retrain for future operations on the continent. The greatest amount of co-operation between the Air and General Staffs since the beginning of the war emerged in these discussions, demonstrating just how seriously the threat of invasion was taken at the time. The Air and General Staffs agreed in August to place an army officer in charge of the experiments and that he was to be supplied with sufficient staff to conduct the trials. Despite the improvement in relations between the two Staffs, the Air Staff still stuck to their ideas about when close air support should be used on the battlefield: 'It was agreed … that support for the Army by means of Close Support Bombing was not the normal method of support and should not be regarded as such in the future.' The object of the experiments and training was to discover:

(1) The most suitable form of organisation for close support bombers.
(2) Appropriate tactical methods for close support bombers.
(3) Signals installations required for control.
(4) The establishment of Royal Air Force and Army personnel required for a close support bomber organisation.
(5) Methods to be employed by Army formations in obtaining close bomber support.
(6) Times in which support under various circumstances can be given.
(7) Methods of controlling close support bombers and directing them on to targets.[68]

This would be the largest joint training exercise of the war to date. Woodall, the army officer given the responsibility of organising and conducting it had been a member of Barratt's staff in France and was, due to this, highly experienced and versed in the difficulties associated with providing close support for ground forces.[69] That the Air Staff were willing to agree to appoint an army officer demonstrates the pressure they had been placed under over the development of tactical air power. It also highlights the willingness of the General Staff to work more closely with the RAF to improve its capabilities in this area. Despite Woodall being a relatively junior officer, a Lieutenant Colonel, he was in fact one of the foremost experts in the field and was actively endorsed for this role due to his experience—further demonstrating how far the army's attitude had changed since the end of the Battle of France.

Woodall set out some basic thoughts on close support bombing in a memorandum that also contained the ideas that the experiments were to investigate. He identified the critical role of close support bombing as providing 'what is in effect, fire support to the infantry or AFV [Armoured Fighting Vehicle]'. In order to conduct close support effectively, Woodall identified two things that were essential: 'attacking or defending Infantry or AFV [having the ability to] indicate to the close support bomber what it is they wished attacked by them and when', and 'That close support bombers in sufficient concentration can be directed to the objective within the time available, which may be extremely short'.[70] Woodall had identified the crucial aspect missing from BAFF's capabilities in France. The time element had been vital during the fighting in France when information received by the ACAB was often out of date once it had been analysed and the necessary orders given.

This time element also caused difficulties in terms of the risk of friendly fire casualties if friendly ground forces had not been able to advance to a previously determined timetable. Woodall, however, kept to the RAF line with regard to when close support should be utilised on the battlefield. He argued that artillery was better for attacking targets known about or encountered at initial planning stages of set-piece attacks. Close support should be kept back in order to engage targets that 'could not be foreseen when the attack was planned or for giving support when the Infantry of AFV had advanced beyond the powers of artillery to assist them'. This had been and was a fundamental principle in the RAF's doctrinal thinking about the application of close support. Through his experiences in France, Woodall was able to identify that the simplest and easiest way to control requests for impromptu support was through the utilisation of W/T or R/T. These requests for support would be received by a central Close Support Bomber Control (CSBC), similar in composition and working practice to the ACAB.[71] Forward communications formations would accompany advanced ground forces to provide the communications link between these formations and the ACAB in a similar fashion to Phantom.

Woodall also made suggestions about how to improve the efficiency and capabilities of the ACAB, based on the problems they had faced whilst in France. Having troops communicate with advanced headquarters was not an original suggestion to improve communications as it had been identified in the interwar army co-operation exercises. The methods employed whilst in France to inform aircraft already in the air where the support was required and in what quantity had been subject to varying results. Woodall suggested that this was mainly down to a lack of clear procedure understood by both airmen and ground troops. Such a procedure should be developed through the experiments to indicate 'the targets to be attacked, our own troops and the timing of the support to be given'.[72] Woodall still had to deal with the most contentious issue that had surrounded aerial troop cover since the formation of the RAF: who commanded the aircraft designated to close support. With the army continuing to argue that they should have overall control, Woodall appeared to concur when he accepted that 'On broad principles the military commander fighting the battle is responsible for the appropriate allocation of all his resources of which the close support effort may be an important part.' As he continued, however, he noted that

> just as *the military commander fighting the battle controls his artillery response to sudden calls by directives issued before the battle rather than saying how many rounds should be fired on a given target when an emergency arises, so the minute to minute control of close support bombers may have to be delegated to a more subordinate officer who can concentrate exclusively on that task in accordance with the higher commander's policy* [emphasis added].[73]

Similarly, as the military commander did not have direct control over other subordinate arms within the army, such as artillery, the army's demands for the control of close support by the highest military commander was not reflected in their willingness to allow other arms to be controlled by subordinates. Woodall suggested a solution to this problem that contained such a degree of common sense that it had probably never occurred to either of the services as they fought to gain or retain control of tactical air power. It would allow the military commander to lay down the overall policy for the battle but the decision in answering impromptu requests for support would be left to the joint staff at each individual CSBC. The staff officers would be briefed on the overall plan and would be able to direct air resources accordingly. Each CSBC should also be created in such a way as to make it as mobile as possible.[74] Woodall also reiterated a suggestion that had been made several times in the army co-operation reports. Each CSBC 'should be adjacent to the headquarters of the Military Commander fighting the battle'.[75] That this was repeated as a recommendation again calls into question how much attention had been paid to the army co-operation exercises of the interwar period.

Woodall also spent a lot of time considering the training for crews that would be necessary prior to the experiments beginning. The focus of Woodall's thinking was something that proved to be a consistent problem while he was in France and would require dramatic improvement if air support was to function effectively in the future: the rapid briefing of crews whilst they were in the air. Woodall believed that the issue lay not in how the pilots were briefed, but by improving the observational skills of the pilots themselves. In Woodall's thoughts, the issue could best be resolved by training pilots to a standard where they could conduct the missions they had been assigned after they had been given the co-ordinates of the target and the approximate position of the ground forces requesting the support. Woodall also considered how the new CSBC should look organisationally, and he felt that the experiments themselves, where several organisational types would be trialled, would show which was the most effective. As a basic guideline framework, however, he suggested that each CSBC should include a 'senior army officer who can interpret a general directive of the amount of support to be given to successive calls for assistance as these come in' and 'a senior Royal Air Force Officer who can implement demands by ordering bombers from appropriate stations to attack'.[76] This was to be a joint service approach, at the mid-level of command, to improve the air support capabilities of the RAF in preparation for future operations on the continent.

The experiments were to be conducted with two squadrons of Battle aircraft that were stationed in Northern Ireland.[77] Given that this was primarily an exercise to trial new signals arrangements the choice of aircraft mattered little, despite the Battle's obsolescence being fully demonstrated in France. A joint memorandum written by the Air and General Staffs confirmed Woodall's foresight on appropriate concentration of firepower within potentially short time frames[78] The pressure felt by the Air Staff is once again demonstrated by the fact that they were willing to allow the use of the term dive-bomber in a joint publication, despite the reluctance to sanction the development of such an aircraft. It also highlights that in order to foster better relations between the two services it was perhaps pointless to argue about terms used for aircraft in a joint publication.[79] It is, however, interesting to note that in a draft memorandum written by the General Staff in mid-August 1940 with a subtitle of 'The Task of Dive Bombers in Land Operations', the word 'Dive' had been replaced with 'Close Support' in the final version, again demonstrating the change in attitude in the War Office as a whole as well as within the Air Ministry.[80]

Woodall's RAF partner for the experiments that took place between 17 and 28 September 1940, was Group Captain A. Wann. Wann would have been well known to Woodall as they had both served as part of Barratt's staff in BAFF.[81] One of their first joint statements made in their final report on the exercises makes for very interesting reading and is particularly instructive in demonstrating how the two approached the exercises. Both were reluctant to look to the recent fighting in France lest it led to 'superficial lessons being learned … and as a consequence too much being expected from close support bombing'.[82] Despite this statement, certain presumptions, based on a study of the *Luftwaffe*'s close support technique were incorporated into the experiments. Woodall's study of the German methods had led him to conclude that, unlike what both the General and Air Staffs believed, the Germans did not have the ability to call for impromptu air support once they had begun their attack. Any close support attacks conducted were based on plans drawn up the previous evening with the *Heer*. Planning and good staff work were the key to planned air support and this goes some way to explaining why close support had only been available for one German crossing of the Meuse. This was where the *Wehrmacht* planned on placing the bulk of its forces and it, therefore, required all available support from the *Luftwaffe*.

Woodall wanted to take his ideas about German tactical, communication and planning methods and combine them with the RAF's development of Phantom to create a system that functioned similarly to the *Luftwaffe*'s but which also had a far better capability. Woodall believed that the key to impromptu air support lay in a good signals communication system. Wann and Woodall were at pains to point out in their final report that due to the difficulties of conducting air support operations, they should not be considered by the army as a standard procedure. Artillery should form the basis of support for land forces and close support should only be considered when formations had outrun artillery cover. By utilising air support in this way certain dangers, such as the potential for friendly fire, would all but be removed. It would also increase the margin of safety for pilots in what could still be a very dangerous role to conduct. Close support was unique as an attacking form, but relatively brief when compared to the sustained attack that could be delivered by artillery.[83]

The biggest development that emerged from the experiments was the creation of the CSBC. The experiments had, however, shown that in principle it was far more economical, both in terms of manpower and equipment, to allot squadrons to specified forward formations. The reason why this was not done was due to the lack of available aircraft. As this was not going to be resolved in the short or medium term, it was not practicable to put into place.[84] When the numbers of aircraft were available the most efficient system had already been discovered and so could be put into practice with little trouble. To allow what close support aircraft were available to attack targets that would assist the overall plan the most, requests received from front line units would be passed to a centralised organisation, the CSBC. The CSBC would then weigh up each request and allot available squadrons to the most important targets.

The experiments also highlighted what the real Allied weaknesses were. The major failing was a lack of defensive capability both on the ground and in the air: 'German aircraft were able to operate over a wide area in which there were no defences'. The *Luftwaffe*'s control of the skies over France was also highlighted as one of the key reasons for their success in supporting the *Heer* and the completeness of their victory in such a short space of time. By attaining air superiority, the *Luftwaffe* had been allowed to 'attain both rapidity and precision in support which would have been quite impossible in a campaign in which the enemy possessed defences against aircraft and our own attacking aircraft were limited in numbers'.[85] Wann and Woodall were able to explain the effects of not having air superiority, and the impact it had not only on friendly air forces but on friendly ground forces operating in the way in which they would like. This report on the experimental training in Northern Ireland released some of the pressure faced by the RAF in the wake of France and the Bartholomew Report by confirming one of the basic principles of air power.

The report also gave details of how close support functioned—its capabilities and its limitations in the field. This was mainly aimed at the ground forces so that they would be fully aware of what to expect from close support and would restrict fatuous requests for support allowing it to be applied in the most efficient manner possible.[86] By highlighting the limitations of close support, particularly when applied in a defensive role, the Air Staff hoped to demonstrate how inefficient the General Staff's idea of having aircraft continually over the battlefield as a protective umbrella for the land forces distributed in penny packets was.[87] That idea, if employed, would have removed the inherent flexibility that air power had to conduct attacks on any part of the battlefield within a reasonable amount of time, as the Wann–Woodall trials were attempting to achieve.

The trials themselves consisted of a series of signals exercises that would demonstrate the most efficient communication system to allow forward formations to request close support on an impromptu basis. One of the problems with the Phantom and ACAB system used in France was that it was one-way only—there was no reverse communications system in place to notify troops making support requests if they had been successful. This was vital for troops to know—acceptance or denial might have serious repercussions for their situation on the ground. To achieve this, a closed loop system was required. During the trials, mobile forward formations were attached to advanced formations. These mobile forward formations could communicate with the CSBC and pass on requests for support. Information was kept as brief as possible to improve speed and efficiency—the nature of the target that was to be attacked and when the support was required.[88] The communications system was to be flexible enough to 'permit of the bomber effort being at the disposal of formations being varied throughout operations'.[89] The report also considered the problems that excess traffic on the communications network might cause and how far this would restrict the efficiency of the system as a whole. To prevent this and to allow the system to function at maximum possible efficiency on what was designed to be a special system of wireless communications, traffic that did not originate from the forward 'tentacles' requesting support, had to be kept to a minimum.[90]

With the CSBC appearing to be the most efficient system available given the wider strategic circumstances, the requirement to establish a number of mobile forward formations meant that CSBC required the means to request this support in the field. Wann and Woodall felt that 'a pool of some twelve Army wireless sets belonging to the Control to permit of nine lower formations being given the means of indicating targets (these forward formations were described as tentacles)'.[91] One CSBC could handle the requests of several tentacle formations with relative ease. This added to the efficiency of the system as a whole as one CSBC could decide the air support requirements for a single zone of operations in line with the overall plan laid down by the senior military commander.

Through their trials in Northern Ireland, Wann and Woodall had 'identified the fundamental weakness of the British air-support method as insufficient contact between Army and RAF staffs, exacerbated by the physical separation of headquarters and the lack of a reliable communications network.'[92] The major recommendations that came out of the their experiments were 'the need for specially trained and equipped units for close support; a specially trained army staff able to act as liaison officers between air and army headquarters; some joint type of command post; and a reliable communications system'.[93] The report and the results and developments that emerged from it, have been described as 'one of the outstanding successes of the war'.[94]

In a further example of the change in attitudes at the Air Ministry and the War Office, both accepted the main recommendations of the report almost as soon as it was completed.[95] The most important of these was the creation of the CSBC. Carrington expanded the system by suggesting that reconnaissance aircraft should be placed on the same signals network already being used by the CSBC. This would provide a further aerial tentacle offering more information on targets and identifying potential new ones that could be attacked.[96] These trials were refined and continued under the aegis of Army Co-operation Command and conducted in Northern Ireland with squadrons of 75 Wing.[97] The Wann–Woodall report was the blueprint for close support development in Britain and provided the theoretical basis to guide the initial developments that had been made in the Western Desert. Further discussions and trials took place regarding the signals to be used for communication between forward formations and the CSBC, and the CSBC and aerodromes. Responsibility for providing the equipment had also been settled—the army organised radios between the tentacles attached to forward formations and the CSBC, and the RAF supplied equipment used between the CBSC and aerodromes. Again, neither service disputed this recommendation. As the system began to be created in Britain, it was agreed that appropriate RAF and army staff could be attached to the CSBCs as they were formed and that those created in England 'should be attached for administration and training to No. 71 Group Army Co-operation Command.[98] The conclusions of the Bartholomew committee allowed the War Office and General Staff to go on to the offensive over air support and force the Air Ministry to face a fait accompli. The work done by Wann and Woodall and the impact of the Battle of France meant that the RAF now had to at least appear to take more seriously requests from the General Staff for the development of tactical air power to be given a higher priority. This included the potential design of specialist aircraft to conduct this role.[99] The Air Staff were willing to compromise to a great extent on this issue in order to prevent the creation of an army air arm, which the RAF still feared was the thin edge of the wedge with regard to its disbandment as an independent force. The General Staff made their arguments for the creation of an army air arm in a detailed note that argued such a force could be created from the War Office's own factories and that they would train their 'own officers, crews and ground personnel' to man the force. The General Staff's opinion was that this new force would in no way make 'inroads on RAF resources'.[100] This belief was naïve at best and disingenuous at worst. The timeframe involved in creating such a force, as well the time needed to acquire the necessary expertise, was the same as when the idea had first been proposed in 1939.

Eden looked for the solution to the army co-operation issue in the settlement that had been reached between the Air Ministry and Royal Navy in the interwar period over naval aviation. He argued that, 'The creation by the Air Ministry of an Army Co-operation Command comparable in status to the Coastal Command would, I believe, be the most effective step which could be taken to ensure the concentration of effort which is required.'[101] The Army Council put forward a suggestion along these lines in order to ensure that the General Staff's requirements regarding the development of army co-operation could be met through the creation of a formation that had the authority of an RAF Command.[102] This is demonstrated in the proposal by the General Staff noted below where the first question asked by the Air Staff was, 'Do we agree with the concept of an Army Co-operation Command?'[103] As this was a matter to be decided by the Air and General Staffs and relations between the two services had improved to such an extent that discussions on the issue were progressing with little problem, the matter never needed to be referred to the War Cabinet.

An Air Staff proposal on the issue began by laying out the responsibilities of the RAF formation that was, at the time, responsible for army co-operation in Britain, No.22 (Army Co-operation) Group. The Group had wide-ranging responsibilities including the following: the administration and training of tactical reconnaissance squadrons with Home Forces; the command of Nos. 1 and 2 Army Co-operation Schools; supervision of the development of the Air OP; and command of No. 111 (Army Co-operation) Wing. The discussions on the General Staff proposal for an Army Co-operation Command mainly focused on the organisation and structure of the command itself. There was little discussion as to whether such a command should be created and so it must be assumed that the Air Staff were, in principle, comfortable with the suggestion. The major issue to be decided was whether this new command should consist of two or three groups. The three-group structure would consist of 'an operational group comprising the army co-operation squadrons [already within the RAF], a training and development group and the proposed Photographic Reconnaissance Group (PRG). The two-group structure would be the same but minus the PRG.'[104] The Air Staff dismissed the idea put forward by Eden that the AOC-in-C of this new Command should be an adviser to both the Air Ministry and War Office on army co-operation matters. This shows the Air Staff's thinking about how the new Command would function within the wider RAF command system. They argued that the

> proper and logical procedure is for the Commander-in-Chief to advise their own Ministries and for the Ministries to each other. An AOC-in-C should not usurp the responsibility of the Air Ministry for advising the War Office on air matters. The established procedure is well-founded.[105]

The Air Staff were attempting to control the flow of information that reached the War Office regarding the developments of tactical air power in Britain by restricting the access they would have to a new Army Co-operation Command. Through this, and by creating the command to be as toothless as possible, they would prevent the creation of an army air arm. It is also entirely possible that the Air Staff were attempting to sideline this new command by controlling what advice the War Office were to receive and preventing their direct access to it.[106]

The Air Staff did not want to create a specialist command for tactical air power and were determined to make it as powerless as they possibly could whilst still appearing to act on the War Office's demands for greater resources in this area. As the service that was responsible for the creation of such a new command, the RAF was best placed to ensure that this was the result of the discussions between the Air and General Staffs.

There were two possible organisational options for the new command. The first suggested

> That No. 22 Group and the Air Staff at GHQ Home Forces should be combined into one headquarters, the Air Officer Commanding being the air adviser to the C-in-C Home Forces, and under his control for operations.

The second option was

> That there should be an Army Co-operation Command (independent of Home Forces) under an AOC-in-C, with two Army Co-operation Groups, one operational and one for training. The three headquarters thus formed would be established on orthodox lines, and should contain a proportion of Army Staff Officers. The operational group would be under GHQ Home Forces for operations.[107]

The operations that this new force would undertake were focused on anti-invasion. There were no implications or suggestions that it would be used in an offensive capacity overseas. This would severely limit the role and influence of the new organisation.

That the focus of the RAF was on anti-invasion operations, the creation of Army Co-operation Command was somewhat of a distraction. With British armed forces no longer having access to bases on the continent from which they could launch operations, and a hostile enemy in control of the Channel ports and the French Channel and Atlantic coasts, Britain faced its ultimate strategic dilemma. The all-important focus was now on continuing the fight against Germany from Britain and ensuring that the whole nation was determined to withstand the onslaught that would be coming. The only way in which the fight against Germany could be taken up proactively was through the application of air power at the strategic level against targets in the German homeland. At this time very little thought was given to the conduct of operations on the continent as this appeared to be a remote possibility in late 1940. There was also the belief that the economic warfare policies embarked upon by Britain at the start of the war would begin to have an impact on the German ability to continue the conflict by the summer of 1941.[108]

The new strategic outlook also meant a radical change in industrial policy. The major focus for the aviation industry was the replacement of the aircraft that had been lost during the Battle of France and Battle of Britain, and not the creation and development of a new army co-operation aircraft. The demand for replacement aircraft had to be found on top of the rearmament programmes that had been put in place prior to 1939. The official history of British war production notes how far the bleak strategic outlook impacted on industrial policy between 1939 and 1941:

> In the minds of the men responsible for the strategic plans of the spring and summer of 1939 the first three years of the war were to be a time of prepara-

tion. The need for preparations equally protracted also followed from the strategic ideas of 1940 and 1941, even if the character of the preparation was no longer the same. In the summer of 1940 as in the autumn of 1939 the country was still compelled to hold back from active operations while its striking forces were still being built up.[109]

As suggestions (outlined above) for the creation of a new Army Co-operation Command were deliberated, their advantages and disadvantages were discussed by the Air Staff. The advantage of the first proposal was that it would be economical in staff and involve little reorganisation. However, it was argued that the AOC would be in a very difficult position as his authority in certain areas would be confused and also undermined. Under this proposal, the commander would be 'responsible in part to the C-in-C Home Forces (namely for Army Co-operation squadrons), and would therefore in a sense be subordinate to him; whereas a large part of his duties (i.e. those in connection with the training units) would lie outside the responsibility of the C-in-C Home Forces'. The commander would find the locating of his headquarters difficult. It would be impracticable for his headquarters to be close or actually within GHQ. Part of the staff of the new command would have to be attached to GHQ and, due to this, his time would have to be divided equally between what was effectively two headquarters.[110]

The advantage of the second proposal was that it fulfilled the requirements that had been put forward by the General Staff that the commander should hold the position and have the powers of an independent commander. It also fitted into the mono-role command structure of the RAF in Britain in which each individual Command was responsible for a separate aspect of air fighting.[111] This structure would allow the commander free reign over the whole administration of army co-operation interests and would be able to focus on the Command's primary role, which was the 'development of tactics and techniques of air co-operation and support of the army'. A Command structured and organised in this way would, in the Air Staff's opinion provide 'a solid framework capable of expanding to meet any further Army Co-operation requirements'. For such a Command to function efficiently, however, it would require a large expansion in the numbers of officers within the RAF and an increase in the numbers of army officers on its staff.[112] Debates within the Air Staff regarding the structure and organisation of this potential new Command had refined their thinking on the issue and allowed them to create it in such a way that its abilities were severely restricted. An operational army co-operation group would be placed under GHQ Home Forces, and not Army Co-operation Command. A training group of army co-operation schools, the Central Landing Establishment, and the Anti-Aircraft and Searchlight Co-operation units would be formed into a training group. The AOC-in-C of such a Command could only exert complete control over the Army Co-operation Schools that formed part of the Training Group.

The new Command, created under these ideas, would only be administrative and advisory in function. It would have no operational responsibility, it would restrict the powers of the AOC-in-C and the Command would find itself low on the list in terms of aircraft and equipment. Concerns were expressed over the creation of such a Command by the AOC-in-C of Bomber Command, Air Marshal Sir Charles Portal.[113] He was concerned that

> one of the tasks of the new Command would be to advise on types [of aircraft]. If this led to the arming of certain units under Bomber Command not suitable for bombing operations against Germany, then he would deplore the arrangement.[114]

It was clear, particularly among senior commanders of the Air Staff, where the RAF's priorities lay.

The Air Staff were also at pains to counter the concerns of the General Staff regarding the status of a new Army Co-operation Command within the RAF as a whole. The General Staff thought the Army Co-operation Command would have a similar status to that of Coastal Command, but this was not the case—Coastal Command was a fully operational Command in its own right. Its AOC-in-C was responsible for conducting operations in the Atlantic Ocean against the German Navy attacking Allied shipping. The Air Staff argued that, given the strategic outlook, no such comparable operational role existed for Army Co-operation Command. The Air Staff shut the door on Army Co-operation Command being upgraded to an operational Command if a successful invasion of Britain was launched by the Germans, by arguing that air support would be conducted by army co-operation squadrons already attached to the army. If further support was required it would be provided by Bomber, Fighter and Coastal Command squadrons as all resources would be required to defeat the invasion and not to attack the German homeland or protect Allied shipping. There would be no need for an Army Co-operation Command in this scenario.[115] Army Co-operation Command found itself in this unusual position for an RAF Command, and its ability to develop tactical air power in Britain would be severely hampered as a result.

It was agreed that the head of the Command 'would be responsible for implementing the policy decided upon by the Air Ministry and War Office for the development of all forms of air support for the Army'. The General Staff believed that air support fell into two distinct categories: reconnaissance and close support bombing. Under the proposals for Army Co-operation Command the General Staff felt that reconnaissance development would 'be well catered for'. It was on the evolution of close support bombing techniques and communications that Army Co-operation Command would need to focus. Despite plans in these areas being well developed already, it was felt that further improvements could be made through 'tactical reconnaissance group[s] and schools'. By being 'under the command of the Air Officer Commanding-in-Chief [they] will do all that is required'.[116] The General Staff did not have the same confidence for the improvement of close support capability and this, they believed, was the *raison d'être* of the new Army Co-operation Command. They felt that if the Command was not given the necessary powers and organised in the most efficient way there was a very real chance it would fail in this. They were willing to concede that if the RAF focused too much on tactical air power development, it could only be at the expense of ongoing strategic operations. In order to allow Army Co-operation Command to have the powers they felt were necessary the General Staff argued that the AOC-in-C should either be responsible for 'training medium bomber squadrons on close support duties or to incorporate a small bomber formation into the new Command'. If the AOC-in-C was given these responsibilities, he would have direct access to a certain amount of Bomber Command resources and AOC Northern Ireland, to arrange training exercises. This was seen to be a better system for squadrons that were stationed in England and Scotland. If an operational bomber force was formed within Army Co-operation Command it

> would give the necessary weight to the close support side of the proposed organisation. The Command would be in the fullest sense an Army Co-operation Command.[117]

This was something that the Air Staff were reluctant to agree to as they wanted to restrict the resources dedicated to tactical air power development as much as possible.

By the end of October 1940, both the Air and General Staffs had reached a position where they were able to sit down and finalise the organisation and responsibilities of a new Army Co-operation Command. It was agreed that the new Command would be organised with an operational Group under GHQ Home Forces, with Army Co-operation Command having full control over the training group.[118] This set-up favoured the Air Staff's position at the expense of the General Staff's demands and this would place it at a severe disadvantage throughout its existence. With the emphasis being placed upon developing army co-operation by the Army Council, the Air Staff's motivations for creating what was a non-operational Command that only had responsibilities for experiments and training must be called into question. The commander of this new organisation would find himself disadvantaged, due to his Command's non-operational nature, in calls for resources against more established, operational Commands. The disagreement that existed between the two services over the basic concepts of air power had also not been resolved during the discussions to create Army Co-operation Command.

In a directive to the AOC-in-C of Army Co-operation Command, it was laid out that this Command would 'comprise all RAF units specifically engaged in Army Co-operation duties in Great Britain'. His main responsibility was to 'implement the policy decided upon by the Air Ministry for the development of all forms of air support for the army'. There was no mention of this being a joint policy decision of the Air Ministry and War Office as had been discussed and agreed upon previously. To facilitate the implementation of this policy, the commander was to 'liaise with [the] Commander-in-Chief and Commanders of other RAF Commands and Commanders-in-Chief Home Forces and Northern Ireland'.[119] The potential for difficulties in these relationships have been detailed above.

The new Command was officially formed on 1 December 1940 and Barratt, former commander of BAFF was installed as AOC-in-C.[120] Its headquarters was established at Bracknell and the staff was '"integrated"— a new vogue word—being composed of Army and RAF staff officers'.[121] Army Co-operation Command's initial responsibility was simply the administration of a dozen Lysander reconnaissance squadrons whose obsolescence had already been effectively demonstrated in France.[122]

One of Barratt's first actions upon being appointed was to familiarise himself with the work that had already been conducted in close support development. He authorised the distribution of the Wann–Woodall report to all squadrons within his Command[123] and suggested that it be adopted by other commands in overseas theatres as standard operational practice. The report had been codified as basic close support doctrine and, due to the joint nature of the trials, should be considered the first piece of joint doctrine produced by the RAF and army. However, Barratt's suggestion was refused—the reason being the RAF's institutional distrust of theoretical solutions—and the very real threat of invasion occupied their minds.[124] The Wann–Woodall experiments were, however, used as 'inspiration and guidance after unsuccessful operations in the Western Desert and Churchill's intervention on air support in this theatre in September 1941'.[125]

Alongside the creation of Army Co-operation Command, the Air Staff also looked to the Directorate of Military Co-operation to improve relations between the two services. It was argued that such a directorate would allow army co-operation 'to have strong representation in the Air Ministry' and it would be directly responsible to the CAS and not Army Co-operation Command. The DMC was to work primarily with the War Office to frame policy for the development of army co-operation, despite this already being part of Army Co-operation Command's remit. Its duties would cover the following areas: 'provision for army air requirements; co-operation with the army at home and abroad and preparation for plans for the formation of air components for field forces as requisite Air Staff/Army matters affecting the Directorate of Combined Operations'. The DMC would also be responsible for some parts of operational planning and would have no executive function in relation to operational Commands.[126] Some of the responsibilities of the DMC appear to be those that would have been given to an operational Army Co-operation Command—having previously insisted on restricting Army Co-operation Command activities, the Air Staff's motives in agreeing to this must be questioned.

Despite the formation of Army Co-operation Command, the development of tactical air power in Britain was still not easy to facilitate—in the first year of its creation Army Co-operation Command's contribution to army support was of great significance, but the Command found itself hamstrung by many factors almost from day one of its inception.

Notes

1. David Ian Hall, 'Lessons Not Learned: The Struggle between the Royal Air Force and the Army for the Tactical Control of Aircraft and the Post-Mortem on the Defeat of the British Expeditionary Force in France 1940', in Gary Sheffield and Geoffrey Till (eds), *The Challenges of High Command: The British Experience* (Palgrave Macmillan: Basingstoke and New York, 2003), p. 113. David Ian Hall, 'Creating the 2nd Tactical Air Force: Inter-Service and Anglo-Canadian Cooperation in World War II', *Canadian Military Journal*, 3: 4 (Winter 2002–2003), p. 42.
2. David Ian Hall, 'The Long Gestation and Difficult Birth of the 2nd Tactical Air Force (RAF)', *Air Power Review*, 5: 3 (Autumn, 2007), p. 26.
3. TNA WO 106/5167, Note by MO7 on the War Office point of view regarding Close Support, 22 July 1940.
4. Byford, 'Fair Stood', p. 51.
5. Imperial War Museum (IWM), Carrington Papers 8/11/4.
6. Carrington, *Soldier at Bomber Command*, p. ix.
7. TNA AIR 20/2811.
8. Gladman, *Intelligence and Anglo-American Air Support*, p. 39.
9. TNA CAB 65/7, WM 151 (40) 14 pp. 354–9. TNA CAB 65/13, WM 151 (40) 14 Confidential Annex, 1 June 1940.
10. TNA CAB 106/246, Despatches of the Operations of the British Expeditionary Force, 3 September 1939–19 June 1940.
11. Hall, *Strategy for Victory*, p. 55. The names of those who sat on the Committee can be found in the report itself. TNA CAB 106/220, The Bartholomew Committee Final Report: Lessons of the Operations in Flanders, 1940.
12. TNA CAB 106/220, Bartholomew Committee Final Report, pp. 7–8. Hall, *Strategy for Victory*, p. 57.
13. David French, *Raising Churchill's Army: The British Army and the War against Germany 1919–1945* (Oxford University Press: Oxford and New York, 2000), p. 174.
14. Jordan and Sheffield, 'The British Army and Air Power', p. 76.
15. Jacobs, 'Air Support', pp. 175–6.
16. Hall, *Strategy for Victory*, p. 56. Byford, 'The Battle', p. 68.
17. Hall, *Strategy for Victory*, p. 56.
18. Blount had been the AOC of the RAF Component. TNA CAB 106/220, Bartholomew Committee Final Report. Hall, *Strategy for Victory*, pp. 56–7.
19. For further details of the history of the *Luftwaffe*, see Matthew Cooper, *The German Air Force 1933–1945: An Anatomy of Failure* (Janes: London, New York and Sydney, 1981).

20. TNA CAB 106/220, Bartholomew Committee Final Report, pp. 5, 14.
21. Ibid., p. 15.
22. Syrett, 'The Tunisian Campaign', p. 158.
23. TNA AIR 20/4447, Note on Air Operations in Support of the BEF in France during the period 10–31 May, Phase II, c.June 1940.
24. TNA CAB 106/220, Bartholomew Committee Final Report, p. 15.
25. Byford, 'The Battle', p. 68.
26. May, *Strange Victory*, pp. 286–305. Murray and Millett, *A War to be Won*, p. 82. Citino, *Quest for Decisive Victory*, p. 275.
27. For more details of how the British viewed German tactical and operational methods, see T. Harrison Place, 'British Perceptions of the Tactics of the German Army, 1938–40', *Intelligence and National Security*, 9: 3 (July, 1994), pp. 495–519.
28. Hall, *Strategy for Victory*, p. 57.
29. TNA CAB 106/220, Bartholomew Committee Final Report, p. 5.
30. Ibid., pp. 5–6.
31. Ibid., p. 9.
32. TNA CAB 106/220, Bartholomew Committee Final Report, p. 5. Hall, *Strategy for Victory*, p. 57.
33. Ibid., p. 58.
34. TNA CAB 106/220, Bartholomew Committee Final Report, p. 5.
35. Ibid., p. 14.
36. Hall, *Strategy for Victory*, p. 59.
37. MO7 was aware that the *Luftwaffe* was a fully independent force and stated this in a note dated 22 July 1940. They were, however, unable to counter prevailing opinion of the War Office on this.
38. TNA WO 106/5167, Note on the War Office point of view regarding Close Support by MO7, 22 July 1940. Ian Gooderson, 'Doctrine from the Crucible: The British Air-Land Experience in the Second World War', *Air Power Review*, 9: 2 (Autumn, 2006), p. 1.
39. TNA CAB 106/220, Bartholomew Committee Final Report, p. 14.
40. Buckley, 'The Air War', p. 111.
41. Muller, 'Close Air Support', p. 183.
42. TNA WO 106/5167, Note on the War Office point of view regarding Close Support, 22 July 1940.
43. TNA AIR 20/3/06, Note on the Army Air Arm, c.July 1940.
44. TNA AIR 41/15, AHB Narrative, 'The Defence of Great Britain Vol: II: The Battle of Britain, 1945'. Stephen Bungay, *The Most Dangerous Enemy: A History of the Battle of Britain* (Aurum Press: London, 2000).
45. TNA 23/3706, Note on the Army Air Arm, c.July 1940.
46. TNA AIR 19/233, Letter from the Secretary of State for War to the Secretary of State for Air, 28 June 1940.

47. Sir Edmund Ironside, *Time Unguarded: The Ironside Diaries 1937–1940* (Constable: London, 1962), p. 354. Basil Collier, *The Defence of the United Kingdom* (HMSO: London, 1957), pp. 123–4, 127–8.
48. TNA AIR 20/4447, Letter from CIGS to DMC, 1 June 1940.
49. Ibid.
50. TNA AIR 20/4447, Letter from Festing to DMC, 15 June 1940.
51. TNA AIR 20/4447, Memorandum on the Co-operation of Air Forces with the BEF during the period 10 May to 31 May 1940, c.June 1940.
52. Gooderson, 'Doctrine from the Crucible', p. 4.
53. TNA AIR 20/4447, Memorandum on the Co-operation of Air Forces with the BEF during the period 10 May to 31 May 1940, c.June 1940.
54. TNA AIR 10/5547, AHB Narrative Air Support.
55. Winston Churchill, *The Second World War Vol. II: Their Finest Hour* (Cassell: London, 1949), p. 405.
56. TNA AIR 20/4447, Memorandum by DMC—Direct Support by Bombing, 1 June 1940. Hall, 'The Challenges', pp. 118–19.
57. Carrington, 'Army/Air Co-operation', p. 38.
58. TNA AIR 20/4447, Direct Support of the BEF in France 10–31 May 1940.
59. TNA AIR 10/5547, AHB Narrative, Air Support.
60. TNA AIR 39/139, Draft Air Staff Requirements for a Light Bomber for Close Support Duties with the Army, 19 August 1940.
61. TNA AIR 2/7336, Letter from the Secretary of State for War to the Secretary of State for Air, August 1940.
62. TNA AIR 20/3706, Army Air Requirements Conference—Appendix B, Notes on the Employment of Bombers with the German Army, 2 June 1940.
63. IWM Carrington Papers, 8/11/4.
64. TNA AIR 10/5547, AHB Narrative, Air Support.
65. TNA AIR 23/3706, Training in Close Support Bombing, 2 August 1940. Hall, 'The Challenges', p. 121.
66. Arthur Coningham, 'The Development of Tactical Air Forces', *JRUSI*, 91 (February/November, 1946), p. 213.
67. Ian Gooderson, *Air Power at the Battlefront: Allied Close Air Support in Europe 1943–45* (Frank Cass: London and Portland, Oregon, 1998), p. 24.
68. TNA AIR 20/3706, Agenda for a Conference at the Air Ministry to discuss the Organisation necessary to conduct Experimental Training in Close Support Bombing, 15 August 1940.
69. TNA AIR 2/5201, Letter from Sholto Douglas to AOC RAF Northern Ireland, 24 August 1940. TNA WO 106/5162, Letter from Lieutenant-General H. J. Huddlestone, General Officer Commanding (GOC), British Troops in Northern Ireland, 12 August 1940.

70. TNA AIR 20/3706, Memorandum by Lieutenant-Colonel J. D. Woodall to GHQ Home Forces, Certain Problems in the Organisation of Close Support Bombing, 13 August 1940.
71. Ibid.
72. Ibid.
73. TNA AIR 20/3706, The Exercise of Judgement on Relation to Answering Requests, August 1940.
74. Ibid.
75. TNA AIR 20/3706, Location of Control Centres, August 1940.
76. TNA AIR 20/3706, Organisation and Composition of Control, August 1940.
77. TNA AIR 2/5201, Summary of Decisions made at a Meeting held at the Air Ministry to discuss Army Air Requirements, 2 August 1940.
78. TNA AIR 2/5201, Close Support Bombing Trials in Northern Ireland, 21 September 1940.
79. TNA AIR 19/233, Dive Bombers Advantages and Disadvantages, undated.
80. TNA WO 106/5162, General Staff Memorandum on Certain problems in the Organisation of Dive Bombers, 13 August 1940.
81. Wann had been the commander of the Battle squadrons during the Battle of France. Carrington, *Soldier at Bomber Command*, pp. 10–11.
82. TNA AIR 39/142, Experimental Training in Close Support Bombing, 5 December 1940.
83. IWM Carrington Papers, 8/11/4.
84. TNA AIR 20/3706, Memorandum by Lieutenant-Colonel J. D. Woodall on Certain Problems in the Organisation of Close Support Bombing, 13 August 1940. TNA WO 106/5162, Letter from Flying Officer R. Waddell, 1st Armoured Division to Major R. M. Bray MO7, regarding Bomber Support, 27 September 1940.
85. TNA WO 106/5162, Report on Close Support Bombing Trials, Experimental Training in Close Support Bombing by Wann and Woodall, 5 December 1940.
86. Ibid.
87. Muller, 'Close Air Support', p. 185.
88. TNA WO 106/5162, Report on Close Support Bombing Trials, Experimental Training in Close Support Bombing by Wann and Woodall, 5 December 1940.
89. TNA AIR 39/142, Report on Experimental Training in Close Support Bombing by Wann and Woodall, 5 December 1940.
90. TNA WO 106/5162, Report on Close Support Bombing Trials, Experimental Training in Close Support Bombing by Wann and Woodall, 5 December 1940.

91. TNA AIR 39/142, Report on Experimental Training on Close Support Bombing by Wann and Woodall, 5 December 1940.
92. Byford, 'The Battle', p. 69.
93. TNA AIR 39/142, Report on Experimental Training in Close Support Bombing by Wann and Woodall, 5 December 1940. Muller, 'Close Air Support', p. 184. Byford, 'The Battle', p. 69.
94. Carrington, *Soldier at Bomber Command*, pp. 10–11.
95. Gooderson, *Air Power at the Battlefront*, p. 24. Carrington, *Soldier at Bomber Command*, pp. 10–11.
96. Carrington, *Soldier at Bomber Command*, p. 11.
97. Gooderson, *Air Power at the Battlefront*, p. 24. TNA AIR 2/5201, Summary of Decisions made at a Meeting on Certain Questions in Connection with Close Support Bombing, 4 December 1940.
98. TNA AIR 39/140, Summary of Decisions made at a Conference regarding certain Questions in Connection with Close Support Bombing, 4 December 1940.
99. TNA AIR 2/7336, Letter from the Secretary of State for War to the Secretary of State for Air, August 1940.
100. TNA AIR 20/3706, Note on the Army Air Arm, *c*.June/July 1940.
101. TNA AIR 20/2811, Memorandum by the Secretary of State for War—Air Support for the Army, 23 September 1940. Coastal Command has been the subject of several studies, the most prominent of which are Christina Goulter, *A Forgotten Offensive: Royal Air Force Coastal Command's Anti-Shipping Campaign, 1940–1945* (Frank Cass: London and Portland, Oregon, 1995) and Andrew W. A. Hendrie, *The Cinderella Service: Coastal Command 1939–1945* (Pen & Sword Aviation: Barnsley, 2006). Also of interest is John Buckley, 'Air Power and the Battle of the Atlantic, 1939–1945', *Journal of Contemporary History*, 28: 1 (January, 1993), pp. 143–61. As will be demonstrated in subsequent chapters, the title of Cinderella Command could just as equally be applied to Army Co-operation Command.
102. TNA AIR 2/5224, General Staff note on Training in Close Support in the proposed Army Co-operation Command, 2 October 1940.
103. TNA AIR 20/2811, Proposal to form a new RAF Command at Home for Army Co-operation, 3 October 1940.
104. Ibid.
105. TNA AIR 20/4301, Proposals for an Army Co-operation Command, 10 October 1940.
106. Byford, 'Fair Stood', p. 51. The Air Staff's thinking on the creation of an Army Co-operation Command can be seen at TNA AIR 20/4301, Proposals for an Army Co-operation Command, *c*.October 1940.

107. TNA AIR 20/4301, Proposals for an Army Co-operation Command, *c.*October 1940.
108. Butler, *Grand Strategy Vol. II*, p. 342.
109. Postan, *British War Production*, p. 119.
110. TNA AIR 30/4301, Proposals for an Army Co-operation Command, *c.*October 1940.
111. Byford, 'Fair Stood', pp. 35–60.
112. TNA AIR 20/4301, Proposals for an Army Co-operation Command, *c.*October 1940.
113. Air Vice-Marshal Sir Richard Peirse took over as AOC-in-C Bomber Command, on 5 October 1940 when Portal was appointed as CAS.
114. TNA AIR 20/2811, Proposal to form a new RAF Command at Home for Army Co-operation, 3 October 1940.
115. TNA AIR 20/2811, Proposals for an Army Co-operation Command, 9 October 1940.
116. TNA AIR 2/5224, General Staff note on Training in Close Support in the proposed Army Co-operation Command, 2 October 1940.
117. Ibid.
118. TNA AIR 20/2811, Agenda for discussion on the Formation of Army Co-operation Command, 20 October 1940.
119. TNA AIR 20/2811, Directive to AOC-in-C Army Co-operation Command, undated, *c.*November 1940.
120. The decision to form Army Co-operation Command had eventually been made in November 1940. Hallion, *Strike from the Sky*, p. 152. Henry A. Probert, 'The Determination of RAF Policy in the Second World War', in Horst Boog (ed.), *The Conduct of the Air War in the Second World War: An International Comparison* (Berg Publishers: New York and Oxford, 1992), p. 684.
121. Carrington, *Soldier at Bomber Command*, p. 26.
122. IWM Carrington Papers, 8/11/4. TNA PREM 4/14/9, Proposal for the Re-organisation of Army Co-operation with the RAF, *c.*November 1940.
123. TNA AIR 39/139, Letter from AOC-in-C Army Co-operation Command to Air Commodore R. V. Goddard (Director of Military Co-operation (DMC)), 1 December 1940.
124. Byford, 'Fair Stood', p. 52. Byford, 'The Battle', p. 69.
125. Hall, *Strategy for Victory*, pp. 105–6, 102.
126. TNA AIR 20/4301, Proposals for an Army Co-operation Command—Responsibilities of the Directorate of Military Co-operation, *c.*October 1940.

CHAPTER 4

The Work of Army Co-operation Command, 1941

As Army Co-operation Command began the overall role assigned to it in 1941, it experienced, as should be expected with any newly created organisation, a degree of teething problems. Major modifications were required both to the Command's internal organisation and its position with regard to non-RAF military organisations within Britain. This was particularly the case with the army's Home Forces. The roles, responsibilities and even location of some of Barratt's subordinate commanders required a major overhaul as they were unworkable in the form that had been agreed between the Air and General Staffs prior to Under the present arrangement th's creation in the autumn of 1940. There were also still high-level tensions between the Air Ministry and War Office over the development of tactical air power in Britain. One area of particular worry was how Army Co-operation Command and the War Office would communicate, especially over progress on developing operational procedures.

Despite these many issues, Barratt and his staff set about confronting some of the major issues that had plagued tactical air power prior to and during the Second World War to date. They used First World War experiences and interwar exercises to guide them in this process. The British strategic outlook in 1941 gave Army Co-operation Command the necessary time to reorganise and prepare further tactical air power developments—with the continent dominated by Germany after the defeat of France, the U-Boat threat in the Atlantic hampering British communications with the US and the empire, and the Italian invasion of North Africa, the country's focus was on non-European theatres of operation. The focus of the RAF as a whole at this time remained on the strategic air offensive against Germany and not tactical air power—this was the only effective way of carrying the fight to the German homeland and also keeping friendly but neutral powers such as the US interested in events in Europe. The fear of invasion had receded to a degree with Fighter Command's victory in the Battle of Britain but was still a real concern and no plans were being made to launch a seaborne invasion against the French coast in the near future.[1]

In 1941, Army Co-operation Command continued its most fruitful experimentation in the refining of artillery reconnaissance and spotting that had been postponed during the Battle of France. Its work was a prime example of how to operate effectively and smoothly with branches of the army, overcoming differences and improving relations, and showed promise for further co-operative ventures. As will be discussed below, however, Army Co-operation Command's operational restrictions also prevented this positive opportunity for expansion.[2] These restrictions were primarily due to the way in which the Air Staff had created Army Co-operation Command—it straddled the awkward and difficult position between the tactical and operational levels of war. The focus of the Command should have been, and indeed was, on the refinement of tactical activity to enable air power to be delivered more efficiently at the lowest level of war but the effects of these refinements would be more greatly felt at the operational level and would act as a force multiplier.

The creation of Army Co-operation Command relieved some of the pressure on the Air Ministry to develop air support techniques, and work began on trials and further experiments in earnest—ideas that emerged formed part of joint RAF/army training exercises. The exercises also demonstrated to a greater degree the sound advice that had emanated from the interwar exercises for the command and control of air support. Both services' understanding of how to conduct air support, its operational limitations and the most effective command and communications structures were slowly improved— Army Co-operation Command was at the heart of this process.

Considerable tension still existed between the two services over the allocation of air resources for trials and training. The RAF, for example, still lacked the resources to be able to conduct both strategic air offensives and army co-operation training—aircraft had to be taken off active operations to partake in exercises, something the RAF was reluctant to do at this point in the war. The impotent status of Army Co-operation

Command and its inability to successfully claim air resources for training, was made clear to the army early in 1941, contributed to continuing tensions between the two services,[3] and prompted the General Staff to continue their calls for a separate army air arm. The fear of a German invasion of Britain was still very much in the forefront of military and political minds and more effort was made to better co-ordinate support for an armed defensive force if the worst fears were realised in the summer of 1941. This co-ordination, however, did not include utilising the knowledge or expertise contained within Army Co-operation Command—the organisation was largely sidelined due to its non-operational status.

Mainly as a result of the tensions that continued over the allocation of aircraft to the close support training role, discussions continued between the CAS and CIGS, particularly over aircraft requirements necessary for a successful cross-Channel invasion. Barratt and Army Co-operation Command's role in this process will be discussed later in this chapter and what will become apparent is how Army Co-operation Command was viewed differently by the RAF and army. To the RAF it was nothing more than a necessary evil to be endured for as short a time as possible until either air power had done such damage to the German ability to prosecute the war that land forces were simply required to mop up small areas of resistance, or the army had given up on demands for their own army air arm. In order to achieve this, the Air Ministry sidelined Army Co-operation Command in terms of aircraft, equipment and personnel. Barratt would also find himself excluded from discussions on such subjects as 'the employment of bomber squadrons in close support of Home Forces'.[4] For the army, Commander-in-Chief of Home Forces, General Sir Alan Brooke, whilst not necessarily looking to create a separate army air arm, was still pushing hard to have squadrons formed specifically to only provide air support to land forces without air superiority having been gained in the first instance.[5] It must be questioned how much the War Office had learnt about modern warfare and the principles of air power since the Battle of France if basic concepts such as this were still being misunderstood by those at the head of the army in Britain. It must further be questioned how much the RAF felt that they could, or indeed should, educate the army on this issue. The responsibility for this would eventually fall to Army Co-operation Command. Major events in the Western Desert, most notably the disastrous (particularly in terms of air support) operations of Brevity and Battleaxe will form a small section of this chapter in order to provide the wider historical context of events in theatres that would also develop an impromptu air support system and the troubles they faced in this area.

The first major issue that confronted Barratt and Army Co-operation Command was raised just two months after its creation. The problem was the relations and communications between the War Office and Army Co-operation Command. As the AOC-in-C of Army Co-operation Command, part of Barratt's role was to implement in conjunction with Home Forces a training policy to further develop army co-operation. The commander at No. 71 (Operations) Group was to act as Barratt's representative and advisor on all matters regarding co-operation including anti invasion measures that were being discussed and developed at this time.[6] One of the major issues for Army Co-operation Command was that no one within the RAF was certain about its place within the overall service command structure. The Air Staff regarded Army Co-operation Command as the appropriate department through which the General Staff and War Office should address their concerns as, despite appearances in the wake of the Battle of France, they still had no real interest in this area. High-level policy decisions were, however, taken without any direct reference to, or consultation with, Army Co-operation Command. The War Office also had high hopes for the development of tactical air power in Britain with the creation of the new Command. The War Office expected more than the Air Ministry were willing to give. It is highly debatable, and indeed unlikely, that the War Office saw Army Co-operation Command as a backdoor means to the creation of their own army air arm, but they certainly expected the status of the command to be raised to that of an operational command as the possibility of a return to the continent increased. These issues, along with others, were highlighted to Barratt almost as soon as Army Co-operation Command had been created.[7]

Barratt acted as soon as it was practicable to do so and wrote to the Under-Secretary of State for Air, Harold Balfour, regarding the command structure of Army Co-operation Command and the location of the commander of No. 71 (Operations) Group. The way in which these issues were resolved demonstrates further how the RAF and Air Ministry viewed Army Co-operation Command—Barratt's concerns deserve to be quoted at length:

> The AOC 71 Group has, in his role of the Home Forces Air Component, the dual function of commanding his Group and acting as air adviser to the C-in-C [Home Forces]. To permit him to fulfil the latter function, his own

office and that of the Air Branch of his Staff is located at GHQ, while the remainder of his Staff remains at his rear Headquarters at Sunningdale.

A very great number of questions affecting air matters, many of which have no direct bearing on the component, arise daily at GHQ, and since the Air Branch of No. 71 Group Staff has in effect become the air section of the General Staff at GHQ these problems are invariably passed to it to deal with.

Arising from this, the AOC 71 Group finds himself and his Air Staff officers tied to GHQ and unable to exercise the necessary supervision over his widely dispersed Command. To relieve this situation I propose the AOC 71 Group, and his Air Branch should regard Sunningdale as their main Headquarters, and that a liaison staff from my Headquarters should take their place at GHQ.

The C-in-C Home Forces has previously discussed with me the defects of the organisation by which 71 Group was saddled with too many tasks outside its providence.

In addition, I am convinced that a Liaison Section of my Headquarters at GHQ Home Forces is essential to permit me to perform fully ... my directive which charges me with the responsibility for the supervision of all air training in co-operation with the Army and with the development of the tactics and techniques of Army co-operation including close support.[8]

What Barratt was suggesting was confirmed by GHQ Home Forces after Exercise Victor, when they stated that it was necessary to make changes 'in the existing methods of liaison between GHQ and RAF Commands'. GOC-in-C Home Forces further believed that the Commander of No. 71 Group could not 'act as the Senior Air Staff Officer [SASO] at GHQ Home Forces before or after "Action Stations" and at the same time carry out his duties as Group Commander'.[9]

Part of the problem was the sheer volume of workload that would be placed upon the AOC No. 71 Group if the call to action stations was ever made. If this did happen his focus would be on acting as SASO to Home Forces and he would be unable to give any real attention to commanding his group. There was a shortage of experienced army co-operation officers of a senior enough rank to undertake one of these two roles thereby resolving the issue. The major stumbling point, however, was that this particular role had not been fully thought through due to the speed at which Army Co-operation Command had been designed and created. This was partly due to the War Office wanting such an organisation to be created but more so by the Air Staff's desire to relieve the pressure they had faced to do something in the wake of the Battle of France. Brooke proposed the following suggestion in an attempt to resolve and streamline what was a very cumbersome and confused command system for all involved:

> The AOC-in-C Army Co-operation Command to be available to act as my RAF adviser, assisted by: A RAF liaison Staff of one Group Captain and permanently located at GHQ. A RAF map room staff to maintain 24 hours watch in the combined Navy-Army-RAF Map Room. The Liaison Staff will: (i) Receive information from all RAF sources and pass it to GHQ branches, combined map room and any RAF Headquarters concerned; (ii) Transmit naval and military information from all sources to [the] RAF Headquarters concerned; (iii) Transmit any requests for support to AOC-in-C RAF Commands; (iv) Issue orders to strategical reconnaissance units working directly with GHQ.[10]

What Barratt and Brooke were suggesting was what would be termed today a joint force, combining air and ground resources in a single command. Such an idea would not have been tolerable to the Air Staff or the Air Ministry during this period as they believed it would violate one of the fundamental principles of air power—that air resources should be centralised under a single air commander. The proposal put forward by Barratt and Brooke would have been eminently workable in principle but might have seen Barratt working under the operational control of Brooke and would have created a de facto army air arm. What would have made this even more intolerable to the Air Staff was that this army air arm would in fact have been a part of the RAF and might have led to the army claiming even more air resources for themselves, preventing the strategic air offensive being prosecuted with the rigour it was felt necessary.

Barratt received a response to the letter he had sent to the Air Ministry about the difficulties he was facing in his new position from the DMC Air Commodore R. V. Goddard, who stated that he would be required to negotiate with GHQ Home Forces in order to 'find out how best their requirements could be met'.[11] This was despite Barratt having already discussed the issues in depth with Brooke. As has been noted, Brooke had also written a detailed memorandum on the issue setting out how he thought the problems could be best resolved. That the Air Ministry felt they also had to do this demonstrates the real position of Army Co-operation Command within the RAF command structure. They were not able to resolve this issue through direct discussions with Home Forces lest it create a type of joint formation that the RAF were desperate to avoid creating. A draft of a letter sent to Barratt from the Vice Chief of the Air Staff (VCAS) Air Chief Marshal Sir Wilfred Freeman, which was actually written by Goddard, stated that

It was realised when your Command was created, that it could not be quite like other Commands, and that its activities must be fairly rigidly confined. It was for that reason that a carefully thought-out directive was given to you, in the hope that some of the difficulties which have since cropped up might be avoided. I'm afraid it won't do to have an Air Marshal alongside C-in-C Home Forces, it might interfere with his direct contact with other operational C-in-C's or with DCAS [Deputy Chief of the Air Staff]. That is why your relations with C-in-C Home Forces were limited to co-operation on matters of training, tactics and technique ... It was feared when we agreed to form Army Co-operation Command that the War Office and Home Forces might be inclined to expect more from you than we agreed upon. The War Office knows very well what it is not entitled to ask your advice on Army Co-operation matters. The same applies to GHQ, except on matters defined in your directive. I have discussed with CAS the difficulties which have arisen and he considers that it would be inadvisable to modify your responsibilities. If the associations you already had with GHQ make it difficult to retract without something being said by CAS to CIGS or to C-in-C Home Forces, perhaps you will let me know what you would like done to clarify your position.[12]

The Air Staff were setting down in writing their deliberate policy of restricting the flow of information on the development of army co-operation to the service that would benefit from it the most. This was based on the spurious idea that closer ties between Army Co-operation Command and Home Forces would somehow restrict the communications Brooke and his successors would have with other RAF Commands and the Air Staff. At no point are Barratt's concerns over his command structure directly addressed and the solutions proposed were rejected out of hand and the blame is placed almost entirely on potential War Office motives. The fear of the creation of an army air arm through closer ties between Army Co-operation Command and Home Forces is evident to see. There had also clearly been crossed wires between the Air and General Staffs as to what could be expected from Army Co-operation Command during the discussions about how best to advance the development of tactical air power in Britain. This adds further weight to the argument that the Air Staff felt pressured to create Army Co-operation Command and were only willing to endure it as a necessary evil until it could be disbanded.

Agreement was reached with Home Forces as to how Army Co-operation Command could best be reorganised and the changes were implemented. To resolve the command issues faced by No. 71 Group, the air staff were moved from GHQ Home Forces to the headquarters of the group. In order to fulfil the representation aspect of the Group's role an air staff officer remained at Home Forces as an SASO. This new arrangement, however, meant that Home Forces could no longer receive advice on air matters and a decision on how to resolve this new issue was postponed until after the new structure had had time to bed in.[13] Barratt's role was also subject to greater restriction and reinterpretation. He was now to be adviser to GOC-in-C Home Forces 'on Army Co-operation policy in its narrowest sense' except 'the operational employment of the Army Co-operation Units of 71 Group'.[14] The SASO that was to be appointed to Home Forces was to be of the rank of either Air Commodore or Group Captain. This move diverged from the ideas originally laid down in RAF doctrinal manuals. The new SASO was to responsible 'to the C-in-C for advice on air matters; consequently the responsibility of the AOC 71 Group to the C-in-C, Home Forces, will no longer be that of an AOC Air Component as defined in Air Publication 1300'.[15] This SASO was Air Commodore J. L. Vachell, and he began his duties on 19 March.[16]

For a newly created Command to experience teething problems is nothing unusual, and that an organisation as politically charged after the interservice arguments suffered to a greater extent should be expected. The way in which the problems were resolved, however, demonstrates Army Co-operation Command's standing within the RAF. Despite suggesting a solution to the issues facing him, and having discussed this with Brooke, Barratt was not consulted about how best to change the command structure of Army Co-operation Command and the Air Staff consulted Home Forces separately. Barratt also had to refer the matter to Goddard continually instead of being able to resolve the issues in conjunction with the Air Staff. Barratt went into depth about this in a letter to Balfour:

> I agree that there should be a representative of my Headquarters and of Headquarters of 71 Group located at GHQ Home Forces, and I have already, after consultation with GHQ, agreed to leave Major C. C. Oxborrow, MC to act in that capacity. I suggest that as AOC-in-C, the Army Co-operation Command, *this matter of representation is one for mutual arrangement between myself and the C-in-C Home Forces*, should circumstances require any subsequent adjustments in the question. I am convinced that the interposition of such an intermediary organisation [DMC], owning no responsibility to me, between the Army in this country and the RAF Command set up expressly to co-operate with it, can only lead to friction, delay, uncertainty of council and inefficiency [emphasis added].[17]

To resolve the structural command problems of 71 Group it was disbanded in August and six Army Co-operation Wings were created and placed at Army Command Headquarters. Each wing was to be commanded by an RAF officer. The officer 'commanding the Wing Headquarters will have executive control under the army commander of all army co-operation squadrons within the command'. He would also 'act as air adviser to the army commander'.[18] This reorganisation created a more joint command structure which would allow greater co-operation between the army co-operation wings and the army command headquarters.

Arguments between the War Office and Air Ministry over the function of Army Co-operation Command and the advice it could give came to a head during discussions about how to resolve the structural command issues. In February 1941, the CIGS aired the War Office's frustrations in detail:

> Under the present arrangement the Army Co-operation Command sends reports, advice and opinions on all matters only to the Air Ministry. The War Office suggests that they should have full access to Army Co-operation Command's opinion … The War Office feels itself greatly handicapped by this restriction … The Command works for the good of both Services. It is fully understood that the resultant policy is a matter purely for the Air Ministry and War Office to decide. But it is difficult for the War Office to help towards forming a joint policy when it is not in possession of all the facts. The War Office may agree or disagree with the Command's opinion but it would at least like to know what that opinion is. It is suggested, therefore, that the War Office should have full access to Army Co-operation Command's opinion, written or verbal, copies of written matter being sent direct to the War Office at the same time the originals go to the Air Ministry. A considerable speeding up of business will result, and better co-operation between the two Ministries will be possible.[19]

The Air Staff had previously rejected out of hand this proposal for greater communication between the War Office and Army Co-operation Command and the minutes of the meeting demonstrate the true intentions of the War Office. They wished to 'establish personal contact with AOC-in-C, and the Air Staff at Army Co-operation Command'.[20] Barratt was personally against the idea of sending all of Army Co-operation Command's papers to the War Office. This could have been due to worries about his Command being subsumed and becoming a de facto army air arm, but given the ideas he had discussed with Brooke over the reorganisation of his own Command, his reluctance could be put down to two other reasons: (1) the potentially overwhelming amount of work this would involve for both parties, and (2) preventing flawed or incomplete ideas being viewed outside of Army Co-operation Command before they had been fully developed. If he was allowed greater discretion over what the War Office received he was willing to increase the flow of information sent.[21] That the War Office wanted greater communication with the organisation created to foster an improved spirit of collaboration and further the development of army co-operation in Britain is fully justifiable, particularly given their recent experiences in France.

Barratt also felt that the position of the Directorate of Military Co-operation placed Army Co-operation Command in a difficult position with regard to fostering better relations with the War Office; he felt that the DMC further hamstrung Army Co-operation Command in its attempts to fulfil its role. Barratt's opinion was that 'there seemed no need for a DMC, since Director of Plans is responsible for planning for Army requirements and the [AO]C-in-C Army Co-operation Command is responsible for advising the Air Ministry of Army Co-operation requirements'.[22] Barratt felt that the DMC was an unnecessary bureaucratic step for army co-operation development in Britain. As head of the DMC, and finding his position under attack, Goddard felt that Barratt's opinion on this was driven because

> he does not wish his activities to be limited by his existing directive. All the difficulties which have arisen have related to matters of future policy or future arrangements, in which he has either gone ahead of Air Ministry authority, or acted upon what he believed to be Air Ministry policy before it had been communicated to him.[23]

Barratt's wider motives in questioning the need for a DMC within the RAF are open to wide-ranging interpretation. He may have been deliberately trying to usurp the position of Goddard and his Directorate in order to simply create difficulties for the Air Staff. Barratt was well known within the RAF for this.[24] It is difficult, however, to marry Goddard's opinion about Barratt's actions with the available evidence. Barratt had raised structural command issues that would not only have caused problems for his Command in the future but were causing issues at the time. He wanted to reorganise his Command in order for it to function effectively as quickly as possible. Through increasing the role, responsibilities and status of Army Co-operation Command, and potentially transforming it into an operational Command, he would stand a greater chance of being successful in his role. Barratt saw Army Co-operation Command as the best way to further the development of army co-operation within Britain and because of this he was not always willing to toe the Air Staff line.

Further moves were made to alter the fundamental makeup of Army Co-operation Command later in 1941. Churchill wrote to both Sinclair and CAS regarding certain appointments within the RAF in his capacity as Minister of Defence. A vacancy in the US ferry service had arisen and Churchill's first choice for the post, Sir Hugh Dowding, had been deemed unsuitable. Churchill's second choice was Barratt and he felt that 'the best arrangement would be to send Air Marshal Barratt there, and replace him with Sir Hugh Dowding who will give confidence to the Army that they will have their interests fully represented'.[25] Barratt's position at Army Co-operation Command was defended by both Sinclair and CAS.

> Neither I nor the Chief of the Air Staff would be prepared to recommend the changes suggested in your minute. Air Marshal Barratt was appointed to Army Co-operation Command only 6 months ago at the suggestion of the War Office and knows more about Army Co-operation than any other officer of his rank in the RAF. He has done his work very well and his knowledge and experience would be wasted in charge of the Ferry Organisation for which he has no special qualifications.[26]

John Ray has argued that Churchill 'still held Dowding in high esteem and did not want a man of such great achievements and undoubted, although sometimes individual abilities, to be dropped'. Churchill saw Army Co-operation Command as a way of rehabilitating Dowding after the Battle of Britain and retaining him at a high level Command within the RAF. When the first calls had been made to remove Dowding from Fighter Command, Churchill had left the matter undiscussed for over two weeks.[27] The question must be raised as to why Churchill had not put forward Dowding to take charge of Army Co-operation Command when it was first created.

Given his vast experience in army co-operation, both the Air Ministry and War Office felt that Barratt was the right man to be head of Army Co-operation Command. If Dowding had been appointed as head, the development of army co-operation would have been severely hampered— Dowding was due to retire in April 1942 and a new commander would have had to be appointed, potentially causing great disruption at a time when greater coherence and unity was required. Also, Dowding's experience had been in Fighter Command and research and supply, and not army co-operation.[28] The issue of Dowding's appointment is not mentioned in the literature available on Dowding and the aftermath of the Battle of Britain.[29] The majority of these works were published before academic focus had turned to the development of tactical air power. Without the work that has previously been done highlighting the development of tactical air power, Army Co-operation Command had been seen as a peripheral issue. In a bizarre turn of events, six months after Churchill's moves to replace Barratt with Dowding, Sinclair sent a minute to Churchill regarding the expansion of the RAF that was taking place. In this minute he recommended removing Barratt from Army Co-operation Command and replacing him with Air Marshal Richard Peirse:

> For some time I have been contemplating a change in that Command and I have discussed it with Portal ... I with Brooke ... mentioned Peirse and Brooke seemed to prefer it. Barratt does not possess the wide experience of Peirse, nor is he as strong a personality. He is, however, extremely hard-working and is a good commander.[30]

No changes were made and Barratt remained at Army Co-operation Command. In 1942, however, Sinclair sent a minute to Churchill stating again that he wanted to remove Barratt from Army Co-operation Command and replace him this time with Air Marshal Sir Alfred Garrod. The Prime Minister discussed this proposal with Brooke, who was now CIGS, and the new GOC-in-C Home Forces General Sir Bernard Paget. Both men felt that Barratt should remain at Army Co-operation Command. Sinclair, disappointed by this response from the General Staff replied,

> Sir Arthur Barratt is an officer of great ability and long experience. That is why I refused the request of the Secretary of State for War [David Margesson] to move him last summer and why I want him as Inspector-General now. On the other hand now is the time to make a fresh start in Army Co-operation Command. The [AO]C-in-C should be of unusual energy and imagination who will make the most of the Command's new equipment and vigorously press its claims on the Air Ministry and the Army. Barratt is not, in my judgement, the right man for this job.

THE WORK OF ARMY CO-OPERATION COMMAND, 1941 131

This chapter has clearly demonstrated that rather than Barratt not pressing the claims of Army Co-operation Command as Sinclair suggested, he had in fact done this and been sidelined in the process by the DMC and Air Ministry who had deliberately kept his brief as AOC-in-C Army Co-operation Command as limited as possible. Churchill replied to Sinclair asking for proof that the army wanted Barratt removed:

> I find on enquiry that both the CIGS and C-in-C Home Forces, would very much regret the departure of Air Marshal Barratt. In view of the complaints that are made [of the way] that the Army has been treated by the Air Ministry in respect of co-operation, and that they have now got an officer whom they like and trust ... Let me see the papers on which you base your statement that the Secretary of State for War requested you to move Air Marshal Barratt last year. My own recollection is that the military opinion was very much in his favour and that was why the move was not made.[31]

Sinclair was forced to admit that the papers to which he had referred did not in fact exist and that there had been no move by the War Office to remove Barratt. The attitude emanating from the Air Ministry regarding Army Co-operation Command, and as a direct result its commander, must be called into question. Within fourteen months of its creation both the Prime Minister and the head of the political and military aspects of the RAF had attempted to remove Barratt from his position. The final attempt to remove Barratt took place just after Sinclair had been forced to defend Army Co-operation Command in the House of Commons. He stated that Army Co-operation Command was in no way inferior to any other RAF Command, despite its non-operational status. This embarrassing statement had to be made whilst the 1942 Air Estimates were being announced to the House of Commons.[32] The feelings of the Air Staff towards Army Co-operation Command are clearly demonstrated in a letter from Freeman to the then AOC No. 5 Bomber Group, AVM Slessor.[33]

> I was lunching with Boom [Lord Trenchard] the other day and he raised the question of the present arrangements for army co-operation. I am afraid that I had not thought about it much recently, but I have a feeling that the present system is not right and that the present Army Co-operation Command, which we organised in rather a hurry last autumn, largely in order to satisfy the army's inferiority complex, is not the right answer.[34]

This letter demonstrates the ambivalent feelings of the Air Ministry towards army co-operation and, as a result, their attitude towards Army Co-operation Command had, in reality, changed little since the Battle of France—whoever was head of Army Co-operation Command would have found the job difficult. This resulted in the attempted leadership changes described above, as well as Barratt pushing for greater powers and responsibilities. The attempts to change the commander also led to a degree of instability within Army Co-operation Command—some reorganisation did take place, handled by the Air Staff in-house. Whilst the War Office was consulted on certain aspects of this, the majority of the decisions were taken by the RAF alone as they were the service responsible for the Command.

While the discussions over the structure of Army Co-operation Command were continuing in Britain, air power at the tactical level was being deployed against the German and Italian forces in the Western Desert, but 1941 saw ground support effectiveness fall to its lowest ebb in this theatre.[35] Two major operations involving tactical air support were conducted in an attempt to relieve the German siege of Tobruk, codenamed Brevity and Battleaxe.[36] The relief of Tobruk was a strategic necessity as its continued occupation threatened Egypt and the Suez Canal,[37] the latter being one of the most important assets for Britain—if this fell under hostile control, communications with the empire would be severed and Britain's grand strategic position would be severely undermined.[38] The head of the RAF in the Western Desert, Tedder, was willing to sacrifice some of the principles of air power so strongly held in Britain in order to foster better relations in the theatre. Previous operational failures had been blamed on air support as had happened in Britain after the Battle of France.

The air support aspect of both of these operations was an unmitigated disaster. Brevity demonstrated the differences that existed between the two services in the Western Desert over the types of targets that were best attacked from the air. As had happened in Britain in 1940, the army, through Brigadier W. H. Gott, felt that air support was best applied once the attack had begun by bombing immediate tactical problems facing ground forces, such as enemy armoured formations. The major problem, not encountered in France due to the speed of the German breakthrough and advance, was the identification of friendly forces in close proximity to the enemy. The RAF, through Air Commodore Raymond Collishaw, argued that ground forces could best be supported from the air by attacking interdiction targets. Both services were, however, willing to work closely together at the highest level in order to resolve the issues that conducting air support presented, which was not the case in Britain. This increased co-operation can be explained by the fact that the forces in the Western Desert were involved in active operations against the enemy and the necessity of gaining victory or avoiding defeat was more important than arguing over principles of command or ownership of resources.[39]

The air plans for Battleaxe were made on a joint basis between Tedder and the General Officer Commander-in-Chief Middle East, General Sir Archibald Wavell, and incorporated the lessons identified from Brevity. There were still, however, basic conceptual differences between the two services over the employment of the WDAF. Wavell wanted the air resources to be used as a protective umbrella and to have bombers on standby to answer calls for support from land forces. Whilst these concepts had been dismissed by the RAF several years before, Tedder was willing to allow it to demonstrate that the WDAF was willing to provide support and 'because the air units involved were only required for a short time'.[40] Battleaxe failed in its objective to drive the German forces under General leutnant Erwin Rommel from Tobruk but Hall has noted that this failure was not necessarily due to a lack of, or inability to provide air support by the WDAF, highlighting that Rommel 'was both forewarned and well prepared'.[41] The prearranged signals system put in place to allow the army to request support had only been used once and this led to calls from Wavell for an army air arm in the Western Desert. The explanation for why the system had failed differed depending on the service: the army felt that the opportunities to request close support had been limited, if not non-existent, during Battleaxe; the WDAF felt that the army had been inadequately trained in how to use the communications system and that it suffered from many failures during the operation.[42] The same erroneous idea that emerged from the Bartholomew Committee with regard to German close support abilities was raised in the Western Desert—the army believed that German land forces had the ability to immediately summon the *Luftwaffe* when they encountered difficulties during their operations.[43]

Following Battleaxe, a number of exercises were held over the summer of 1941 in order to 'determine the most suitable targets for air attack and the ideal method of reconnoitring, engaging, and destroying them'.[44] The exercises also tested the correct tactical methods of conducting attacks, experimenting with bombing from various altitudes and with different sized bombs, as well the use of machine-guns and cannon for ground strafing.[45] After the completion of these exercises, a joint conference was held to develop a policy acceptable to both parties—in the deliberations that followed, the Air Support Committee that had been established used the work of Wann and Woodall, refined by Army Co-operation Command, to guide their thinking on an impromptu air support capability. The only major area of contention that still existed between the WDAF and Eighth Army was the defence of ground forces against air attack. The argument of Eighth Army was the same as that agreed upon in the Bartholomew Committee Report: that a fighter umbrella should be maintained to protect them. Neither service was willing to back down and it took the intervention of Churchill to resolve the issue, stating that 'Nevermore must the ground troops expect, as a matter of course, to be protected from the air by aircraft. ... Above all, the idea of keeping standing patrols of aircraft over moving columns should be abandoned.'[46] In addition to this, Churchill also settled the issue of ownership of air resources and the independent standing of the RAF in the Western Desert.[47]

On 30 September a new edict, the Middle East (Army and RAF) Directive on Joint Air Support was released detailing the techniques for 'target selection, recognition and attack', as well as 'the procedures for the transmission of information between the Army and RAF up and down the entire chain of command'. It worked in a similar manner to the CSBC concept that had been developed in Britain. This has been described as 'an innovative joint command structure'. Its origins, however, can be found in the ideas that emerged from the interwar army co-operation exercises.[48] The only real difference between the British and Western Desert joint headquarter concepts was the level of command at which they functioned. In the Western Desert it was established at the Corps level. This was not possible in Britain at the time as a formation of this size did not exist.

In Britain, one of the first moves by Army Co-operation Command to improve the abilities of the RAF to support the army in the field was in the development of new artillery reconnaissance procedures based on the ideas that were to have been trialled in France in 1940. Barratt's ideas on this demonstrated the refreshingly new attitude he brought to working with the army in Britain. Writing to Balfour, he noted that 'it is desirable to set out the problem as the Army sees it'.[49] In order to allow as many squadrons as possible to conduct this role any new system that was to be developed had to be based on simplicity of training.[50] Despite D Flight being the formation dedicated to conducting the trials under Army Co-operation Command, its operational work was the responsibility of Fighter Command. Those who had championed the development of the Air OP concept

> Were faced with the greatest challenges ... The most pressing being asked was, 'how much risk was too much for an airborne OP pilot to survive while flying at low level in the face of enemy ground formations, or in a sky filled with enemy fighters?'[51]

One of the biggest issues that had plagued artillery observation in France was the aircraft used in the role. The Lysander had proved itself to be slow and obsolescent in the face of the *Luftwaffe* and the few attempts that had actually been made to conduct observation had resulted in either the destruction of the aircraft or them being driven off by the enemy.[52] The Air Staff were reluctant to see the creation of specialised formations for this role unless there was strong evidence for it, again demonstrating the prevailing attitudes and fears within the RAF. In a joint trial, Army Co-operation Command and the School of Artillery set about finding the best design of a suitable aircraft—they used a low-wing monoplane (the actual aircraft is not mentioned in the trials report) to conduct observation to discover if the problems in France were due to the design of the high-wing Lysander itself or simply that it was the wrong type of aircraft. The results showed that a low-wing monoplane could be positioned to conduct artillery observation and reconnaissance. Experiments were also conducted on the procedure that had been used. When artillery batteries were registering their precise location with observation aircraft, the call to fire was answered by two instead of three salvos 'since it was considered to be too difficult to make three observations during one run over the target'.[53] The Lysander was also used to conduct more trials where aircraft corrected rather than simply observed the fall of shot and advised the battery of this information as had occurred previously. The fact that the Lysander was used for this type of trial was not of great importance as, despite its obsolescence, it was the procedure being trialled and not the aircraft.[54]

A conference was held at Army Co-operation Command's headquarters to discuss how best to further develop artillery reconnaissance procedures, during which it was suggested that the clock code system developed during the First World War should be replaced by another used by the gunners of the Royal Artillery. The gunner system, it was argued, would allow the required volume of fire to be produced more quickly and would also give the pilot greater freedom in target selection as, due to the higher vantage point, he would be able to judge the importance of the target. It was claimed that the gunner procedure would allow a pilot, untrained in anything else, to conduct an impromptu shoot through the use of R/T.[55]

Barratt was personally sceptical of this potential change, fearing that pilots would have a greater burden placed upon them. He did 'not consider from the nature of the trials conducted there is any justification for the recommendation that the Artillery method of correcting fire should be introduced in place of the Clock Code System'.[56] Barratt's views were confirmed by the senior artillery officer of Eastern Command, Brigadier Duncan. Duncan was of the opinion that the Air OP, using the clock code system, could provide a useful, but limited function, supplementing the information that was already gained through normal artillery reconnaissance channels such as the Land Observation Post. Barratt was willing to concede that a pilot who had been extensively trained had always been able to conduct a shoot using the gunner procedure, but his belief in the clock code system stemmed from three considerations: such extensive training could not be given to every pilot; the gunner procedure was more complex and placed a greater degree of responsibility on the pilot; and the experiments that had been conducted had been brief in nature. Barratt was not against the new system due to any sense of conservatism about changing procedures or an unwillingness to co-operate with the Royal Artillery.[57] Further limited trials were held in April and reached similar conclusions to the previous ones:

> [The] artillery methods of ranging by corrections to line and range are simpler, quicker and more efficient than any method based on the clock code. They lend themselves more readily to observation from a low altitude behind our own lines, and are more in accordance with modern air fighting and AA [anti-aircraft] defence.[58]

It was felt that by adopting the artillery procedure for air observation there would be a simplification of training problems 'for both … the R[oyal] A[rtillery] and RAF'.[59] This opinion was voiced by a formation within Army Co-operation Command, but was still not enough to convince Barratt or the Air Staff of its utility—all were particularly reluctant to see the clock code system replaced unless they were presented with overwhelming evidence to do so.[60]

The army had lost total confidence in the clock code system to support their artillery in the field after their experiences in France and against the Italian Army in Libya.[61] Barratt's opinion was that it was not the system used that was at fault but that, particularly in France, British aircraft had been attempting to conduct shoots in the face of intense enemy opposition. His major concern with the trials that had been so far conducted with the artillery method of correction was that they had been too few in number and deliberately skewed to provide particular results. Barratt's insistence on retaining the old clock code system could be interpreted as simple preservation of RAF autonomy of the role, a favouring of tried and tested methods. But when we consider Barratt's attempts to work more closely with the army in general, however, combined with his previous experience as an artillery officer prior to joining the RFC in the First World War, as well as his willingness to codify new solutions such as the Wann–Woodall experiments, we can reach a different judgement.[62] The system did not have to be developed and refined to meet a deadline for use in active operations and so Barratt had the luxury of time to fully test these new ideas to ensure that they were not only robust enough, but also suitable for use in several different theatres. The evidence of the co-operation between Army Co-operation Command and the School of Artillery in the development process leads to the conclusion that Barratt considered the system unsatisfactory in its present form and he wished to see the results of more balanced trials before he would approve its use. Barratt was still also not convinced that army co-operation pilots could be trained in the artillery method and that when faced with enemy opposition, they would be more concerned with their own safety rather than the situation on the ground.[63] The results of further trials were overwhelmingly positive and with this Barratt's scepticism disappeared. He was now convinced not only of the effectiveness of the new procedure but also the ease with which army co-operation pilots could be trained to use it. The new system came into effect from 15 June 1941.[64]

The work for Barratt and Army Co-operation Command did not finish with the implementation of the new reconnaissance system. It was still necessary to refine the necessary communication system to allow it be rolled out across army co-operation squadrons and for them to be trained. To achieve maximum communication efficiency between aircraft and artillery batteries, it was agreed that a two-way R/T system should be used. This involved two different types of radio sets. The ground equipment was the Army No. 11 Set and the airborne unit in Tomahawk army co-operation aircraft initially used in this role, the Army No. 19 Set. A problem was identified very quickly during the initial training phase—the allotment of frequencies for the role. Barratt wrote to Balfour to explain the problem and argued that 'this promising suggestion should not be turned down because of the frequency difficulty but that the War Office should be pressed to review the allotment of frequencies so as to permit its adoption'.[65] In response to this letter, the army's Director of Telecommunications wrote to Barratt assuring him that the War Office saw no difficulty in 'allotting suitable frequencies to Squadrons for Artillery Co-operation'.[66] The development and refinement of the Air OP concept would continue into 1942 and 1943.

The possibility of invasion in early 1941 still loomed large over Britain as it was not clear what German intentions were since the end of the Battle of Britain and a series of exercises were conducted with this specific scenario in mind and with two overriding aims. The first was to increase the number of co-operation squadrons, including appropriate signal and control staff that would be able to provide the support required. The second was to make ground troops in Britain aware of the limits of close air support and not to see it as the panacea to all of the difficulties they might face in the field, as well being fully versed in the procedure to request impromptu aerial backup. If these aims could be achieved as quickly as possible, it would lead to a more efficient and effective air support system with which to help defeat any attempted invasion. A wider advantage would be that a critical mass of troops from both services would be trained in conducting air support and that they would be best placed to consider further improvements. The biggest of these exercises was Bumper, conducted during the traditional army exercise period of July and August, although smaller exercises were conducted throughout the year. One major issue affected these exercises and ensured continuing tensions between the Air Ministry and War Office—the release of Bomber Command's medium bomber squadrons from active operations.[67] Peirse, AOC-in-C Bomber Command, made it clear that in his opinion no reliance should be placed upon anti-invasion exercises involving the use of close air support as such methods would be unsuitable in defence of an amphibious landing.[68]

The first exercise of 1941, Dragon, took place in January. The most striking remark to emerge from the report was not about how successful, or not, the exercise as a whole had been, but that the close support tactics used had previously been 'evolved and practised … for joint operations in Palestine and in Air Control operations elsewhere'.[69] The Air Ministry were at pains to state what the priority for medium bomber squadrons was in order to avoid confusion between themselves and the War Office:

> Owing to the nature of these exercises it may be possible that misconceptions have arisen as to the role of medium bomber squadrons against invasion. In their anti-invasion role the medium bomber squadrons form part of the flexible organisation of Bomber Command and it would be uneconomical to keep them unemployed waiting to support the Army when a role could be found for them within the task of the Bomber Command.[70]

The full resources of the RAF would be deployed in an air support capacity in the event of any successful landing by German forces, but even during what would be a grave emergency, the RAF still wanted to maintain its mono-role command structure. This did not, however, apply to Army Co-operation Command as it was a non-operational command and did not have access to operational resources. The idea for using medium bomber squadrons in a close support role had first emerged during discussions regarding the Wann–Woodall experiments. Slessor, who was the then Director of Plans, believed that all medium bomber squadrons should be trained to conduct close support. Freeman highlighted to Slessor that certain squadrons had already been earmarked to conduct a close support role and that these squadrons would be made available for training in this role whenever they were not required for strategic operations against the German homeland. The availability of these squadrons was to be a running issue for both Army Co-operation Command and the War Office and led to the continuing bad relations between the Air and General Staffs.

A major factor in the availability of these medium bomber squadrons was that the staff who were responsible for deciding their training programmes and availability was changed shortly after the decision had been made to make them available to Army Co-operation Command. The new staff officers had, in Barratt's opinion, different priorities about the utilisation of these aircraft and the importance of the close support training exercises and to close support in general.[71] This was vehemently denied by the Air Staff, and the denial highlights further why Army Co-operation Command had been created. Goddard wrote to Barratt stating that 'it is most improper to suggest that [the then DCAS AVM] Douglas, agreed to the close support doctrine because he was anxious to *appease* the War Office' (emphasis in original).[72] That this had to be denied suggests that the Air Staff felt they had to defend the decisions they had made so far (to give tactical air support a greater profile in Britain) in order to prevent the accusation that they were simply acting in this way to relieve the pressure placed upon them by the War Office since the end of the Battle of France.

When the Air Staff reviewed what they saw as the potential future needs of the army in terms of air support they felt that it was necessary to repeat their doctrinal thinking of how best the army could be supported in the field. This was that 'the principal aim of bomber support for the army is to isolate the battlefield … i.e. direct support'.[73] The fundamental issue that had divided the two services since the end of the First World War about the role of aircraft in support of ground forces was no nearer resolution as the army still saw close support as the best method. The War Office was also increasingly unhappy with the Air Ministry over the training of medium bomber squadrons in any form of air support. Brooke wrote of the situation and re-emphasised the army's ideas about the correct form of air support:

> Close support of the Army is not only *not* the primary role of medium bomber squadrons, it is a role which they hardly consider or practice. Out of the proposed trial of 500 sorties of medium bombers for training, only 45 took place [emphasis in original].[74]

Brooke also made clear his feelings on the best possible solution to this problem:

> he was not satisfied with the amount of support he was receiving from the Royal Air Force. He had always been opposed to the formation of an Army Air Arm, but his experiences in recent months had driven him to the conclusion that some form of this, that is, some RAF resources under the direct control of the Army was essential.[75]

Due to the strategic situation that confronted Britain at this point in the Second World War, with a hostile power dominating the Channel ports and Atlantic coast and British land forces unable to launch operations on the continent, the RAF were the only service that could conduct operations that directly targeted the German homeland, and so they were able to dismiss the War Office's concerns with more ease than had been possible in 1940.

Barratt raised the concerns of Brooke and the War Office in general with Portal, who was now CAS. Barratt was well versed in the War Office's opinion on the development of air support in Britain as he had discussed the matter at length with Brooke. Barratt highlighted that Brooke did not see any failings in the co-operation between Army Co-operation Command and the General Staff or War Office but that the issue was one of the policy of the Air Staff. Barratt was also well aware that the RAF did not have the resources available 'to set aside any large proportion of air forces for the exclusive support of the Army which was not actually engaged in a land campaign'.[76] If the resources were not available for large-scale support of operations they were definitely not available for training exercises. There were two major issues with this however. First, the exercises being conducted focused upon anti-invasion operations and not the support of ground troops in an offensive capacity. As the strategic outlook for Britain hopefully improved the focus for training and development would move from anti-invasion to offensive operations. Second, with the still limited resources available to Bomber Command to conduct its strategic air offensive campaign against Germany, the medium bomber squadrons were essential to increase the fire-power being deployed over Germany. The medium bomber squadrons involved in these operations suffered from high casualty rates and turnover of personnel, which meant that little continuity and advancements could be made in the training. Barratt felt that there was no advantage to be gained in continuing to train Bomber Command squadrons in close air support for this reason.[77] He must surely have felt frustrated with this situation—training was under his control but he was unable to run a programme that could do more than impart the basics of close support operations.[78]

The training that had been conducted with the medium bomber squadrons of 2 Group had highlighted certain areas that could be developed further as the training season continued. The first was that 'The highly trained medium bomber squadrons ... were capable of adapting to this form of support given a short period of extensive training'. The second was that 'such training lies more in ground organisation, rapid briefing, correct interrogation, quick get-away and turn around, and knowledge of the system'.[79] These limited training exercises had shown where improvements and training needed to be focused. The basic system designed by Wann and Woodall and codified by Army Co-operation Command had been shown to be effective and was relatively easy for those involved in deploying it to master after a brief but intensive period of training. It was still to be seen, however, whether it could work when deployed on a larger scale, as the Director of Bomber Operations, Air Commodore J. W. Baker, commented: 'It remains ... to test the army air support organisation as a whole, and for this purpose it will be necessary for a number of 2 Group Stations to be exercised simultaneously'.[80]

The problems of organising training exercises with the medium bomber squadrons of Bomber Command was fully demonstrated when an exercise scheduled for March had to be cancelled due to the aircraft being required for raids over Germany. This was not, however, the only factor in the rise in tensions between the Air and General Staffs. The principal object of this training was 'to perfect the organisation for the provision of air support, including the method of control' and 'To train the RAF in army support, and incidentally the army in the widest use of this support'.[81] The preliminary training exercises were designed in such a way as to provide basic information regarding 'the amount of ground training required, gauge the type and extent of the exercises which were subsequently to be conducted by the other stations in No. 2 Group and [further] study the organisation for army air support in general'.[82] The developing strategic outlook and the time required to develop as robust an air support system as possible would be a major factors affecting when any British expeditionary force could return to the continent. In actual fact, the strategic outlook would now be fundamentally dictated by events on the Eastern Front after the German invasion of the Soviet Union in the summer of 1941, actions in North Africa and US reaction to the Japanese attack on its fleet at Pearl Harbor.

Further training exercises would also be planned, directed and controlled by Barratt with the staff at Army Co-operation Command.[83] Barratt was given a further deadline of 1 September to have completed the training of No. 2 Group. This would be no easy task to accomplish with the conflicting priorities for the group and Barratt's position and status within the RAF as a whole. The officer who was given responsibility for devising the system of training was Barratt's representative at Home Forces, Oxborrow and he 'fostered' the Command there. Oxborrow also negotiated 'between 2 Group and the Corps with which it was successfully trained and ... superintended the formation of the CSBCs'. Oxborrow must take the credit for the continued development of the CSBC concept originally devised by Wann and Woodall.[84]

The training so far conducted by No. 2 Group was seen by the Air Staff as 'an unqualified success', despite the issues that had and would continue to plague it.[85] They also felt that the preconceptions the War Office had regarding the RAF's ability to provide air support had been dispelled:

> The army have always doubted the ability of bomber squadrons, firstly to find battlefield targets, and secondly to get off the ground quickly. Last week's exercises have certainly proved these doubts to be unfounded.[86]

The summer of 1941 saw the first large-scale army co-operation exercise involving squadrons of No. 2 Group. Before the exercise was conducted, however, there were some slight modifications made to the original Wann–Woodall system. The use and development of the CSBCs had stalled due to confusion over the terminology that was used by the air and ground staff within them, leading to a real lack of efficiency. The War Office felt that the role and remit of the CSBC should be extended to include the ability to 'operate offensive action by both fighter reconnaissance squadrons and bomber reconnaissance squadrons when these are employed in the attack of targets on the ground in Army Air Support.'[87] The confusion over terminology affected this aspect of the CSBC's work, and stemmed from the use of the terms 'close' and 'direct' support, 'as no clear line of demarcation [between the two terms] is possible'.[88] In Barratt's eyes, part of the problem was due to the bombing tasks that the CSBC was meant to help aircraft undertake. It again demonstrated the army's inability to consider that the CSBC might be a force multiplier at the operational level of war—they simply saw it operating at the tactical level. There was a great deal of

> misconstruing [of the term] close support [which is] far too narrow, and in regarding the CSBC as exclusively the instrument for arranging the attack of targets pointed out by forward formations, and not as it should be, the advanced headquarters of the Royal Air Force formation providing intimate support for the land battle.[89]

In an attempt to resolve the problems caused by the terminology, Brooke suggested that a simplification of terms was the best way to resolve the difficulties. He felt that the terms causing the confusion 'should be abolished and that all bombing carried out by aircraft under the control of army authorities should be known by one name such as "Army Support"'.[90] Whilst the air support resources would never come under the army's control, it was agreed that the terms caused unnecessary confusion and so they were abolished. The CSBC was also renamed to reflect this change in terminology and became the Army Air Support Control (AASC).[91] The function of the AASC remained unchanged.

The Air and General Staffs expected the majority of large-scale training in army co-operation to take place in September and October 1941, and Exercise Bumper was the largest of the year. In terms of the air aspect of the exercise, it was intended to use Bumper to 'study the employment of aircraft in army air support of large formations in offensive operations', as well as the 'employment of army co-operation squadrons in their reconnaissance role when working with Corps and Armoured Divisions'.[92]

Bumper also gave the RAF the opportunity to deploy the AASC in circumstances that resembled active operations as far as was possible and the two deployed units utilised different communications systems. No. 1 AASC was allotted to Southern Army, who played the role of British forces, and placed rear links at the aerodromes of the formations that were to provide the support for their ground forces. No. 2 AASC was allotted to forces tasked as the German IV Army and as with No. 1 ASSC placed rear links to the aerodromes but also added another communications link between the headquarters of No. 2 Bomber Group, to allow it to remain in contact with its aerodromes.[93]

The exercise was also used as a chance to retest one of the ideas that had originally been discarded during the Wann–Woodall experiments, as it was now feasible to allot support aircraft to ground formations. The idea had received theoretical approval from Wann and Woodall but could not be tested at the time as the RAF did not have the resources available. Barratt's report on the air aspect of the exercise demonstrates how this might function during active operations as it is similar to

> the control of any other supporting arm. Squadrons are each equipped with their own 'means' and are allotted in support of forward formations in the same way as long range artillery might be allotted. The 'means' transmits the forward command's demands direct to the squadron. The army command and RAF command can re-allot squadrons, allot the reserves, to formations using the normal communications.[94]

Barratt weighed up the advantages and disadvantages of allotting squadrons to ground formations based on the experience of Bumper and the opinions put forward by Wann and Woodall, and came to the conclusion that it was the quickest available and the simplest in terms of set-up. It also allowed training to be simplified. Further advantage would be gained as the local commander would know what forces were currently available to provide support and the pilots would be more knowledgeable about their specific area of operations.[95]

Given an extended period of working and resting together a better relationship would be developed between the airmen and ground forces, as had happened with the artillery observation pilots and artillery batteries in the First World War. This would increase the efficiency of the air support system as pilots would have greater empathy for the forces they were supporting. The exercise also provided confirmation of the basic ideas that had emerged to conduct air support and provided avenues for further trials and training, particularly with regard to the efficiency of the AASC:

> The broad principles on which we have been working have survived the tests of training to which they have been submitted remarkably well. For further progress we need two things—aircraft of the right type in the requisite numbers, and available for the tasks of army air support as a first priority—and secondly, experience in actual operations.[96]

The report on the AASC was written by the War Office and not the Air Ministry and highlighted another issue that continued to sour relations between the two organisations for the majority of the Second World War: the allocation, design and delivery of aircraft, from Britain and the US, to fulfil and expand the RAF's ground support capacity in Britain. The COS Committee were advised of the average timings for aircraft taking off once the information from the AASC had been received at the aerodrome. For the No. 2 Group bomber exercise this figure was nine minutes and nine seconds. In BUMPER it was fifteen minutes.[97] These times were a vast improvement over those seen during the Battle of France, and even the Wann–Woodall experiments, even if it was not under active operational conditions.

Bumper had also further clarified the role of the AASC when it was deployed during operations. It was 'to act as a clearing-house for calls for air support initiated by forward army elements' and 'to despatch air support sorties against targets selected as a result of information received from tactical reconnaissance and other sources of intelligence available at army headquarters'.[98] The issue of the amount of AASC's that would need to be deployed when large ground formations were in contact with the enemy and at what level of command the decisions should be made, was also resolved during Bumper:

> The scale of one AASC per army means that the control will normally be held at army headquarters until such a time as the army commander is in possession of information sufficient to enable him to decide with which of his lower formations he intends to strike the decisive blow.[99]

Whilst Bumper had been a resounding success for the furthering of army co-operation in Britain, it did cause tensions between the Prime Minister and the Air Ministry over the extended period that the squadrons of No. 2 Group would be unable to conduct active strategic level operations, despite their removal from the role receiving the agreement of the COS Committee. Churchill was anxious that the fight should be carried to Germany in any way and as hard as possible. That No. 2 Group had been prevented from being involved in these operations was of great concern. These tensions increased as bad weather prevented the conduct of major operations against Germany after the Group's return from Bumper.[100]

Alongside the development of army co-operation training, much work was also done to prepare the RAF and army to operate in anti-invasion operations. The communications and tactics that were to be used in this worst-case scenario increased the tensions between the Air Ministry and the War Office despite the best efforts of Army Co-operation Command to improve them. Army Co-operation Command's role in anti-invasion planning, due to its non-operational status, had little to offer outside the realm of ideas and experimentation and it was sidelined in terms of resources and influence. Despite this, it was still important as an organisation—it had a role within the wider RAF Command network and demonstrated the innovations that were occurring in other departments. Army Co-operation Command was also consulted on some of the ideas that were being put forward to support the army. In developing anti-invasion plans both services were more willing to work together through Army Co-operation Command to find common solutions and also to dedicate sufficient resources as the survival of the nation was at stake:

> There can ... be no possible conflict of aims between the army and the air force and the army will be fully and directly served by all classes of aircraft. It will in fact, be supported by the whole of the Bomber and Fighter Commands.[101]

The RAF were at pains to highlight that in the case of a national emergency, such as defeating a successful invasion, there would be no need for specialist army co-operation squadrons to support the army as any and all resources would be deployed in a support role. Even in this, however, they still kept to their doctrinal thinking, arguing that as the army could only be involved in either defensive or counter-attack operations in such a situation, the best way to support them would be an interdiction role, meaning 'the prevention of the arrival of enemy reinforcements and not the direct attack of his forward troops'.[102] Goddard went even further when giving the RAF's opinion of the best use of air resources in this context:

> The Air Ministry is strongly of the opinion that, in the event of invasion, the opportunities for *direct* support by bombers will be so great and advantageous that it is likely to be uneconomical to employ bomber squadrons in close support.[103] [emphasis in original]

It is highly unlikely that in the event of a successful invasion by German forces that the RAF would not have given all forms of air support to the army in order to repel it, but it does highlight that in doctrinal terms, the thinking of the RAF had advanced little since the Battle of France. The commander of No. 71 Group, Army Co-operation Command, commenting on a memorandum on bomber support for the army stated that 'in the event of invasion all bomber aircraft shall remain under the control of C-in-C Bomber Command'. The War Office agreed that this was the most sensible place for bomber resources to be controlled from but still had misgivings over how they were to be controlled: Any 'success was dependent upon the maintenance of landline communications' and 'The average time factor involved will not allow the reasonable possibility of effective attack on close support targets, and in fact is such as to reduce all air bombardment to direct support.'[104] Whilst the Wann–Woodall experiments had decreased lead times for impromptu air support, the system was not robust enough nor very widespread within the RAF for it to have a major impact and so both services would be reliant on the ideas used in France to provide air cover.

Barratt's opinion on the anti-invasion measures being prepared was sought only the once and concerned what the army's requirements would be in this event. He believed that 'given an adequate scale of army co-operation squadrons, the fighter and bomber requirements of the army should be capable of being met … by Fighter and Bomber Commands'. For Bomber Command to be able to fulfil these requirements Barratt suggested 'that it will be necessary [for] detailed arrangements for both direct and close support to be put into operation in the event of the enemy securing penetration into this country'.[105] There is no evidence to show if this was done and the situation where it would have to be employed never emerged.

As has been demonstrated by the fact that the RAF had to move squadrons from Bomber Command for army co-operation exercises on a temporary basis, they were ill-equipped for this role and the War Office pushed hard for the aircraft of Army Co-operation Command to be upgraded, and also for the development of a specialist dive-bomber. The RAF believed, correctly, that this increased attention on dive-bombers was the result of a fundamental misreading of the Battle of France and the impact of German air power.[106] At this time the Air Ministry was only willing to concede that resources had not been dedicated to air support in the past.[107] Army Co-operation Command was in an almost impossible situation regarding resources—given the problems that still existed within the British aircraft industry, the difficulties of receiving regular supplies of aircraft from America, its non-operational status, and the standing of army co-operation in general within the RAF in Britain, Army Co-operation Command would always be at the bottom of the list for equipment.[108] Despite these pressures and the strategic outlook (operations on the continent could not yet be considered feasible due to the pressure being exerted by the *Kriegsmarine* on British shipping), it was agreed to re-equip Army Co-operation Command with either Brewster or Vultee aircraft, both of American design.

However, Army Co-operation Command was to be disappointed once again, as shown by a letter Barratt wrote to the Deputy Director of Plans at the Air Ministry, ACM Sir Ronald Ivelaw-Chapman:

> In the view of the shortage of pilots and the necessity for concentrating on all economies possible to permit the expansion of the bomber effort, I am aware that it is now not possible to carry out the expansion of army co-operation squadrons by the forecasted date, that is to say, May.[109]

Bomber Command was, rightly, the most important part of the RAF at this time and so demanded ever increasing resources at the expense of Army Co-operation Command who would have to make do with the scraps that were left over. It is difficult to see how this situation could have been resolved any differently to allow Army Co-operation Command greater access to resources. It is doubtful, however, that even if these additional resources had been available that they would, in fact, have been used to re-equip Army Co-operation Command. The situation was not helped by demands from the War Office that were unrealistic in both the amount of aircraft they felt was needed and the timeframe for them to be built and available for operations.[110] To their credit, and despite the production difficulties still plaguing the industry, the RAF had committed to and provided eleven medium bomber squadrons specifically for use in a close support capacity by February 1941.[111] It is not clear if these were newly built aircraft or machines that were not required by other squadrons. As a non-operational Command, Army Co-operation Command would not actually have seen these aircraft (they would have been registered as part of the Army Co-operation Command structure within Home Forces) and would only advise on how they could best fulfil their designated role.

Eden was particularly satisfied simply to have persuaded the Air Ministry to create an extra eleven medium bomber squadrons for close support.[112] His reasons for seeing this as a small but important victory were expressed in a letter written to Sinclair: 'It is particularly satisfactory to me to find that the Air Staff agree to the necessity of providing close support aircraft for the army.'[113] A statement such as this from Eden demonstrates just how deeply the experience of defeat in France had affected the army in Britain as a whole—and that partly to shirk their own responsibility they continued to blame the RAF.

The General Staff's proposals for an air support force capable of providing support to ground forces in the field was a minimum of fifty-four squadrons. They believed, as was almost inevitable with the directive that had been issued to Barratt when he took charge of Army Co-operation Command, that these squadrons 'should be allotted to Army Co operation Command and trained primarily for army support work'.[114] Fearing that this was yet another attempt by the army to create a de facto army air arm by the back door, the Air Staff argued that if these squadrons were to be created and placed within Army Co-operation Command, the fifty-four squadrons would be 'much less efficient as fighters and bombers (which would doubtless be their actual role in conjunction with land forces) than they would be if their primary role was in Fighter and Bomber Commands'.[115] They further claimed that, were these squadrons allotted to Army Co-operation Command for training, their time would 'be taken up in learning tactical reconnaissance detail not essential to close bomber and fighter support'.[116] It is difficult to see the Air Staff's case, particularly in the second part of their objections. The squadrons would, rightly, have to undergo a brief period of tactical reconnaissance training in order to enhance their role when providing close support but the focus of the training need not have necessarily been on this area and could have been centred on close support. A man with Barratt's command, leadership and administrative experience, could have ensured this was the case. It is also difficult to see just how being in Army Co-operation Command would have made these squadrons any less efficient than if they were in Bomber and Fighter Commands. These objections again lead to the conclusion that the Air Staff saw Army Co-operation Command as a necessary evil, but one that could not be allowed to expand too far or to gain too much power or influence. The Air Staff also employed the oft-used argument that their ability to prosecute the strategic air offensive would be weakened if this proposal was implemented.[117]

In order to prevent relations falling to an even lower level, the Air Staff countered the General Staff's fifty-four squadron proposal with one of their own. This proposal was that six new squadrons should be created from scratch and allotted to the army, through Home Forces, 'for tactical bomber and fighter reconnaissance roles'. This would bring the number of army co-operation squadrons in Britain up to a total of twenty.[118] In addition to this, twenty-four squadrons currently within Bomber and Fighter Commands were also to be trained in army co-operation in the widest sense, 'to provide bomber and low attack support in the battlefield areas'. With the difficulties already being experienced in trying to train No. 2 Group in army co-operation, it is difficult to see how these extra squadrons could be trained in a manner that would satisfy both parties.

The War Office's expectations of Army Co-operation Command were crushed with these proposals.[119] It became clear that Army Co-operation Command had only been created as a tactical measure to relieve some of the pressure the RAF had faced in the aftermath of the Battle of France and the Bartholomew Report. Army Co-operation Command's real power and ability to effect change had been seriously curtailed by the Air Ministry from the outset but this did not become clear to the War Office until now. It was moves such as this by the Air Staff, combined with the years of stalling that led Brooke to claim, 'The situation is hopeless and I see no solution besides the provision of an army air arm.'[120] The new aircraft that were to form the six army co-operation squadrons, whether placed within Army Co-operation Command or Bomber and Fighter Commands, were another source of tension, this time not just between the Air Ministry and

War Office, but also between the British and Americans regarding deliveries of aircraft.[121]

During 1941, Army Co-operation Command was in the process of replacing their obsolete Lysanders with Tomahawks from the United States.[122] The army felt that, as this had already been discussed in February, the decisions reached bore 'little relation to the fact, because no satisfactory steps have been taken to implement the agreed policy'. The actions of the RAF in re-equipping Army Co-operation Command had, for the War Office at least, been too little too late and done at too slow a pace. Paget went further in his criticism and the effect it had. 'I am convinced that far from progressing, co-operation between the army and RAF has slipped back seriously during this period ... There has been no mention of the provision of the suitable close support bomber, which was stated as under consideration last December.'[123] Paget's views were not a direct criticism of Army Co-operation Command or the work that it had so far done but reflected an increasing frustration felt within the War Office that the RAF were still not taking the development of tactical air power as seriously as the War Office felt it should have been.

Delays in replacing the Lysander, first with Blenheims and then with Tomahawks, was due to aircraft supply problems, specifically the Baltimore, which had been ordered from the United States. Until these arrived to re-equip other squadrons the Blenheims could not be released for army co-operation tasks. There were also serious delays with the Tomahawk. The Air Staff believed that there was no need to produce a specialist dive-bomber aircraft as most of the specification could be 'closely met by various types in existence, though not necessarily in production'.[124] There was also disagreement about how aircraft should be allotted when used in a close support role. The War Office believed that there should be three squadrons per Corps and three per armoured division. Half of these aircraft were to be fighter reconnaissance and the other half bomber reconnaissance aircraft.[125] They also felt that army air support squadrons should form

> an air component which should be an integral part of the corps of the army to which it was allotted. They must be specially trained and the machinery for their control must be organised and trained with the squadrons.[126]

This again demonstrates that the army had not considered the operational level implications of a force organised in this way and were still viewing the problem of air support from the tactical level. Such a force organised in this way would be limited in the effect it could have at the operational level as its focus would be on the basic tactical problems faced by the army in the field. Considering the size of the RAF in 1941, the War Office demand for fifty-four squadrons was wildly optimistic and this was part of the reasoning put forward by the RAF when dismissing the army's ideas. At this time, the RAF also regained its confidence and felt able to stand up to the army's demands. Portal stated that

> The Army Air requirements set out in COS (41) 89 (0) call for the allotment of an air component and specialised types of aircraft amounting to a total of 3,888 aircraft. This total should be compared with our current first-line strength of the RAF which is 3,585 and the total of 5,623 which was our expansion figure for the Spring of 1942. If these requirements were to be met in the form in which they have been stated it could only be at the expense of the bomber and fighter expansion. The general effect of meeting these requirements out of the contemplated Air Force programme would be a reduction of 36 long-range fighter squadrons, 12 light bomber squadrons, 37 medium bomber squadrons and 130 heavy bomber squadrons.[127]

It cannot be denied that the army exaggerated their requirements for air support during 1941. If they had received all the squadrons they had requested more problems would have been created rather than solved as it would not have been possible for either the army or Army Co-operation Command to make full use of them. Through exaggerating their requirements, the army was hoping to have a fraction of their request fulfilled. Production problems meant that the RAF would not have been able to meet these overblown requirements. Even if this had been possible, the RAF's overall attitude towards army co-operation meant that a minimum number of army co-operation squadrons would have been agreed to in order to appear to be taking the development of army co-operation as seriously as the army believed was necessary.

The army continued to push for as large an air component as possible to act as a de facto army air arm. The RAF continued to refute these claims and in October outlined the following reasons why:

> At a time when the air offensive is a vital factor in our plans the Air Staff believe it to be wrong in principle that a substantial part of our air resources should be placed in a role where training is wholly subordinate to fighting. The Air Staff agree that a high standard of training is necessary. No difficulty arises about such training with the army co-operation squadrons which are

permanently allotted to the army. But the balance of fighter and bomber squadrons required for army support must in their view be provided from RAF formations and not be permanently allotted to the army ... the Air Staff proposals on the question of army support squadrons are as follows:— Twenty squadrons of army co-operation aircraft will be formed and placed in Army Co-operation Command at the disposal of the army.[128]

Whilst the number of squadrons had not increased, the decision to place them within Army Co-operation Command is of interest—still keeping to the principle that air resources should be centralised and under the command of an RAF officer, the army would now have greater access to this force than they had previously. The proposal to form these new squadrons in Army Co-operation Command would be a source of heated discussion and argument in 1942.

The state of army co-operation in Britain and in the Western Desert was particularly poor at the end of 1941. Relations between senior commanders had, if anything deteriorated further during the year and there was little sign of improvement. Army Co-operation Command was still waiting to be re-equipped, and discussions on the best way to achieve this would continue well into 1942. Army Co-operation Command was, however, to find itself sidelined to an even greater extent in the calls for resources and the ability to develop ideas beyond the experimental stage.

Notes

1. Butler, *Grand Strategy Vol. II*, pp. 342–53. Postan, *British War Production*, pp. 119–22.
2. This argument is made in great depth in Carrington, *Soldier at Bomber Command*, Chapter 3. Also see Peach, 'A Neglected Turning Point', pp. 150, 167. Probert, 'The Determination of RAF Policy', p. 684.
3. Carrington, *Soldier at Bomber Command*, p. 43.
4. TNA AIR 10/5547, AHB Narrative, Close Support.
5. Liddel Hart Centre for Military Archives, Alanbrooke Papers 11/15. Alex Danchev and Daniel Todman (eds), *War Diaries 1939–1945: Field Marshal Lord Alanbrooke* (Phoenix: London, 2002 [Weidenfeld and Nicolson: London 2001]), p. 268. The entry referred to above is dated 18 May 1941. Arthur Bryant, *The Turn of the Tide 1939–1945* (Collins: London, 1957), p. 237.
6. TNA AIR 10/5547, AHB Narrative, Close Support.
7. TNA AIR 39/28, Letter from Headquarters No. 71 Group to AOC-in-C Army Co-operation Command, 22 December 1940.

8. TNA AIR 39/20, Letter from AOC-in-C Army Co-operation Command to the Under-Secretary of State for Air regarding the Adjustment of Duties between Headquarters Army Co-operation Command, and Headquarters No. 71 Group in relation to General Headquarters Home Forces, 5 February 1941.
9. TNA AIR 39/20, Memorandum by GOC-in-C Home Forces, regarding Liaison between GHQ Home Forces and RAF Commands, 13 February 1941. Exercise Victor was series of army/air exercises to test communications and signals methods. TNA PREM 3/496/1, 3/496/2, 3/496/4.
10. TNA AIR 39/20, Memorandum by GOC-in-C Home Forces regarding Liaison between GHQ Home Forces and RAF Commands, 13 February 1941.
11. TNA AIR 39/20, Letter from DMC to AOC-in-C Army Co-operation Command, 20 February 1941.
12. TNA AIR 39/20, Draft Letter written by DMC on behalf of VCAS, c.February 1941. As this is in response to the communications from AOC-in-C Army Co-operation Command and GOC-in-C Home Forces the letter dates after 20 February 1941.
13. TNA AIR 39/20, Letter from Headquarters No. 71 Group and GHQ Home Forces to Army Co-operation Command, 11 March 1941.
14. TNA AIR 39/20, Memorandum on the organisation of RAF Staff, GHQ Home Forces, 11 March 1941.
15. TNA AIR 39/20, Letter from DMC to AOC-in-C Army Co-operation Command, 16 March 1941.
16. TNA AIR 39/20, Letter from I. R. Hardman to AOC-in-C Army Co-operation Command, 19 March 1941.
17. TNA AIR 39/20, Letter from AOC-in-C Army Co-operation Command to Under-Secretary of State for Air, 23 April 1941.
18. TNA AIR 20/327, Memorandum on Disbanding No. 71 Group and the Formation on Six Army Co-operation Headquarters, 9 August 1941.
19. TNA AIR 20/2812, Meeting between CIGS and CAS on Army Co-operation Matters, 19 February 1941. TNA AIR 2/7336, Letter from the War Office to DMC on relations between the War Office and Army Co-operation Command, 18 February 1941.
20. TNA AIR 20/2812, Notes on the Agenda for a meeting between CIGS and CAS, c.February 1941. TNA AIR 20/2812, Minutes of a meeting held to consider Army Co-operation matters, 19 February 1941.
21. TNA AIR 2/7336, Minutes of a meeting to discuss Army Co-operation matters, 19 February 1941.
22. TNA AIR 39/28, Letter from DMC to AOC-in-C Army Co-operation Command, 29 January 1941.

23. TNA AIR 2/7359, Minute from DMC to CAS, 29 January 1941.
24. IWM Carrington Papers, 8/11/6.
25. TNA AIR 19/562, Minute from the Prime Minister to the Secretary of State for Air and CAS, 1 July 1941.
26. TNA AIR 19/562, Minute from the Secretary of State for Air to the Prime Minister, 1 June 1941.
27. John Ray, *The Battle of Britain: Dowding and the First Victory, 1940* (Cassell Military Paperbacks: London, 2000 [Arms and Armour Press: London, 1994]), pp. 166, 160.
28. Orange, *Dowding*, pp. 238–9.
29. Jack Dixon, *Dowding and Churchill: The Dark Side of the Battle of Britain* (Pen and Sword: Barnsley, 2008), p. 147. Martin Gilbert has noted how Churchill wanted to 'give Dowding command of Army Co-operation Command in Britain'. This statement is, however, made in a footnote and no further analysis is given. Winston S. Churchill, *Vol. VI: Finest Hour, 1939–1941* (London: Heinemann, 1983), p. 1040, footnote 3.
30. TNA AIR 19/562, Letter from the Secretary of State for Air to the Prime Minister, 20 December 1941.
31. TNA CAB 101/136, Draft of Grand Strategy Narratives, Army Air Co-operation Part III, undated.
32. TNA AIR 19/562, Letter from the Prime Minister to the Secretary of State for Air and CAS, 2 June 1941. Hansard HC Deb, 4 March 1942, Vol. 378, Cols. 656–749, http://hansard.millbanksystems.com/commons/1942/mar/04/sir-archibald-sinclairs-statement. Accessed 24 November 2012. TNA CAB 101/136, Draft of Grand Strategy Narratives. IWM Carrington Papers, 8/11/6, Formation of Army Co-operation Command.
33. Slessor's rank at this time was temporary and would not become permanent until April 1942. Vincent Orange, *Slessor: Bomber Champion: The Life of Marshal of the Royal Air Force Sir John Slessor* (Grub Street: London, 2006), pp. 80, 90.
34. TNA AIR 20/4446, Letter from Air Chief Marshal Sir Wilfred Freeman to John Slessor, 27 July 1941.
35. For further details on the fighting in the Western Desert see I. S. O. Playfair, *The Mediterranean and Middle East Vols. I–IV* (HMSO: London, 1954–1966). Philip Guedalla, *Middle East 1940–1942: A Study in Air Power* (Hodder and Stoughton: London, 1944). P. G. Griffith, 'British Armoured Warfare in the Western Desert', in J. P. Harris and F. H. Toase (eds), *Armoured Warfare* (D.T. Batsford: London, 1990). Kent Feorowich, 'Axis prisoners as sources of British military intelligence', *Intelligence and National Security*, 14: 2 (1999), pp. 156–78.

36. TNA AIR 41/44, The Middle East Campaigns Vol. 1, p. 155. Hallion, *Strike from the Sky*, p. 153. Gladman, *Intelligence and Anglo-American Air Support*, pp. 59, 76.
37. Weinberg, *A World at Arms*, p. 223.
38. TNA CAB 53/35, COS (65) JP Egypt: Combined Defence Plan, 17 December 1937. TNA CAB 53/36, COS (674) JP Defence of Egypt, 4 February 1938. TNA CAB 53/37, COS (691) Mediterranean, Middle East and North-East Africa Defence Appreciation 21 February 1938. Hall, *Strategy for Victory*, p. 68.
39. TNA AIR 41/44, The Middle East Campaigns Vol. 1, p. 155. Hall, *Strategy for Victory*, p. 82.
40. TNA AIR 10/5547 AI IB Narrative Close Support. Lord Tedder, *With Prejudice: The War Memoirs of Marshal of the Royal Air Force Lord Tedder* (Cassell: London, 1966), pp. 124–8. Hall, *Strategy for Victory*, pp. 82–3.
41. Hall, *Strategy for Victory*, p. 83.
42. TNA AIR 41/44. The Middle East Campaigns Vol. 1, p. 174. TNA AIR 10/5547, AHB Narrative Close Support. Hall, *Strategy for Victory*, pp. 83–4.
43. TNA AIR 10/5547, AHB Narrative Close Support. Alan Moorehead, *The Desert War* (Hamish Hamilton: London, 1965 [Sphere: London, 1989]), p. 151.
44. Hall, *Strategy for Victory*, p. 105.
45. TNA CAB 101/136, Army Air-Co-operation, p. 26; Hall, *Strategy for Victory*, p. 105.
46. Portal Papers Folder 2, Correspondence between the Prime Minister and the CAS, 19 August–5 September 1941; TNA AIR 41/25, The Middle East Campaigns Vol. II, p. 20; I. S. O. Playfair, *The Mediterranean and Middle East Vol II*, pp. 287–8.
47. More details of Churchill's intervention on this issue can be found in Hall, *Strategy for Victory*, pp. 107–8.
48. Ibid., p. 109.
49. TNA AIR 39/47, Letter from AOC-in-C Army Co-operation Command to the Under-Secretary of State for Air regarding air force co-operation with the Royal Artillery, 29 January.
50. TNA AIR 39/47, Memorandum regarding Artillery/Air Co-operation, 6 February 1941.
51. Darrell Knight, *Artillery Flyers at War: A History of the 664, 665 and 666 'Air Observation Post' Squadrons of the Canadian Air Force* (Merriam Press: Bennington, Vermont, 2010), p. 32.
52. Parham and Belfield, *Unarmed Into Battle*, p. 17.
53. TNA AIR 39/47, Artillery Reconnaissance in a Single Seater Fighter Type, *c*.March 1941.

54. TNA AIR 39/47, Letter from the Under-Secretary of State for Air to AOC-in-C Army Co-operation Command, 5 April 1941.
55. TNA AIR 39/47, Artillery Co-operation Trials—Part I, April 1941.
56. TNA AIR 39/47, Conference held at Army Co-operation Command on Artillery Reconnaissance, 9 April 1941. TNA AIR 39/47, Letter from AOC-in-C Army Co-operation Command to Headquarters No. 70 Group, 12 April 1941.
57. TNA AIR 39/47, Letter from AOC-in-C Army Co-operation Command to Headquarters No. 70 Group, 12 April 1941.
58. TNA AIR 39/47, Artillery Co-operation Tests—Part II, April 1941
59. TNA AIR 39/47, Report from Headquarters No. 70 Group to Army Co-operation Command, 15 April.
60. TNA AIR 39/47, Letter from the Air Ministry to J. D. Woodall, 26 April 1941.
61. TNA AIR 39/47, Letter from Major-General Otto Lund, GHQ Home Forces to AOC-in-C Army Co-operation Command on Artillery Reconnaissance, 5 April 1941.
62. Liddell Hart Centre for Military Archives, King's College London, http://www.kcl.ac.uk/lhcma/locreg/BARRATT.html. Accessed 25 April 2013.
63. TNA AIR 39/47, Letter from ACO-in-C Army Co-operation Command to Major-General Otto Lund, GHQ Home Forces in response to a letter from CGS on Artillery Reconnaissance, 10 May 1941.
64. TNA AIR 39/47, Minutes of a Meeting held at the School of Artillery, Larkhill, 2 June 1941.
65. TNA AIR 39/48, Letter from AOC-in-C Army Co-operation Command to the Under-Secretary of State for Air regarding Artillery Co-operation, 15 August 1941.
66. TNA AIR 39/48, Letter from the Director of Telecommunications to AOC-in-C Army Co-operation Command, 9 October 1941.
67. Jacobs, 'Air Support', p. 176.
68. TNA AIR 2/7410, Letter from AOC-in-C Bomber Command to the Under-Secretary of State for Air. 14 February 1941.
69. TNA AIR 20/5840, Remarks on Close Support Bombing and other Air activities in Anti-Invasion Co-operation prepared for use at a final conference at GHQ Home Forces on Exercise Dragon, 5–8 January 1941.
70. TNA AIR 2/5524, DMC's draft of an Air Staff Memorandum on the use of Close Support against invasion, 23 February 1941.
71. TNA AIR 39/16, Memorandum by AOC-in-C Army Co-operation Command on Close Support Development, c.May 1941.
72. TNA AIR 39/16, Letter from DMC to AOC-in-C Army Co-operation Command, 22 May 1941.

73. TNA AIR 20/4446, The Employment of Bomber Aircraft in Support of Land Operations, 1 April 1941.
74. TNA WO 32/9836, Memorandum by CIGS on co-operation between Army and RAF, 3 May 1941.
75. TNA AIR 39/16, Minutes of a Conference held at the War Office to discuss certain proposals for improving Army–Royal Air Force Co-ordinations, 12 May 1941.
76. TNA AIR 39/16, Letter from AOC-in-C Army Co-operation Command to CAS, 13 May 1941.
77. Ibid.
78. TNA AIR 23/1762, Training of Squadrons of 2 Group in Army Air Support—Report on preliminary period by AOC in C Army Co-operation Command, 4 July 1941.
79. TNA AIR 23/1762, Training of Squadrons of 2 Group in Army Air Support—Second Report by AOC-in-C Army Co-operation Command, 4 July 1941.
80. TNA AIR 20/5840, Letter from J.W Baker to AOC-in-C Bomber Command, 20 August 1941.
81. TNA AIR 2/5224, Minutes of a Meeting to Discuss the Training of the Squadrons of No.2 Group in Army Air Support, 2 July 1941.
82. Ibid.
83. TNA Air 2/5224, Minutes of a meeting to discuss the training of the squadrons of No. 2 Group in Army Air Support, 2 July 1941.
84. TNA WO 233/60, Draft of Plan for Development of Air Support for the Army 1939–1945 by P. Browne Director of Air (War Office), 25 May 1945.
85. TNA AIR 8/580, Letter from Director of Plans to CAS 1 July 1941.
86. TNA AIR 20/2173, Letter from Deputy DMC to CAS, 20 July 1941. The letter is not signed by the Deputy DMC to identify this person.
87. TNA AIR 39/95, Letter from AOC-in-C Army Co-operation Command to Officers Commanding Nos. 32–37 Wings, 21 August 1941.
88. TNA AIR Memorandum by CIGS to Under-Secretary of State for War 19 May 1941.
89. TNA AIR 2/5224, Essence of comments by AOC-in-C Army Co-operation Command on GHQ draft paper on Air Support, *c*.May 1941.
90. TNA AIR 2/5224, Memorandum by CIGS to Under-Secretary of State for War, 19 May 1941.
91. TNA WO 32/9836, Letter from GHQ Home Forces to Under-Secretary of State for War, 7 June 1941.
92. XXX
93. TNA AIR 39/80, Report by AOC-in-C Army Co-operation Command on the Air Aspect of Bumper, 28 October 1941.

94. Ibid.
95. Ibid.
96. TNA WO 32/10403, Report on Army Air Controls, 16 October 1941.
97. TNA AIR 8/986, Army Air Requirements (COS (41) 206 (0)), 5 November 1941. The codename of the exercise of the bombers of No. 2 Group is not given in the report.
98. TNA AIR 2/5224, Memorandum on Army Air Support Controls, c. October 1941.
99. TNA WO 32/10403, Report in Army Air Controls, 16 October 1941.
100. TNA PEM 3/80, Minute from CAS to Prime Minister, 11 November 1941. Carrington has argued that the fact that 'Army Co-op[eration] Command persuaded Bomber Command to take nine squadrons of Blenheims off real operations ... [was] a triumph for Army Co-op[eration Command] and a defeat for Bomber Command'. Carrington, *Soldier at Bomber Command*, p. 43.
101. TNA AIR 20/950, Army Air Requirements by the CIGS, 4 June 1941.
102. Ibid.
103. TNA IR 20/4446, Remarks on Close Support Bombing and other Air Activities in Anti-Invasion Operations by DMC, 8 January 1941.
104. TNA AIR 39/140. Comments on Bomber Support for the Army by C-in-C No. 71 Group, 1 February 1941.
105. TNA AIR 39/16, Notes by AOC-in-C Army Co-operation Command on the agenda for a meeting on air co-operation with the army to be discussed, 27 May 1941.
106. TNA 39/16, Memorandum by VCAS Slessor, 6 May 1941. TNA AIR 39/139, Draft of Air Co-operation with the Army—Policy—Notes for CAS prior to discussion with CIGS, c.January 1941.
107. TNA AIR 20/950, Army Air Requirements by the CIGS, 4 June 1941.
108. TNA AIR 20/4301, Letter from Group Captain J.D.I Hardman to Air Vice-Marshal H. Edwards, AOC-in-C RCAF Overseas, c.May 1942.
109. TNA AIR 2/7336, Letter from AOC-in-C Army Co-operation Command to Deputy Director of Plans, 5 February 1941.
110. Denis Richards, *Portal of Hungerford* (Heinemann: London, 1977), pp. 205–6.
111. TNA AIR 32/9836, Memorandum by C-in-C Home Forces on Co-operation between the Army and RAF, 3 May 1941. Towards the end of 1940 the RAF had also actively considered the specifications of a twin-engine aircraft that also had 'diving qualities', but this concept was not pursued (TNA AIR 2/7336, Note from the Secretary of State for War on the Close Support Bomber situation, c.December 1940.
112. David Ian Hall, *Learning How to Fight Together: The British Experience with Joint Air-Land Warfare* (Air Force Research Institute: Maxwell Air Force Base, Alabama, 2009), p. 13.

113. TNA AIR 2/7336, Letter from Secretary of State for War to the Secretary of State for Air, *c.*August 1940.
114. XXX
115. XXX
116. XXX
117. TNA AIR 8/986, War Cabinet COS Committee –Army Air Requirements COS (41), *c.*July 1941.
118. Ibid.
119. TNA AIR 39/16, Minutes of a Conference to discuss certain proposals for improving Army–RAF co-ordination, 12 May 1941.
120. Danchev and Todman, *War Diaries 1939–1945*, p. 258. The entry quoted is dated 18 May 1941.
121. TNA WO 32/9836, Minutes of a meeting held at the War Office to discuss army–air co-operation, 30 June 1941.
122. TNA AIR 39/16, Minutes of a Conference to discuss proposals for improving army–RAF co-ordination, 12 May 1941.
123. TNA WO 32/9836, Memorandum by C-in-C Home Forces on Co-operation between the army and RAF, 3 May 1941.
124. TNA AIR 39/139, Army Air Requirements (COS (41) 39 (0)), 8 June 1941.
125. TNA AIR 39/16, War Office Memorandum of Army Air Requirements, 12 June 1941.
126. TNA AIR 20/950, Summary of Air Requirements, 12 June 1941.
127. TNA AIR 20/950, Army Air Requirements—Memorandum by Portal, 12 June 1941.
128. TNA AIR 20/950, Army Air Requirements—Note by Portal, undated, *c.*October 1941.

CHAPTER 5

The Beginning of the End of Army Co-operation Command, 1942

The very existence of Army Co-operation Command was at the heart of the debate over the structure of air support between the Air and General Staffs. In 1942 the Air Staff proposed the air support organisation that they had wanted to create since 1940. That they had not done so then was due to the interservice political pressure they faced after the Battle of France. The debates between the two services in 1942 provided the Air Staff with an ideal opportunity to create an air support structure outside of Army Co-operation Command and make its future role almost redundant. Despite the arguments of the General Staff, and Brooke in particular, there was never any real thought given to upgrading Army Co-operation Command to operational status and instead the Air Staff looked to Fighter Command for the future operational development of air support in Britain.

Part of the reason for this, aside from the Air Staff's general feelings towards Army Co-operation Command and the risks involved in upgrading it, was that Fighter Command allowed air support to have an effect at the operational as well as tactical level of war, something that some members of the General Staff were beginning to understand. That is not to say that Army Co-operation Command did not have an influence on army co-operation development during this year. Further development of the Air OP took place in 1942 as well as additional exercises highlighting the impact of tactical air power at the operational level. The focus of all services in 1942 turned to the invasion of the continent

© The Author(s) 2016
M. Powell, *The Development of British Tactical Air Power, 1940–1943*,
DOI 10.1057/978-1-137-54417-9_5

after it had been agreed between America and Britain that the defeat of Germany should take priority over the defeat of Japan in the Pacific. The tide was turning against the Germans in the Battle of the Atlantic and North Africa and fighting on the Eastern Front was proving to be a vast drain on their resources. These events made the Allies more confident of launching European operations in the medium term and the RAF began to look at how best land forces could be supported from the air. With this renewed focus on Europe and the work undertaken in the Western Desert it was becoming increasingly clear that the mono-command role in Britain could not provide the necessary support. This change of direction combined with the developments emerging from the Western Desert made Army Co-operation Command's existence increasingly untenable.

The status of Army Co-operation Command within the RAF fell even further after discussions between the RAF and army were held to decide where twenty newly created squadrons were to be placed. The original decision, made by Brooke, was for these to be placed with Army Co-operation Command and not Fighter Command as suggested by the Air Staff. This decision was, however, reversed by Portal causing great consternation within parts of the War Office. The establishment of army co-operation squadrons within the Fighter Command framework was a significant additional responsibility to its air defence role for which it had originally been established. Poor relations between Army Co-operation Command and the army continued throughout 1942. Despite the deterioration of No. 2 (Bomber) Group throughout 1941, discussions regarding its continued training in air support and its overall composition continued.

With the RAF establishing its own forces for conducting army support operations, Army Co-operation Command's status within the wider RAF framework was again clearly demonstrated and, with hindsight, its creation in 1940 might be questioned as superfluous—Army Co-operation Command was simply a stopgap solution to the situation the RAF found itself in after the Battle of France. The Air Staff never regarded Army Co-operation Command as a part of the operational force that would accompany and support the army across the Channel—it was created in a rush and at the behest of the Army. This chapter will highlight how far the thinking of the two services over the application and impact of tactical air power still differed wildly. To the Air Staff, Army Co-operation Command was a placebo with which to placate the War Office. To support these arguments Barratt's visit to the Middle East, the events taking place there in 1942 and the discussions held between the

Air and General Staffs over the organisation of air support formations will be discussed in depth. This will include the rise of Fighter Command due to its superior signals organisation and operational experience. The reports written by the SASO at GHQ Home Forces, Air Commodore Henry Thorold, and Slessor about the most effective and efficient method for providing air support will also be analysed.

One of the major areas where the thinking of the services differed was just where army co-operation forces should be placed within the RAF. The discussions that took place between the two demonstrate just how divergent this thinking was and also that the War Office had still not understood how to fight at the operational level of war. To the War Office the most sensible place for these forces was in Army Co-operation Command; for the Air Ministry, it was Fighter Command. A series of discussions between Portal and Brooke took place on this issue, without the involvement of Barratt or any of Army Co-operation Command's staff officers. At the same time, ongoing experimentation and development of air support was underway in the Western Desert, but it is difficult to see just how far, if at all, these operations may have influenced the discussions—the differing strategic conditions of both theatres make this influence unlikely. Victory in the Western Desert was vital to maintain communications with the Empire and also as a base for operations against Sicily and Italy. All aircraft in the Western Desert could, in an emergency, be used to support ground forces in either an offensive or defensive capacity and so made any discussion of composite air support groups there redundant.[1] This was not the case in Britain due to the RAF's mono-role command structure. Tacit agreement between the RAF and army on the issue of the composite groups and their placement within the RAF was only reached through the intervention of Churchill.

The non-operational status of Army Co-operation Command was also subject to wide-ranging discussions. There were further calls for it to be re-equipped, which would have transformed it into a fully operational Command. These calls were once again rejected by the Air Staff and added further weight to the argument that Army Co-operation Command was not essential to future RAF plans. Despite the changes that were being discussed and implemented at the command level above it, the work of Army Co-operation Command continued. One significant aspect of this was a visit by Barratt to the Middle East theatre during active operations against the enemy. This visit allowed Barratt to gain a greater insight into the application of army co-operation based upon the operational experience, in isolation from Army Co-operation Command but based on the ideas that had been developed by them after the Battle of France.[2] Barratt's visit highlighted the fact that the problems faced by the RAF in both theatres regarding air support were still not fully resolved. The raid on Dieppe does not form a part of this book as, despite the use of some Army Co-operation Command squadrons in the operation, its impact did little to affect the work done in 1942.[3]

The British forces in the Western Desert launched Operation Crusader in 1941/2 in order to relieve the German siege of Tobruk and prevent any further advance by Rommel's forces. During this operation a new air support system based on integrated planning was first trialled—developed after Battleaxe, it demonstrated the importance of air superiority and the co-location of headquarters.[4] The latter was an idea that can be traced back to the interwar army co-operation exercises in Britain, and in the experiments conducted by Wann and Woodall. Crusader also saw the implementation of a new piece of military hardware unavailable to Army Co-operation Command: the fighter-bomber.

However, several problems were encountered during Crusader. The fluid nature of the battle meant that there was confusion about the location of friendly and enemy forces and communication problems abounded. The air power historian Richard Hallion has noted that 'the *average* time for requests for air support to the actual attack on enemy forces in response to the call was between 2½ *and 3 hours*' [emphasis in original].[5] This was longer than the response time during the Battle of France. The problems encountered during Crusader were expected with the use of a new and unfamiliar system and many of the issues encountered 'could be solved easily enough … with minor adjustments and further joint service practice'. It also highlighted deficiencies in British armoured tactics that added to the problems faced by the WDAF.[6] In order to resolve the problems that had been encountered providing air support, Army Support Controls (ASC), the WDAF's version of the CSBC/AASC C2 system was centralised under Coningham at the Combined Army/Air Battle Headquarters. In the system employed during Crusader, ground troops sent requests to Corps headquarters which were then passed to ASC. This link was removed and forward formations passed their requests directly to ASC headquarters, bringing the system into line with the Wann–Woodall concept. Communications between ground and air forces were improved based on ideas that had been used to enhance air support in the Empire. During daylight, 'landmarks took the form of bold letter of the alphabet

(20 yards in length), and by night lighted petrol cans (a large inverted V sign with sides 100 yards long) pointed directly towards the enemy'.[7]

Barratt visited the Middle East during the summer of 1942, and was able to observe the application of air support during the first three days of the Battle of Alam el Halfa.[8] The purpose of this visit was, over the course of two weeks, to view in detail the air support system in use in that theatre and to identify what could be brought back to enhance the air support capabilities of Army Co-operation Command and, given the precarious position of Army Co-operation Command at this time due to the discussions over the placement of composite groups, the RAF as a whole. During his visit, Barratt was able to observe the system under operational conditions and his report is enlightening insofar as it highlighted the developments that had been made to the original system, but also how effective the doctrinal ideas laid out during the interwar period were when fully embraced and implemented.[9] Alam el Halfa was, for the British, a defensive battle, and 'Rommel's last attempt to conquer Egypt'.[10] The growing importance of the Eastern Front as well as the German failure to occupy Malta in the previous year meant that the Middle East was becoming a neglected theatre for the *Wehrmacht*. Rommel was receiving fewer and fewer supplies from Germany—if this operation around Alam el Halfa failed, the German forces in North Africa would find their position increasingly untenable.

That Alam el Halfa was a defensive rather than an offensive battle for the British forces made the application of air support a relatively easier task to accomplish. In order to conduct air support in an offensive battle, a communications system would be required that was both efficient and flexible enough to meet the demands of the ground forces. These developments in the Middle East and North Africa would not have been possible without the training given to No. 2 AASC by Army Co-operation Command before its deployment with the WDAF. Gooderson has highlighted that No. 2 AASC had been trained in the Wann–Woodall system and was then involved in operations in the Middle East in 1942. This statement is unsupported in the text, but further evidence of this deployment is provided by Shelford Bidwell and Dominick Graham's work on the British Army and the development of theories of warfare. In this work, the authors cite an unpublished history of No. 2 AASC entitled *Notes from the Theatres of War, No. 1* written by Major General J. M. McNeil, who had given the authors access to his papers. Carrington has furthered this argument in an article published in *JRUSI* where he states, 'When the first ASSUs were sent from AC Command, they were at first fitted into the Desert Air Force system, but the Barratt–Woodall–Oxborrow system prevailed.'[11]

Barratt highlighted that, 'In order to obtain the closest co-ordination of both Military and Air Plans the Air Officer Commanding, Western Desert, and General Officer Commanding 8th Army are located in the same camp.'[12] This was, as has already been noted, a basic and often repeated aspect of the many interwar exercise reports.[13] Barratt also highlighted problems with the siting of advanced headquarters that had been resolved through operational experience. These advanced headquarters were based upon the CSBCs first designed through the Wann–Woodall experiments in 1940. Barratt stated,

> In order that the Air Officer Commanding Western Desert, can exercise immediate and direct control over the operations of the Bomber and Fighter Groups, it is desirable that the location of the Air Headquarters should be within reasonable distance of forward aerodromes and adjacent to a landing ground for his own use.[14]

There had, however, been advances made on the Wann–Woodall concept:

> Experience has shown that it is quite impossible to have a camp in the forward area combining the total staff of both Army and Air Headquarters. Accordingly, the splitting of Army and Air Headquarters into Advanced and Air Headquarters, is necessary ... provided direct telephone lines between Advanced and Rear Headquarters functioned well, few administrative difficulties have occurred.[15]

These developments could only occur through operational experience and making mistakes in the face of the enemy. Co-operation in the Western Desert was not limited to the lower levels of command as it was in Britain. This was something that Barratt would never experience. The operational experience gained in the Western Desert allowed Tedder and Coningham to begin to plan for offensive operations against the Germans 'before the defensive battle ... had run its course'.[16] The offensive operations eventually culminated in the Second Battle of El Alamein and ended with victory at Tunis in 1943.[17] This air system was fully accepted and implemented by the Eighth Army.[18]

Whilst the idea that the air support system used in the Western Desert was a creation of that theatre alone is subject to debate within this book, the fact that it was accepted by the Eighth Army was paramount to the development of a workable air support doctrine for future operations in Europe after 1943. The Allied operations of 1943 that culminated in the expulsion of Axis forces from the African continent were the first major operational experience for American forces and they faced a steep learning curve.[19] The RAF looked to the experience and innovations coming from the Western Desert theatre for assistance in resolving the perennial argument that had been taking place between the Air Ministry and War Office since before the Battle of France: who should have operational control of tactical air support resources. In a response to Barratt's report, the new DMC, Air Commodore J. D. I. Hardman, noted:

> One of the main points of contention at home is the problem of operational control of the Army Support squadrons. The soldier says he must have it because otherwise no target will ever be attacked in time. The airman says he must have it because he alone knows the air situation and must provide fighter cover and, if necessary, close escort ... I am convinced that the only sure solution lies in having joint Headquarters and that it is worth having these even at the cost of splitting up Headquarters into advanced and rear echelons at some slight inconvenience and loss of efficiency. If Army and Air Force Headquarters are not split up they will probably be too big to live and work together.[20]

It seems slightly strange that a lack of efficiency would be cited as a possible reason for not splitting up headquarters when no such comment was made by Barratt in his report or had indeed been made those operating the system in the Western Desert.[21]

John Terraine has described the levels of co-operation that were possible in the Western Desert, away from the bitter interservice arguments in Britain and in a situation where co-operation was required to stave off the very real possibility of calamitous defeat. This co-operation came from the realisation that 'at certain times and in certain circumstances Army cooperation would be the function not of "special" aircraft designed and allocated for the purpose, but of *the whole available air power* [emphasis in original]' and that

> The most important difference between England and Egypt at this stage was that [this] principle though perceived in England was not acted upon; in Egypt, under the stress of war, it *was* acted upon. But Tedder did not have to struggle against the rigidities and dogmas of the functional Command

system; he could use the RAF in the Middle East as a single unit [emphasis in original].[22]

In his own words, Barratt was 'fortunate to be present at Advanced Air Headquarters during the first three days of ... battle, and I was able to watch the whole machine in action'.[23] These three days gave Barratt further insights into how the theoretical system, designed prior to the creation of Army Co-operation Command and then refined by it, functioned and allowed him to observe the changes that had been made in the light of operational experience:

> Each evening the General Officer Commanding had a personal meeting with the Air Officer Commanding ... He gave him the clearest possible appreciation of the situation, the information as he knew it, what he intended to do himself, and what he expected the enemy to do. The Air Officer Commanding then said what he could do himself, and a general air plan was agreed upon. A further conversation took place the following morning as a result of events, ground and air, during the night.[24]

The AASC system was also seen to be working well, including when they were located within the headquarters:

> These [the AASC] were reported as being extremely good ... and did not suffer in any way from being back at Army Headquarters ... The target pro forma proved its value, if only enforcing [the] priority of target messages.[25]

Upon receiving Barratt's report, the DMC called into question the emphasis placed upon the ASSC both by those serving in the Middle East and as a consequence Barratt. It also questioned the army rationale for impromptu air support:

> *It is evident that much of the support given is deliberately planned the night before. In other words it is pre-arranged and not dependent upon the AASC organisation at all.* We have always thought this would be so, and all our information points to the fact the Germans do it the same way. We have often been unjustly accused of falling a long way short of the Germans in our system of providing close support. In point of fact what success the Germans have had has never been attributable to any magical quality in their system of air communications, but to careful planning before a battle and the efficient execution of those plans during it [emphasis added].[26]

The conclusion of the DMC, whilst correct in identifying the German method of providing close support to their ground forces, failed to recognise how the AASC system could in fact enhance the RAF's air support capability to a level above that of the Germans and highlights their general thinking on this issue. The DMC was still far more interested in defending itself against army opinion in 1940 than developing an effective air support system in Britain. Barratt was of the opinion that, despite the success of the AASC in the Western Desert, there was still much that could be learned to increase their effectiveness:

> As much education as possible is required in forward formations in the use and possibilities of the tentacles. Too many still regard it solely as a means of receiving air information and do not recognise their responsibility in sending back information vital to the RAF immediately.

In his recommendation for the further development of air support in Britain Barratt noted,

> It is considered that this system [the AASC] for [the] passage of information is excellent. It has worked under battle conditions and should be instituted forthwith.

Barratt also argued for changes in procedure for pilots conducting tactical reconnaissance: 'It is considered that there is a definite requirement to make a report in the air, particularly if the information is of an important character ... so that in the event of their [the pilot] failing to make a return the information will not be lost'.[27]

With the decisions being taken by the Air and General Staff over the development of the Army Air Support Group (AASG) (composite air support groups) leaving the future of Army Co-operation Command in doubt, it must be questioned how far any lessons that could be taken from Barratt's visit could be incorporated. Barratt wanted to continue in the role he had been assigned—to develop an air support system within Britain that was based not only on his own Command's ideas but also those being developed overseas, particularly the Middle East. In a letter to VCAS, Air Marshal M. E. H. Medhurst, he argued that

> A re-write of ATI [Army Training Instruction] 6 is certainly now necessary in the light of experience gained. I am much impressed by the Middle East Instruction on the same subject. It started from our own Command

Instruction and has been brought up to date in the Middle East as a result of actual battle experience. I do not think we in this respect could do better than to use the Middle East booklet as the basis for the new one.[28]

Barratt was able to identify where the basic concepts for the air support system in the Western Desert had originated, and that was from the work done by Wann and Woodall and Army Co-operation Command.

In an attempt to resolve the shortage of bomber aircraft available for close support training in Britain, as well as to expand their overall air support capabilities, the RAF decided to increase the number of aircrews that would be trained in this role by expanding the aircraft type involved. One of the major factors that influenced the decision to involve fighter aircraft in army co-operation training, apart from the good results that had been seen through their use in the Western Desert, was the change in strategic outlook in 1942. The Eastern Front, and in particular the Battle of Stalingrad had been a priority for the *Wehrmacht* and was consuming vast quantities of *matériel*. This meant that the 'Luftwaffe no longer showed much interest in contesting the air space over southern England or northern France unless there was a concurrent threat of RAF bomber attacks'. The *Luftwaffe* had an additional call on its resources as it also had to defend the homeland from RAF attack. Without a new mission Fighter Command would find it difficult to retain its prestige or the call on resources it had previously enjoyed.[29] Experience in the Western Desert had 'shown that Fighters with cannon and machine-guns, have a far greater effect than Bombers'.[30] It was agreed by the Air Staff 'that 15 Fighter Squadrons are to be earmarked for Army support duties and are to be made available for training and exercises in this role'. As with No. 2 Group in 1941, however, the Air Staff placed caveats on when this training could be conducted, again suggesting that they were only willing to do the minimum necessary to prevent a repeat of the situation in 1940:

> It is not intended that these 15 squadrons should be detailed exclusively for Army Support. Operations against enemy aircraft and training for that purpose continue to take precedence before Army support training.[31]

In order to facilitate this training, it was decided that No. 257 Squadron was to be affiliated with 'a suitable Army formation … and general liaison was to take place between them'. The idea behind this was not a new one—it was to encourage good relations between army and air formations and had been very successful during the First World War when Britain's air resources were a fundamental part of the army and Royal Navy. No. 257 Squadron was just one of many squadrons involved in this work. It will be used as an example here as it highlights some interesting ideas that emerged when fighter squadrons were involved in army support training. As relations between the troops and airmen improved and reached an acceptable standard, the squadron was earmarked to take part in army exercises with its affiliated ground formation. When No. 257 Squadron had gained a degree of experience working with the army, the lessons identified would be codified and rolled out on a wider basis so that all fighter squadrons would be able to conduct air support if required.[32] The initial training was to concentrate on aiding 'Army formations in destroying or opposing enemy tanks and mechanised forces, should they effect … a penetration in an invasion'.[33] This was a move that received great support from the General Staff and from Brooke in particular:

> The power of fighter aircraft in attacking ground targets has been clearly demonstrated in operations against the enemy … *The object is now to put this weapon to its most effective use in Army Air Support, and this will be achieved only by continual practice in handling by Army formation Commanders*, by continual practice, map-reading and recognition of targets by the RAF and by whole-hearted co-operation on the part of both services [emphasis added].[34]

The General Staff were again attempting to gain operational control over this new form of air support, and were only looking at the tactical level possibilities for the use of fighter aircraft as they had done in 1941 with No. 2 Group. As the training of No. 257 Squadron developed throughout the early part of 1942, certain suggestions were made regarding the different roles that should be played by fighter and bomber aircraft when engaged in air support: 'Bombers should be used mainly for strategical air support, i.e. indirect air support … Fighters should be used mainly for tactical air support, i.e. direct air support'. The squadron also suggested that a standing patrol of fighter aircraft should be continuously maintained during any major land action. This was a similar suggestion to that proposed by the War Office after the Battle of France. This had been dismissed by the Air Staff as not only being wasteful, but also violating one of the founding principles of air power: the ability to project its strength at any point across the battlefield. No. 257 Squadron, however, argued that 'It is thought that there will be no flying wastage by having a standing patrol because [the] aircraft [involved] will be in constant demand in that section of the front that [it] is allotted [to] by the Army Air Support Control for that particular patrol.'[35] RAF thinking had not changed on the idea of the standing patrol and this suggestion had been put forward after a period of extended training with the army and it is possible that the army's ideas about tactical air power had overly influenced the opinion of the squadron's commanding officer.

Trials were held in May to

> investigate the quickest and most practicable methods of support for fighter aircraft to answer calls for support from the Army Air Support Control and to reduce to a minimum the time lag between the origin of a message at the forward tentacle and the time of take-off of fighters.[36]

The focus of the trials was on the 'defensive use of the Army Air Support Control'.[37] Despite the vast change in the strategic situation of the Second World War as a whole, there was still concern about the possibility of a German invasion at this time. Certain conclusions reached as a result of these trials required the modification of existing ideas. Landlines were to be made available in order to make the fullest possible use Fighter Command's communications system 'to pass demands from the Army Air Support Control to the Group Headquarters'.[38] An Operational Instruction from Fighter Command which looked at the methods for providing air support for the army concluded that, 'Fundamentally, there will be no difference in the organisation and methods used for this task whether the operation be invasion of the Continent, operations further overseas or the defence of this country against invasion.' Those at the head of Fighter Command stated,

> It is not yet decided as to where the responsibility [for air support] shall lie, as between RAF Commands, for the development of Army Air Support, *but it is obvious that close touch must be kept between Fighter Command and Army Co-operation Command on all aspects of this problem ... it is of great importance that Fighter Command, whose personnel will eventually take a major part in Air Operations in support of our armies, should study and train for the task, and it is my wish that the means of giving this support should be the subject of constant study by all Commanders of their staffs* [emphasis added].[39]

It is clear from this statement that the AOC-in-C Fighter Command, Air Marshal Sir Sholto Douglas, was well aware where the future development of army co-operation in Britain lay. Of almost equal importance, however, was that by 1942 the RAF had developed an air support system that would, in theory at least, be able to provide cover for land forces in any of the potential operations that the service might be called upon to undertake. The rise of Fighter Command, and the development of fighter aircraft in an army support role, was to continue at great pace throughout 1942 with the development of the AASG. The Air Staff looked to Fighter Command for the further development of tactical air power in Britain over Army Co-operation Command for several reasons: a large amount of resources had already been allocated to the service and it was less vulnerable to calls from the General Staff for diversion of these resources to the army. Also, with the *Luftwaffe* no longer contesting airspace over Britain and northern France as keenly, its squadrons would be able to engage in greater training compared to those in Bomber Command as there would less call on them for active operations.

The Air Staff set about investigating the air support structure that should be instigated to support the army in the field for future operations. In this respect two separate reports were produced advocating two different structures; one proposal was put forward by the SASO at GHQ Home Forces, Thorold and another by the now Assistant Chief of the Air Staff (ACAS), Slessor. That air support could be looked at in two divergent ways demonstrates how much work had been done by Army Co-operation Command in developing air support thinking within the RAF throughout its existence. The two ideas put forward differed in one major respect:

> the Thorold Plan prescribed a general system of air support without a specific battle or campaign in mind; Slessor's paper was a comprehensive and precise proposal to meet the air requirements of opening a second front in Europe.[40]

The ideas contained within the Thorold proposal, and which the Air Staff actively considered differed little from those that had been used in previous operations. They agreed with the idea that a certain number of army co-operation squadrons should be allotted to the army and be under their operational control to conduct tactical reconnaissance, but disagreed with the General Staff's ideas about how many squadrons were needed to fulfil this role. The Air Staff also agreed with the idea that Army Co-operation Command's aircraft capacity should be increased to twenty squadrons and 'placed at the disposal of C-in-C Home Forces'. No. 2

Group was also to be increased in size by twenty squadrons and train more regularly with the army.[41]

The General Staff were enthusiastic about the potential expansion of Army Co-operation Command, and the resultant increase in their own air resources under their operational control. There was, however, still a great deal of disagreement as to where No. 2 Group should be placed after it had been enlarged. The General Staff felt that placing the Group within the Metropolitan Air Force, which formed part of Fighter Command, was a waste of potentially important air support resources and they felt the best place for these new squadrons was within Army Co-operation Command. If this happened, it would have two major consequences for the RAF in Britain that would violate certain fundamental air power principles and shift the balance of power in the development of tactical air power. Firstly, No. 2 Group would be 'wholly at the disposal of C-in-C Home Forces', in addition to the twenty squadrons earmarked for Home Forces.[42] Secondly, and more importantly however, Army Co-operation Command and, as a result, Home Forces, would have access to operational squadrons. Army Co-operation Command would then become a de facto operational command, with the attendant change in status that would allow it to make greater demands on resources as Bomber, Fighter and Coastal Commands were able to do—Army Co-operation Command would have to be taken more seriously by the Air Staff. This was unacceptable to the Air Ministry and they repeated the argument used in 1941 when they dismissed the idea of moving No. 2 Group to Army Co-operation Command:

> The Air Staff view is that the primary role of this Group must be determined by strategic requirements. Until there is a firm prospect of this Group being needed this year for air support of land forces on the Continent, the Air Staff consider that it would not be justifiable to withdraw the Group entirely from taking part in the air offensive which is the only other means of reducing pressure on the Russian front.[43]

The General Staff felt that moving No. 2 Group to Army Co-operation Command was in the Group's best interests due to the poor condition into which it had fallen in the early part of 1942.[44] Whilst it had been agreed in 1941 between the two Staffs that this Group would undertake the majority of army co-operation training in Britain, its use on active operations had taken its toll and the result of this was that it 'had practically disintegrated'. This was 'due partly to the shortage of aircraft and partly due to casualties incurred in attacks on shipping'.[45] Due to its lack of influence within the RAF as a whole, there was little Army Co-operation Command could do to prevent the Group's almost near destruction. The Army's motives in attempting to gain control of No. 2 Group must be seen from this perspective—the hard training in, and aircrew experience of, close support procedures over the previous twelve months was proving to be pointless as crews died and aircraft were lost. The Thorold Report recommended an organisation similar in composition to that of BAFF and was based upon 'a number of functional commanders of bomber, fighter and army support groups, all interposed in the chain of command'. The Air Staff felt that this system would be too cumbersome to meet the varied demands required of air support in operations on the Continent.[46]

The proposal put forward by Slessor offered a solution that differed to a great extent to that put forward by Thorold and was firmly rooted in providing air support for an expeditionary force active on the Continent. Plans such as this could be made with the entry of the United States into the Second World War and the defeat of Germany being given priority over the conquest of Japan. One major reason why Thorold's and Slessor's ideas differed to such an extent was that Thorold had more contact with Army Co-operation Command and its work than Slessor and so would have been greatly influenced by its thinking. Slessor's ideas were based upon discussions that had been taking place about the creation of composite groups to provide air support. Composite groups would allow the RAF to retain the inherent flexibility of air power and such a group would be placed under the higher operational control of an army commander. The operations of such a force would be directly under the control of an air force commander working closely with the army commander in line with the overall military plan and control would be exerted through the headquarters of an army support wing. In order to allow close support to be conducted, the AASC formation was to be extended to allow it to fit into this organisation.[47] The General Staff's motives in attempting to increase the capacity of Army Co-operation Command reflected their concern to have a force that would be capable of supporting their land forces in resolving tactical level problems they would face in the field. They were unable to conceive the operational level benefits that the composite group could bring. This is clearly demonstrated in their initial reaction to the Slessor report.

The General Staff were not convinced about the abilities of a composite group solution to meet what they saw as their air support needs. This came as somewhat of a shock to Slessor, who 'felt some disappointment to the reaction of the General Staff ... in which I stated plainly my view that the functional system of command was unsuitable'. Slessor reinforced this, claiming 'He [Brooke] cannot, I think, be aware of the well-known fact that Fighter Command has far more practical experience of the realities of air support for the Army than has Army Co-operation Command.'[48] This was a hugely damning comment, not just on Army Co-operation Command and its work, but also on the way in which the RAF had created it. It demonstrates the difficult position that Army Co-operation Command was in as a non-operational Command, and how little it could thus achieve.

Some sections of the army demonstrated a real change in attitude towards the composite group. This can be seen in a letter from Paget, regarding a study week held in November 1942. One day of this study week was devoted to the organisation that would be required to support an army in the field. The principle ideas that emerged from the discussions were that air support forces should be under 'A unified command under a single Air Officer Commanding-in-Chief of all air forces allocated to the support of the field armies in each theatre of operations'. Further to this, 'The RAF organisation within the unified command [was] to comprise a series of composite RAF Groups, each group containing Fighter, Bomber, Reconnaissance and Army Air Support Squadrons.' These groups 'were to be formed on the basis of providing one Group to each Army in the field'. The AASC was to be reorganised in order to provide 'a permanent control element at Corps Headquarters as well as Army Headquarters'.[49] Home Forces was beginning to understand the benefits that could be achieved through the application of tactical air power at the operational level, and part of the reason for this were the ideas developed by Army Co-operation Command and the training they instigated with Home Forces.

The army's planning for the invasion of the continent had grown to such an extent that their thinking regarding the location of air support communications had to be altered to reflect this change. A formation such as a Corps would be on a scale large enough to fully utilise an army air support (composite) group. This goes a long way to explaining why it had not been suggested when discussions about the creation of Army Co-operation Command were taking place. The proposals put forward from these discussions 'received general approval in the course of the discussion from both the Army and RAF representatives, the latter including the C-in-Cs Fighter Command and Army Co-operation Command'.[50]

Writing to Hardman, Woodall offered his opinion on the idea that had been put forward by Home Forces, arguing that it was 'a good straightforward and clear one, but in certain ways it is applicable to a specific operation rather than to all theatres of war'.[51] Woodall added further weight to his argument through an analysis of the idea of unified command, the position of the RAF organisation within this and the potential impact such ideas could have on air support formations, and deserves to be quoted at length. He argued for an

> Air Officer Commanding-in-Chief for all air forces operating in a theatre of war. This, however, is not the same as a single Air Officer Commanding-in-Chief of all air forces *allocated* to the support of the field armies. For example, Tedder is Air Officer Commanding-in-Chief of the air forces in the Middle East, but his responsibilities extend far beyond the support to the field armies. I cannot see in such a theatre a permanent allocation of air forces to the field armies with a permanent Air Officer Commanding in Chief of such allocated air forces ... GHQ recommends a series of composite RAF Groups, each Group containing fighter, bomber, reconnaissance and army air support squadrons. I feel that this is all right and, in fact, most desirable, for the Groups working with armies, but in any given theatre of operations it may well be convenient for the Air Officer Commanding-in-Chief to have under his hand specialist Fighter Groups for the air defence of the area as a whole. This is, in fact, I think the case in the Middle East, where the defence of the Nile Delta is entrusted to such a Group. Although a composite group is ideal for the support of land operations, I do not think that we should lose sight of the advantage of functional groups for specialist purposes, nor do I think we can possibly tie down an Air Officer Commanding-in-Chief as to how the Groups other than with armies are organised [emphasis in original] [52]

Woodall's suggestions regarding some of the problems that may be faced by an AOC-in-C commanding composite groups are of interest as they are from an army officer, but still show a good deal of understanding of how air power could have an impact at the operational level of war. The suggestion put forward was a combination of both the Thorold and Slessor reports and would put a unified command system above that of the composite group organisation. This would result in a system that was unwieldy and suffered from the same complex communications problems that had hampered the work of BAFF in France. That Home Forces wanted to utilise a system that was based around the composite group system under RAF operational control, and not an army air arm, is testament to the work done by Army Co-operation Command and the relationship the two had developed. This relationship was almost non-existent at the Staff level above Army Co-operation Command and Home Forces. It is highly possible that there was some degree of disconnect between the ideas being discussed by the General Staff, despite Paget's presence there, and those at Home Forces. The General Staff were also unwilling to give up on the idea of an army air arm, which had been their aim in this area for many years and more work was required in the coming years for full trust to be established at this level.

Barratt had been advised of the Air Staff's desire to re-equip Army Co-operation Command in January 1942 with fifty American Mustang aircraft.[53] By the spring, the War Office put forward what they believed to be their minimum requirements in air support aircraft, which was again over-exaggerated. Brooke requested sixty fighter reconnaissance squadrons, thirty light bomber reconnaissance squadrons and twelve Air OP squadrons in a memorandum presented to the COS Committee.[54] Discussions between the two staffs on this issue agreed on a figure of twenty new squadrons for Army Co-operation Command in May and this was to be completed by September at the latest.[55] The major development of 1942 that affected Army Co-operation Command was the expansion of AASG, the entity suggested in the report on air support formations presented by Thorold in order to reconcile 'the divergent interests of Bomber, Fighter and Army Co-operation Commands'.[56]

Discussions between the Air and General Staffs over the issue of the AASG highlight the status of Army Co-operation Command within the wider RAF Command framework and the rise of Fighter Command in an army support role. The initial idea behind the AASG was 'to ensure that when Operation Roundup occurred, the Army would have a force of Army Air Support squadrons thoroughly trained in that role'.[57] The Joint Planning Staff for Roundup argued that 'Under the existing set-up there are too many RAF commands concerned—Fighter, Bomber, Coastal and Army Co-operation Command'.[58] Roundup was the plan to invade France in the spring of 1943. These plans were eventually dropped in favour of Operation Torch. A War Office memorandum noted that

> the demands for fighters are numerous, demands for bombers are extremely few. The reason why the demands for bombers are so few is almost certainly because commanders fully realise that 2 Group is weak and fully employed on operations.[59]

The War Office were of the opinion that RAF commanders still saw the training of formations in army air support 'as an additional secondary item to their primary role ... and they deal with it ... on a compromise basis, the given factor being that their permanent organisation and their present roles must not be disturbed'. To attempt to resolve this lack of training, the War Office resorted to its usual method, albeit this time on a smaller scale than had previously been suggested: a part of the RAF should be placed under their operational command. In this case the formation suggested was No. 2 Group. Their reasoning for selecting No. 2 Group was that 'there was no reason why the whole Group or part of it should not be employed on every exercise with the troops'. Under this plan, No. 2 Group was to be redesignated an army air support group and would provide the army with the distinct advantage of having 'an RAF organisation focused entirely on the problems of Army Air Support'.[60]

The War Office believed that by gaining control of No. 2 Group, the following would receive almost immediate attention: 'the squadron organisation would be placed on a mobile footing, training would become standardised on the most suitable lines and there will be a certainty of an irreducible minimum of Army Air Support on the day of the battle'. This situation would also increase the morale of the army in conjunction with planning for future operations by 'altering the Army's present hopelessness about Army Air Support and producing a determination to train itself to make the best possible use of it'.[61]

This training would, however, simply focus on the tactical level problems faced by the army in the field and concentrate on close support rather than the operational level impact interdiction support could have. The morale of the army had dropped greatly when preparations were being made for anti-invasion operations and a return to the continent appeared doubtful. The War Office also feared that the discussions that had been held with the Air Ministry would continue with no significant progress being made if they did not have control of No. 2 Group: 'In the view of the difference of opinion between the two services, and our past experience, one cannot be optimistic of a quick settlement.'[62] In this letter from Paget to Brooke, the fundamental reasons for the differences of opinion between the two Services are not mentioned. The Joint Planning Staff recommended that in order for the air support requirements of the army to be fulfilled, the organisation that existed in Britain required change. The Staff suggested that an Air Striking Command should be created from Bomber Command squadrons and that it should operate from Britain. Further fighter and bomber squadrons would also accompany an invasion force and would be detailed to support it on the Continent.[63] This potential resolution would not satisfy either party—the army would still be without a force that was under their operational control and the RAF would still be too fearful of such a move by the War Office to consider giving it any real operational responsibility. It would also suffer from the same communications and organisational difficulties that an upgraded Army Co-operation Command would face.

Despite these reservations about the creation of such a force, the COS Committee were anxious 'to get the principle of the Air Striking Command going as soon as we can'. The COS felt that, in regard to combined operations, there was 'great difficulty ... being experienced in planning the air side of the Combined Operations, since there is no one big enough to co-ordinate Bomber, Fighter and Coastal Command'.[64] Army Co-operation Command was not included by the COS Committee in this reckoning due to its non-operational nature and also the fact that it possessed a distinct lack of aircraft. Discussions about the possible creation of an Air Striking Command led to debate about the continued existence of Army Co-operation Command. Unsurprisingly, given the close work that had already taken place between them and Army Co-operation Command, the War Office, and the General Staff in particular, were in favour of Barratt becoming the AOC-in-C of the air forces that would be involved in Roundup. The RAF were still of the opinion that Fighter Command was the correct place for the establishment of any new air support formation. The AOC-in-C of Fighter Command, Douglas, argued that 'the present Fighter Command organisation would be the best basis for the formation of an air striking force for operations on the Continent ... The Army Co-operation Command would be under the Commander-in-Chief Expeditionary Force.'[65]

The AASG, which would form part of an Air Striking Command, was to be formed from squadrons who specialised in this work and 'squadrons from the Fighter and Bomber forces of the Air Contingent which may be detached for the purpose'.[66] The AASG idea was encouraged by the Air Staff, and Portal originally agreed to place this force within Army Co-operation Command rather than Fighter Command.[67] Changes in the planning for Roundup, caused partly by reservations on the part of the British about invading the continent in 1943, caused consternation with regard to the organising of the AASG and moves were made by the Air Staff to establish such a formation in principle at the very least. However, the proposals could not be put into place in practice due a lack of available forces.[68] Home Forces were also supportive of the creation of the AASG:

> It would seem reasonable … to press for the immediate formation of the Army Air Support Group, making it clear that the Group should be regarded as a training organisation only [and we should emphasise] our readiness to accept the transfer of the actual squadrons to whatever organisation is jointly agreed in the long run.[69]

Paget was hedging his bets as to what formation would be best placed to support future army operations. The decision to form the AASG within Army Co-operation Command had been made in May 1942.[70]

With the changes being made for the strategic conduct of the war at the COS level, combined with the practical experience already gained in the Middle East, the RAF continued to have a good enough reason to delay making radical alterations to the army air support structures currently in existence in Britain for the time being. If the discussions between the political leaders of Britain and the United States settled on a strategy that did not involve invading Europe through France, the operational expertise was still available and could also be transferred to other theatres. This allowed the RAF extra room to discuss and debate ideas that were now being proposed without having to show they were flatly refusing them out of hand.

This was fully accepted by the army, as the relations between them and Army Co-operation Command had improved greatly throughout 1941 and continued on this path in 1942. The War Office saw Army Co-operation Command as the natural home for the AASG. This issue seemed, to all intents and purposes, to have been settled and Barratt was asked for a recommendation for the commander of the group when it was placed within his Command. Barratt's choice was an SASO who had served under him in the AASF in France as well as having had staff work experience in India, Air Commodore T. W. Williams. Barratt furthered his case, stating that

> he was the power behind the throne in 2 Group, and he knows the Army Air Support business in all its details. The Army likes him, and I know his worth and I think it is time he had command.[71]

Barratt was, however, not to get his man, or indeed control of the AASG. Williams had been allowed to 'go to the Far East at Peirse's special request',[72] and a month after Barratt's recommendation for the commander of the new support group, Freeman wrote in a memorandum to other RAF Commands and the War Office:

> You will be aware that it was recently agreed with the War Office to form an Army Air Support Group in Army Co-operation Command. This decision is now under review and it is probable that the Army Support Squadrons will be formed in 11 Group [Fighter Command] which will subsequently be reorganised to fulfil a dual role of Fighter and Army support in preparation for certain projected operations.[73]

It is hard to explain such a major change in policy, particularly in such a short space of time. Hall has argued that, on this matter at least, Brooke found himself outmanoeuvred by the War Office and the matter was eventually settled by Churchill who looked to the WDAF's air support organisation for guidance.[74] For the majority of the War Office, Army Co-operation Command had turned into the Cinderella of the RAF that allowed them to 'wash their hands of the business [of army support]'.[75] A letter written in the days preceding Freeman's memorandum sheds more light on the issue than is currently available in the literature. In early August, Freeman had written to Douglas stating, 'For the further husbanding of our Spitfire resources, it has been decided that the 5 squadrons which are due to form for the army support role between now and November should not be created *de nove* but should be provided by transfer from Fighter Command.'[76] By creating the AASG under Fighter rather than Army Co-operation Command, the RAF would be able to prevent the potential creation of an army air arm. It would also allow it to manage the production of aircraft more easily by transferring resources already available to a different role than having to wait on the British aircraft industry to build new machines. The aircraft were readily available—modification and training programmes were beginning to emerge, not only from the Middle East but from Army Co-operation Command as well. All that was required was to organise training exercises for the pilots within Fighter Command and allow time for it to have the desired effect. This move would further sideline Army Co-operation Command, especially after the improvement in relations on the whole between the two services.

It was hoped that by expanding the scope of Fighter Command to include an air support role, squadrons would be able to organise exercises with greater ease due to their status within the RAF. In many cases, however, the groundwork had already been laid by Army Co-operation Command during preliminary exercises in 1941 allowing Fighter Command to build on this. The only real area where Fighter Command was superior to Army Co-operation Command, aside from its operational nature, was in its signals network and organisation. This signals network was static and had been thoroughly tested and refined in operations during the Battle of Britain. It also allowed for the control of several squadrons conducting air support missions.[77] Ultimately, it was this signals network that was the key reason for establishing air support formations within Fighter Command rather than Army Co-operation Command. It allowed the centralisation of C2 capabilities to conduct air support at the operational level. This was something that was not possible given the structure and non-operational status of Army Co-operation Command and its lack of experience in conducting active operations, all factors relating again to the way in which Army Co-operation Command had been structured at its formation in 1941.

The postponement of Roundup—partly due to the failure of the joint British–Canadian landings on the beaches of Dieppe—also had a large bearing on Fighter Command becoming the home for air support in Britain. With the delay in operations from Britain, there was now time to allow a more rounded discussion about the form an air support organisation should take. It further meant that exercises could now be conducted to develop the new organisation, as well as to ensure Fighter Command was fully trained and capable of conducting this role.

In a letter to the Under-Secretary of State for Air, Douglas set out in more detail the RAF's arguments for wanting to establish the AASG in Fighter Command, putting forward the same points in more depth:

> it appears to me to be most unwise to form an Army Air Support Group in Army Co-operation Command comprising two of the existing squadrons of Fighter Command plus ten new squadrons equipped with fighter aircraft. By all means let us form these additional ten army support squadrons, but let them, I suggest, remain in Fighter Command where, in addition to intensive training in Army Air Support, they can also receive a modicum of training in fighter duties ... I understand that the main purpose underlying the formation of these Army Air Support Squadrons was to ensure

that, when Operation Roundup occurred, the Army would have a force of Army Air Support Squadrons thoroughly trained in that role and well-practised with the troops which they would actually support in a landing on the Continent … if these 12 Army Air Support Squadrons are placed in Army Co-operation Command, they will, it seems, be condemned to spend almost two years and possibly longer divorced from active operations, concentrating merely on training with a diminished Home Forces. In these circumstances the morale of these squadrons is unlikely to be of a high order when the day of battles come.[78]

Douglas was right in his criticisms of Army Co-operation Command and the possible outcome if the AASG was created within it. What is not acknowledged, however, is why Army Co-operation Command was in this position in the first place. It had effectively been neglected since its creation and the Air Staff wanted to remove it from the RAF framework as soon as possible. Army Co-operation Command was not as effective as it could have been, for the most part due to the way in which the Air Staff had created it, and the discussions over the AASG demonstrate that it had been created as a stop-gap solution to relieve the pressure that had built up during and after the Battle of France. Brooke was firmly of the opinion that the AASG should be created within Army Co-operation Command as had been originally agreed with Portal, failing to understand how the AASG could help his forces fight at the operational level. Portal set out how he and the Air Staff saw the situation and in this context it is worth quoting his deliberations at length:

The basis [for development] was that when the Army is fighting, the effort of the whole air force must be primarily directed to ensure the success of the land operations; and in these conditions the functional organisation of the air force into Bomber, Fighter and Army Co-operation Commands which … has served us well in the past two years when the army at home has not been engaged, is no longer suitable. On the assumption therefore that the Army would be concentrating in the South-East of England for an offensive across the Channel next Spring, my intention was to reorganise No. 11 Group into a Command comprising 3 composite Groups of Fighter, Bomber and Army Support squadrons which would correspond to the number of armies … the re-organisation … is [now] neither necessary nor appropriate; and in particular the organisation for army support in the United Kingdom must primarily cater for training and the development of the technique both in the air force and the army … I have undertaken to form 12 Army Support

Squadrons, and it would be a mistake to postpone their formation until the Spring ... The point to be decided now is how, in the new conditions these Army Support squadrons can best organized ... There are two alternatives, and I propose to leave the choice to you, though I shall advise you which, in my view, would be the more likely to secure the object we both have in mind ... And to help you decide on your choice I suggest you should have a talk to Sholto Douglas ... The first alternative is to form the squadrons in Army Co-operation Command, under an Army Air Support Group as a training organisation ... The second alternative is to form the squadrons in Fighter Command, and to appoint to the Staff of Fighter Command an Air Officer, Air Vice-Marshal to Air Commodore, with a good Brigadier or General Staff Officer I as assistant ... I personally have no doubts that the second alternative would give the best results ... I am convinced it will result in better training and a more enthusiastic interest in Army Support.[79]

Portal's letter to Brooke raises an interesting issue regarding the relative statuses of Army Co-operation and Fighter Commands. With half of the staff of Army Co-operation Command consisting of army officers, could Army Co-operation Command not have been upgraded and reformed to prevent the army from turning it into an army air arm? Portal was willing to transform the operational priorities of one Command, whilst neglecting the organisation that was created specifically for army co-operation. Brooke's response to Portal's proposals highlights this issue and his belief that an operational Army Co-operation Command was the solution to providing support for the army on the Continent:

I have considered the alternative proposals which you suggest ... and I prefer that which places the 12 Army Support squadrons under an Army Air Support Group in the Army Co-operation Command. The Army Co-operation Command has accumulated considerable experience in matters connected with the machinery for Army Air Support and it is a command whose sole responsibility is the study of army requirements with no other conflicting interests. I am anxious to see development within this Command the organisation for Air Support not only for training but also for operations ... I have consistently said that I am anxious that these squadrons should when formed and properly trained, take part in offensive operations ... The mere fact that squadrons become trained in Army Co-operation work doesn't from my point of view, justify their release without replacement ... I assume that we are agreed that the formation of the Army Air Support Group is but an initial step towards this training of a total of 20 light bomber squadrons and a minimum of 15 fighter squadrons.[80]

This decision was made without consulting Douglas, but we can be confident that the advice he would have given Brooke would not have differed from that of Portal. It may, however, have been a chance for Douglas to set out the operational level effects tactical air power could have had when supporting the army. Douglas further argued that

> The Air Officer Commanding-in-Chief, Army Co-operation Command ... has done his best to make arrangements for his army co-operation squadrons to carry out a small amount of active operations with Fighter Command. While this is all to the good, it is not the same thing for the ordinary pilot as being a member of an active operational command and engaged frequently in active operations. For the foregoing reasons therefore I strongly urge that the 12 Army Air Support squadrons should be formed in Fighter Command and remain there at any rate until such time as Operation Roundup appears imminent.[81]

The idea put forward by Douglas was a sound one. Pilots would gain more from being involved in any form of active operation rather than simply training under Army Co-operation Command. Only Fighter Command could provide this as even if Army Co-operation Command was upgraded to an operational Command, it could only conduct active operations once the invasion of the Continent had been launched. Portal's response to Brooke's decision for the AASG to be formed in Army Co-operation Command highlights the RAF's thoughts towards it as well the possibility of having to create a training formation within it that could easily become an operational unit. Even at this point in the Second World War, the RAF still felt that they had to actively consider the General Staff's ideas to avoid the claim that they were not providing enough support to the army and this is why Portal originally allowed Brooke to make the decision on the fate of the AASG:

> I note your preference for the first alternative ... that the squadrons should form in Army Co-operation Command, under an Army Support Group as a training organisation. I am sorry you have made this decision because I am sure far better results would be obtained if the squadrons were formed in Fighter Command. I believe that you would have been impressed with the arguments that Sholto Douglas could have brought forward in favour of that course. However, you have made your decision without hearing them and we will act accordingly ... I am agreeing against my real judgement in the matter, to the formation of an Army Air Support Group as a training

organisation in Army Co-operation Command. I do so because I am anxious to meet you in every way possible and to ensure that the organisation aspect should not be allowed to hold up the formation of the Army Air Support squadrons ... I, for my part, am convinced that the air problem envisaged admits of no other solution. Therefore, with every desire to meet you, I am afraid that I cannot compromise over such a fundamental point.[82]

With the declaration of war on Germany by the US, the strategic outlook of the conflict had altered radically. There were several options available to Britain and the US in conducting their grand strategic ideas. After their experience in conducting the Dieppe raid, Churchill and the War Cabinet preferred to attack the soft underbelly of Europe.[83] These operations would be launched from bases in North Africa using the forces that had previously been fighting in that theatre. This gave the application of air support two distinct advantages. First, the build-up of troops for this role would not be hampered through their possible diversion for operations in other parts of the Continent. Second, those conducting the operations from North Africa against Sicily and the Italian mainland were already well versed in conducting air support through the experience gained in operations in the Western Desert. The system could be further refined to fit into the demands of a European theatre. Discussions regarding the placement of the AASG in Britain would have to be finalised to allow the army to believe that they would receive the necessary support from the air.

Sinclair felt that allowing the decision on the placement of the AASG made by Brooke to stand was incorrect, despite Portal's initial acceptance. At a COS meeting, Portal explained the reasoning behind his thinking:

when the large scale Continental operations came into the foreground of the picture it had become necessary to consider how to organise the RAF to take part in them. It was obvious that the functional organisation of Fighter, Bomber, Coastal, etc. Commands would be inappropriate and that we should have to go in for a system of the same type as that employed by the Germans in their big campaigns ... Each Group would be a mixed force of fighter, light bomber, army support and reconnaissance squadrons. Initially these groups would be operated from Fighter Command sectors in Great Britain ... There would be no place in such an organisation for an Army Co-operation Command. If these ideas were accepted, then it was felt that it would be much better to place the army support squadrons in the

Groups of Fighter Command, so that the latter could begin to train wholeheartedly for their continental role.[84]

The AASG was the type of air support formation that the RAF was looking for in 1940 when Army Co-operation Command was created. It provided a way of developing air support that allowed them to retain operational control of the forces involved with little input or comment from the army. This was not possible under the Army Co-operation Command system. The AHB narrative on close support details how the RAF saw the future of air support and the problems it faced in trying to apply air support on a large battle front with its functional command organisation:

> The existing operational arrangement in England which consisted of functional Bomber, Fighter, Coastal and Army Co-operation Commands was not fully reconcilable with the need for flexibility and rapidity of action which were necessary in order to ensure that the air effort could be applied to support any part of the army front. Furthermore, it was necessary for the army Commander to be able to select objectives and apportion effort for almost any number of supporting squadrons and these had to come under the control of one air force commander in any one area, who could see the air situation as a whole and co-ordinate support, reconnaissance and fighter operations. This postulated a non-functional, composite organisation and it was apparent that Fighter Command offered the best basis upon which to build ... Air Support was no longer to depend upon limited resources but was to give the whole strength of Fighter Command behind it and the elimination of Army Co-operation Command therefore became a logical step in invasion, since it could not and would not be able to command sufficient resources.[85]

The RAF faced two distinct choices in the development of the AASG. These were to convert Army Co-operation Command into a fully operational Command or to transfer the bulk of army co-operation development and training to Fighter Command. Carrington has surmised the army's position in the following way:

> The General Staff ... adhered to the original proposal and plan as modified by the Thorold paper. In short they preferred Army Co-operation Command with all its imperfections to a share in the attentions of 11 Group at such times as it happened to be not another master.[86]

Brooke's fear about placing the AASG within Fighter Command was that it would suffer the same fate as No. 2 Group and not be fully dedicated to the support of the army in the field. It would, however, allow the RAF to fully support the army at the operational level and adequate resources would be available to allow further development that was simply not possible through Army Co-operation Command.

The development of the Air OP concept by Army Co-operation Command and the School of Artillery continued at pace throughout 1942. Woodall confirmed what had happened and what had been developed during the previous year to a staff officer of Southern Command, Brigadier B. C. H. Kimmins: 'With the fighter reconnaissance type and the new procedure by which the pilots actually shoots the battery using two-way radio telegraphy, he can, I think, do most of his work from fairly far back.' Woodall used this opportunity to highlight the biggest factor that was preventing further rapid development of the Air OP.

> Of course the main snag at the moment is the ghastly situation of the aircraft supply position ... In all exercises [the] General Staff want more tactical reconnaissance sorties than the aircraft can do, and as a result artillery reconnaissance comes a bad last in the order of priority.[87]

In early March 1942, a training camp for artillery reconnaissance was held and its benefits went further than simply training artillery and air formations in the new technique. The camp afforded the pilots and artillery officers the chance to spend the week living together in the same areas, just as they had done during the First World War. This increased the camaraderie and the effectiveness of co-operation between the two services. The techniques that had emerged from the trials of 1941 were also subject to greater refinement. One area that had not been considered earlier was the procedure for ending a shoot from the air—this would depend on what type of shoot was being conducted. If it was a neutralisation shoot to destroy the target and the pilot wished the artillery batteries to continue firing, he was to state his reasons for this and he 'should not stop firing in order to record the target'. If it was simply a registration shoot the pilot would end 'the shoot by recording the target'.[88]

Certain problems were also beginning to emerge with regard to the actual training of Air OP pilots: 'It has been apparent that the training of AOP pilots lacks practical experience of operations in the field.' Pilots who passed through the initial training phase had to be trained further once they had reached their assigned squadrons meaning they were still unavailable for operations:

> it is not possible to effect practical training due to ... the short duration (6 weeks) of each course ... the shortage of AOP ground personnel to act as Section Personnel, and ... to the establishment of vehicles and motor cycles which is insufficient to meet AOP training requirements under operational conditions in the field.[89]

The proposed solution to this problem was the formation of an Operational Training Unit (OTU), either as 'a separate unit or ... an enlargement of the present 1424 Flight [the training flight]'.[90] It was also decided that a gunner officer was to pilot the aircraft involved, engaging targets as they would 'from a ground OP, using R/T'.[91] It was also proposed to expand 1424 Flight to allow '30 trained AOP pilots ... to be produced every month'. The location of the flight was also to be moved to Army Co-operation Command's headquarters at Old Sarum to enhance the role it played in the training.[92] The 1941 trails had already established the vulnerability of aircraft conducting this role and as a result pilots were issued with instructions to follow while conducting shoots. They were to be 'no less than 2,000 yards behind our forward troops, at a height not exceeding 600 feet and [utilise] flights of not more than 20 minutes duration'.[93]

The further development of the Air OP was hampered by a lack of clarity over responsibility for administration of the resources. Army Co-operation Command argued that 'the need has been demonstrated for a clear statement defining exactly the spheres of responsibility of the RAF and Army for control and administration of Air OP squadrons'. Although the Air OP squadrons were RAF units, they were to be placed under the operational control of the army formation they were working with. The army was also to take over responsibility for the tactical training of these squadrons. In order to facilitate this in the most efficient and effective way, it was suggested that 'The closest co-operation will be required between GHQ Home Forces and Army Co-operation Command in order that 43 OTU shall be kept fully informed of the operational requirements of Air OP squadrons.' Regarding the training of the Air OP squadrons with artillery batteries, this too was to be the responsibility of Home Forces 'in consultation with Army Co-operation Command'. The School of Artillery was, however, able to call conferences of squadron commanders with the permission of Army Co-operation Command where artillery training had to be co-ordinated with teaching within 43 OTU.[94]

The development of the Air OP, and the subsequent placing of the squadrons engaged in this work demonstrates not only the good relations that existed between Army Co-operation Command and the School of Artillery, but also that, in certain circumstances, it could be beneficial to both services to give the army what they wanted: operational control of aircraft in the field. Aircraft were piloted by gunner officers of the RHA and placed under the control of the local army commander for operational duties. The School of Artillery developed their training programmes alongside Army Co-operation Command, working with rather than against each other, unlike other areas of air support development in Britain. Army Co-operation Command would also continue to work with the School of Artillery to further refine the Air OP concept in 1943, but its future existence was in doubt with the organisation of Fighter Command to provide a ground support function and continuing plans for the invasion of France. The developments started under Army Co-operation Command would also be subjected to rigorous testing.

NOTES

1. David Syrett, 'The Tunisian Campaign', p. 159. Richards, *Royal Air Force 1939–1945 Vol. I*, p. 252. Richard P. Hallion, 'The Second World War as a Turning Point in Air Power', in Sebastian Cox and Peter W. Gray (eds), *Air Power History: Turning Points from Kitty Hawk to Kosovo* (London and Portland, Oregon: Frank Cass, 2002), p. 102. Terraine, *The Right of the Line*, p. 352.
2. Gooderson, *Air Power at the Battlefront*, p. 26.
3. For further details on Dieppe see Ken Ford, *Dieppe 1942: a Prelude to D-Day* (Osprey: Oxford, 2003) and John P. Campbell, *Dieppe Revisited: A Documentary Investigation* (Frank Cass: London, 1993)
4. TNA AIR 20/2812, The Organisation, Function and Control of Air Forces in Support of the Army in an Overseas Theatre of War, 21 May 1942. Ministry of Information, *RAF Middle East: The Official Story of Air Operations in the Middle East, from February 1942 to January 1943* (HMSO: London, 1945), pp. 7, 10. Tedder, *With Prejudice*, pp. 211–12. John Connell, *Auchinleck: A Biography of Field Marshal Sir Claude Auchinleck* (Cassell: London, 1959), pp. 402, 411. Andy Tjepkema, 'Coningham: The Architect of Ground-Air Doctrine', *Air Clues*, 45: 6 (June, 1991), pp. 205–8. Hall, *Strategy for Victory*, pp. 128–31.
5. Hallion, *Strike from the Sky*, pp. 156–8.
6. Hall, *Strategy for Victory*, p. 113.
7. Ibid., p. 116.
8. TNA AIR 10/5547, AHB Narrative, Close Support. Hall, *Strategy for Victory*, p. 139.

9. TNA AIR 2/7880, Barratt's Visit to the Middle East, 27 August–9 September 1942. Written 21 September 1942. TNA AIR 20/2106 and AIR 37/760, Report on Visit to the Middle East by Barratt.
10. Hall, *Strategy for Victory*, p. 138.
11. Gooderson, *Air Power at the Battlefront*, p. 26. Bidwell and Graham, *Fire Power*, p. 307. Carrington, 'Army/Air Co-operation', p. 40.
12. TNA AIR 32/1041, Middle East Training Manual No. 7, Lessons from Operations October/November 1942. Gooderson, *Air Power at the Battlefront*, p. 26.
13. Army Co-operation Reports 1927–1935, TNA AIR 10/1708, AIR 10/1759, AIR 10/1827, AIR 10/1777, AIR 10/1794, AIR 10/1913, AIR 10/1914, AIR 10/1915 and AIR 10/1911, RAF War Manual Part I – Operations AP 1300, AIR 10/1889, RAF Manual of Army Co-operation, 2nd Edition, AP 1176.
14. TNA AIR 2/7880, Barratt's Report, 21 September 1942.
15. Ibid.
16. Hall, *Strategy for Victory*, p. 140. Further details can be found at Vincent Orange, 'Getting Together: Tedder, Coningham and Americans in the Desert and Tunisia, 1940–1943', in Daniel R. Mortensen (ed.), *Airpower and Ground Armies. Essays on the Evolution of Anglo-American Air Doctrine, 1940–1943* (University Press of the Pacific: Honolulu, Hawaii, 2005).
17. Hall, *Strategy for Victory*, pp. 140–1. David R. Mets, 'A Gilder in the Propwash of the Royal Air Force? Gen. Carl A. Spaatz, the RAF and the Foundation of American Tactical Air Doctrine', in Daniel R. Mortensen (ed.), *Airpower and Ground Armies. Essays in the Evolution of Anglo-American Air Doctrine, 1940–1943* (University Press of the Pacific: Honolulu, Hawaii, 2005).
18. Hall, *Strategy for Victory* p. 141.
19. Mortensen *Ground Armies*. Syrett, 'The Tunisian Campaign'.
20. TNA AIR 2/7880, Letter from DMC to VCAS on Report on Visit to the Middle East by AOC-in-C Army Co-operation Command, 3 October 1942.
21. Hall, *Strategy for Victory*, pp. 104–16.
22. Terraine, *The Right of the Line*, p. 352.
23. TNA AIR 2/7880, AOC-in-C Army Co-operation Command's Report, 21 September 1942.
24. Ibid. See also TNA AIR 2/7880, AIR 20/2107, Air 37/760 and Hall, *Strategy for Victory*, p. 139.
25. Ibid.
26. TNA AIR 2/7880, Letter from DMC to VCAS on Report on Visit to the Middle East by AOC-in-C Army Co-operation Command, 3 October 1942.

27. TNA AIR 2/7880, Report on Visit by AOC-in-C Army Co-operation Command's Visit, 21 September 1942.
28. TNA AIR 20/2812, Letter from AOC-in-C Army Co-operation Command to VCAS Medhurst, 18 December 1942.
29. Hall, *Strategy for Victory*, p. 146.
30. TNA AIR 16/776, Notes on Training Fighter Squadrons to Support Army Formations, c.February 1942.
31. TNA AIR 16/776, Letter from Headquarters Fighter Command to Headquarters 9–14, 81 and 82 Groups, 3 January 1942.
32. TNA AIR 16/776, Memorandum on Air Support, 2 February 1942.
33. TNA AIR 16/776, Notes on Training, c.February 1942.
34. TNA AIR 16/776, Memorandum by CIGS on Fighter Squadrons in Army Air Support, c.January 1942.
35. TNA AIR 16/776, Suggestions by No. 257 Squadron in Air Support, undated, c.March 1942.
36. TNA AIR 16/552. Letter from AOC 12 Group to Headquarters Fighter Command, 18 May 1942.
37. Ibid.
38. Ibid.
39. TNA AIR 16/552, Letter from Headquarters Fighter Command to 9–14 Squadrons regarding Army Air Support (Operational Instruction No. 20/1942 sent with letter), 27 September 1942.
40. Hall, *Strategy for Victory*, p. 124.
41. TNA WO 216/127, The Thorold Paper, 1943.
42. Ibid.
43. TNA WO 216/127, COS (42) 271, 20 May 1942.
44. TNA WO 199/334, Memorandum on Army Air Support, undated, c.May 1942.
45. TNA CAB 101/136, Unpublished draft of the Grand Strategy Narrative, undated.
46. Hall, *Strategy for Victory*, pp. 124–5.
47. TNA CAB 80/37, Continental Operations 1943: Operational Organisation and System of Command of the RAF, Memorandum by CAS, 21 July 1942.
48. TNA AIR 75/43, Draft Letter from Slessor to Prime Minister, 4 September 1942.
49. TNA WO 32/10396, Letter from C-in-C Home Forces to the Under-Secretary of State for War regarding the Organisation and System of Control of Air Forces in Support of Overseas Operations, 5 November 1942.
50. Ibid.

51. TNA WO 32/10396, Letter from Woodall to DMC regarding Organisation and System of Control of Air Forces in Support of Overseas Operations, 10 November 1942.
52. Ibid.
53. TNA AIR 39/110, Letter from Director of Operations to Army Co-operation Command regarding the Development of Army Co-operation Command, 24 January 1942.
54. TNA CAB 80/35, COS (42) 164 Army Air Requirements, 10 March 1942.
55. TNA AIR 10/5574, AHB Narrative Close Support.
56. TNA WO 233/60, Draft of Development of Air Support to the Army 1939–1945 by P. Browne Director of Air (War Office), 25 May 1945.
57. TNA AIR 8/894, Letter from Air Marshal Sholto Douglas to the Under-Secretary of State for Air, 18 August 1942.
58. TNA AIR 8/1063, Report by the Joint Planning Staff, 21 May 1942.
59. TNA WO 199/334, Memorandum on the Army Air Support Group, May 1942.
60. Ibid.
61. Ibid.
62. TNA WO 199/334, Letter from Paget to Brooke, 28 June 1942.
63. TNA AIR 8/1063, Report by the Joint Planning Staff, 21 May 1942.
64. TNA AIR 8/1063, COS (42) 162 (0), 26 May 1942.
65. Ibid. Douglas does not mention the issue of the Air Striking Command or the AASG and the discussions he had with Brooke over this in his autobiography *Years of Command*. That an issue such as this, which was subject to much discussion between the two Services does not feature in the autobiography of an officer with the status of Douglas partly demonstrates the status of army co-operation and as a direct result Army Co-operation Command within Britain.
66. TNA AIR 20/2812, Memorandum on the Organisation, Functions and Control of Air Support Forces in Support of the Army in an Overseas Theatre, 21 May 1942.
67. TNA WO 199/334, Letter from Paget to Brooke, 27 July 1942.
68. TNA CAB 69/4 and AIR 8/989, DO (42) 34, 1 April 1942. Hall, *Strategy for Victory*, p. 118.
69. TNA WO 199/334, Letter from Paget to Brooke, 27 July 1942.
70. TNA AIR 20/2812, Memorandum on the Organisation, Functions and Control of Air Forces, 21 May 1942.
71. TNA AIR 20/2812, Letter from Barratt to Freeman, 3 July 1942.
72. TNA AIR 20/2812, Letter from VCAS Wilfred to AOC-in-C Army Co-operation Command, 6 July 1942.
73. TNA AIR 20/2812, Memorandum by Freeman, 10 August 1942.

74. TNA CAB 79/57, COS (42) 138 (0), 5 October 1942. Hall, *Strategy for Victory*, pp. 126–7.
75. TNA CAB 101/136, Army Air Co-operation, Letter from Brigadier L. C. Hollis to Churchill, 19 September 1942.
76. TNA AIR 8/984, Letter from Freeman to Douglas, 3 August 1942.
77. Hall, *Strategy for Victory*, p. 148.
78. TNA AIR 8/984, Letter from Douglas to Under-Secretary of State for Air, 18 August 1942.
79. TNA WO 216/127, Letter from Portal to Brooke, 31 August 1942.
80. TNA WO 216/127, Letter from Brooke to Portal, 3 September 1942. There is no mention of this matter in Brooke's diaries and it is not mentioned in any of the published biographies.
81. TNA AIR 8/984. Letter from Douglas to the Under-Secretary of State for Air, 18 August 1942.
82. TNA WO 216/127, Letter from Portal to Brooke, 7 September 1942.
83. Robert M. Citino, *The Wehrmacht Retreats: Fighting a Lost War, 1943* (University Press of Kansas: Kansas, 2012), p. 14.
84. TNA PREM 3/8, War Cabinet Chiefs of Staff Committee, 5 October 1942.
85. TNA 10/5547, AHB Narrative Close Support.
86. TNA WO 233/60, Development of Air Support, 25 May 1945.
87. TNA AIR 39/48, Letter from Woodall to Brigadier B. C. H. Kummins, Southern Command, regarding Artillery Reconnaissance, 20 January 1940.
88. TNA AIR 39/48, Letter from Army Co-operation Command to 32, 34, 35 and 36 Wings regarding an Artillery Reconnaissance Practice Camp, 26 March 1942.
89. TNA AIR 39/69, Letter from the Commanding Officer No. 651 Squadron to Headquarters regarding the Operational Training of AOP (Pupil) Pilots, 1 July 1942.
90. Ibid.
91. TNA AIR 39/69, AOP Squadrons Memorandum, 26 July 1942.
92. TNA AIR 39/69, Letter from Headquarters No. 70 Group to Army Co-operation Command, 28 July 1942.
93. TNA AIR 39/69, AOP Squadrons Memorandum, 26 July 1942.
94. TNA AIR 39/69, Letter from Army Co-operation Command to Headquarters Nos 32–39 Wings, Headquarters No. 70 Group and No. 43 OTU on the Control and Administration of Air Op Squadrons, 18 November 1942.

CHAPTER 6

The End of Army Co-operation Command, 1943

The air support system for continental operations was radically overhauled in 1943 and the new system was based around the ideas and discussions of 1942. In order to fully test the abilities of the composite group idea within the wider air support framework and give the pilots of these formations the necessary experience, a large-scale exercise was conducted. The air aspect of this was headed by Barratt. The Air OP (its function and placement within the wider framework) was also a major consideration of this exercise. The training operation, code-named Spartan, was vital not only to the further development of tactical air power thinking in Britain but it was also the final nail in Army Co-operation Command's coffin as, in terms of tactical air power at least, the mono-role RAF command structure disappeared and Army Co-operation Command no longer had a function. Despite the adoption of the composite group early in 1943, Army Co operation Command was still a major force in the development of tactical air power in Britain until its disbandment in July 1943.

This chapter analyses in depth the relevant aspects of Spartan and the discussions that followed on the organisation of air support forces, the disbandment of Army Co-operation Command and the creation of the 2nd Tactical Air Force. The RAF did not want to lose the lower formations of Army Co-operation Command nor the expertise that had been cultivated within it. That this was the case demonstrates that Army Co-operation Command had more impact on the development of tactical air power in Britain than had previously been acknowledged. The biggest problem facing the Air Staff

© The Author(s) 2016
M. Powell, *The Development of British Tactical Air Power, 1940–1943*,
DOI 10.1057/978-1-137-54417-9_6

was how best to utilise the expertise that had been garnered within Army Co-operation Command. Many of these formations were not disbanded but were in fact transferred to other areas of the RAF.

The new tactical air support formation created in mid-1943 differed from Army Co-operation Command in two major ways.[1] First, 2nd Tactical Air Force was an operational formation, giving it similar access to resources as Fighter and Bomber Commands. Second, with the changing tide of the Second World War as a whole, the prospect of an Allied invasion of the Continent became an ever clearer reality, giving both 2nd Tactical Air Force and the army in Britain operations for which they could make realistic plans—a greater political impetus was matched by increasing build-up of US troops and equipment in Britain. Despite being the junior partner in the alliance, the British government and services felt that they could not be seen to fall behind in preparations for such an invasion. There was also a greater emphasis on inter-theatre learning. Many of the lessons identified by Army Co-operation Command were combined with operational experience gained in the Western Desert when the final operations in North Africa, following Operation Torch were conducted. Further refinements were also made prior to and during the landings and subsequent operations in Italy.[2]

With the development of the composite group, the AASC would require major alteration. One of the major issues raised by the Air Staff was that of permanently allotting the AASC to the army's corps organisation. Despite the composite group breaking one of the fundamental principles of air power (that of centralising air resources under an air commander), they felt that this was a step too far. The Director of Air at the War Office, P. Browne, wrote to Paget stating that 'the Air Staff are unable to agree to the proposals which you make'. The Air Staff felt that due to its being primarily an air formation, it should remain within the RAF: 'It has always been a cornerstone of the agreed Air Ministry and War Office policy that the A Air SC [Army Air Support Control] should be [the] advanced headquarters of the RAF formation providing Army Air Support.' They further highlighted the experience gained in the Middle East to reject the idea that the AASC should become a permanent part of the corps organisation, arguing that,

> While it is agreed that there may be occasions where it would be desirable to control air support on a corps level (although this apparently has never been the practice in the Middle East) it is considered that these occasions

will be rare and that it would be possible to foresee them well in advance, e.g. before a complete Army is established in a theatre of operations or when a corps is given a completely independent mission. It is considered that on these occasions the group or other RAF commands will detach from his staff a responsible officer and the necessary personnel and equipment to the particular corps headquarters from where the air support will then be controlled in precisely the same way as in the combined RAF/Army Headquarters.[3]

The War Office's moves to gain operational control of the AASC was at too high a command level for the Air Staff and they continued their argument by stating, 'Taking into consideration the rare occasions on which control will be required on a corps level it is felt that this suggested re-organisation is unjustifiably extravagant.' The efficiency of the AASC would not be improved if the War Office recommendations were implemented, as there would be 'no saving of equipment or personnel ... as special channels would still be required'. As a result, 'There would ... appear to be no advantage in relieving the A Air SC of these communications'.[4] Undeterred by the Air Staff's response, the War Office continued to push for changes to be made to the AASC. Fresh proposals were put forward in February 1943 that took into account the Air Staff's arguments. The basic principle that the AASC was to remain an RAF formation was conceded but it was proposed to reorganise it so that it was able to provide '*one section for operational duty at Army* and *one at each of the two Corps Headquarters* (in the event of an Army being composed of more than two Corps, additional Corps sections to be added as necessary) [emphasis in original]'.[5]

The fundamental make-up of the AASC, as originally developed by Army Co-operation Command, was to remain unchanged with it being comprised of a joint RAF and army staff.[6] That this joint staff continued was based upon the principle that 'communications between A Air SC and RAF units should be manned and operated by the RAF and communications between A Air SC and military formations by the Army'. The use of RAF personnel to communicate with RAF formations and army personnel to communicate with army formations would ease communications difficulties that had previously plagued air support. This would also mean the creation of an RAF group headquarters 'with self-contained W/T communications at Army Headquarters, *the A Air SC* [would] *no longer be required to provide W/T communications from Army Headquarters to airfields* [emphasis in original]'. Each AASC section was to have '*wireless equipment to permit direct control of squadrons which may be sub-allotted* [emphasis in original]'. An effort would also be made to standardise wireless equipment 'in order to achieve the greatest possible degree of interchangability [*sic*] and to simplify maintenance'. Gale recommended that an RAF representative should be placed at Corps Headquarters along with the appropriate staff in order to 'act as Air Adviser to the Corps Commander on all air matters'.[7] The recommendations of a joint headquarters and signals organisation pre-dated the experiments conducted by Wann and Woodall and the creation of Army Co-operation Command as they had been put forward during the army co-operation exercises conducted during the interwar period. That it took this long to implement them in Britain, and was only done so after its success was demonstrated in the Western Desert raises questions about how much attention was paid to the ideas that emerged from the interwar exercises. The arguments put forward by the Air Staff regarding the status of the AASC were further challenged in the letter and demonstrate the General Staff's determination to have these units under the highest possible level of command and control.

> If the A Air SC is accepted as a RAF unit, it is logical to regard it as part of the organisation of a Composite Group associated with and parallel to an Army. As such *it would be controlled and administered by its parent formation. The Army Staff, which hitherto has exercised command of the A Air SC and has been shown on that establishment should then be borne on the strength of the military formations concerned*, the officers becoming staff officers for air matters of the formation commanders concerned [emphasis in original].[8]

Gale felt that even though the decisions regarding the future of the composite group had not yet been finalised,

> the availability of a new model A Air SC now is an urgent necessity for training and pending the production of the Army and RAF formations involved, *I recommend that the Air Ministry be asked to form one of these units under the appropriate RAF Command, and affiliated to General Headquarters, Home Forces*, and this should be given temporarily such elements as will make it administratively self-contained, until it can be absorbed within the Composite Group organisation. *During the interim period, the Army Staff should continue to live and work with the A Air SC as before, in order to participate in training and development* [emphasis in original].[9]

The agreement that had been reached between Home Forces and the Air Staff on this issue demonstrated the improvement in relations that had been achieved between the two since the Battle of France. This was in part due to the work of Army Co-operation Command and the confidence that the army in Britain had that there was a senior operational RAF organisation dedicated to aerial army support. Combined with the experience gained in utilising the AASC in overseas theatres, the organisation's form was slowly beginning to take shape.

The decision to hold Spartan was made in early December 1942 and it was scheduled to take place in the first half of March 1943, based on two armies at full strength.[10] The RAF had major problems finding the resources necessary to provide the required composite groups to support such large formations. They were required to provide 'a minimum of twenty-four Fighter and Bomber squadrons' and 'two RAF [composite] groups'.[11] The prospect of Spartan was received enthusiastically by the War Office, and as early as 12 December 1942, when it was being discussed, they were of the opinion that it would 'provide excellent training in Army Air Support'.[12] The cause of this enthusiasm was a combination of the altered strategic outlook and the very fact that major air support exercises were being conducted with the tacit support of the RAF. With the Red Army advancing, particularly after the Battle of Kursk, the *Luftwaffe* diverting ever more resources to the defence of the German homeland as a result of the Combined Bomber Offensive, and the Allied success in North Africa opening up the soft underbelly of Europe, the time was approaching for the launch of a second front on the Continent. This would require a functional air support capability that was acceptable to both services.

Operations on the Continent required an overhaul of the air support command structure in Britain to bring it more in line with that used in the Western Desert. This more joint structure, based around the composite group, would not include Army Co-operation Command as its existence could only be justified through a continuation of the overall mono-role command structure of the RAF. The composite group demonstrated that, in terms of air support at least, the mono-role command structure of the RAF was unsuitable if support for ground forces was to be effective. The War Office could see that the support of their forces in the field was being taken more seriously by the RAF than had been the case to date, despite the creation of Army Co-operation Command. That this exercise was taking place at all demonstrates how far the relations between the two services had been improved since the Battle of France. The work of Army Co-operation Command was vital in this process, explaining air power to the army in Britain and allowing them to gain an understanding of the operational level impact tactical air power could have. Spartan was designed 'to afford a background on which to present certain problems connected with the planning and control of Air Support which would arise at a Group/Army Headquarters, and to provoke discussion in these problems'. The operational situation that provided the context for the exercise was 'the invasion by forces of this country of the European continent'.[13]

The main objective for the air aspect of Spartan was 'to study and practice the handling of Mobile RAF Composite Groups', as the system for their employment in active operations had not yet been decided. The system that was to be trialled in Spartan had first been considered in 1942 and it would now be tested under the control of Barratt. The idea that had been discussed was to have composite groups formed in parallel to, and identifying themselves with, the armies with which they were working. It was intended that the experience gained in Spartan would allow the RAF 'to design a force capable of rapid movement and flexible control.'[14] A survey conducted in January 1943, however, highlighted the lack of suitable available aircraft which meant 'that it is quite impossible to provide for both the British and German sides on a mobile basis'. In order to overcome this shortage and test fully the composite group idea in an invasion scenario, it was proposed to form only the British side on as mobile a basis as possible, with as many groups as possible, 'to try out fully their capabilities and suitability for Continental operations'.[15] For the purpose of the exercise, the organisation of formations for air support was to be based upon the perceived needs envisaged for 'the assault phase of a combined operation'.[16]

Taking the lessons that had been identified from operations in the Western Desert, and which had previously been established during the interwar period by Wann and Woodall and Army Co-operation Command, the composite group commander was to have his headquarters co-located with the army commander.[17] This idea was still not integrated completely into the mindset of either service, as a reminder was made that the group commander was to sit 'jointly with [the] Army Commander, but not subordinate to [the] army.[18] That the equality of commands still had to be emphasised at this stage of the Second World War confirms that this was still very much an issue, despite the amount of discussion that had taken place and the creation of a Command level formation within the RAF that was specifically designed to resolve these problems. This, combined with the evidence that had emerged from overseas theatres, demonstrates that the relations between the two services above Command level were still poor.

The composite group headquarters was also to be divided into two sections in order to increase its overall mobility. Again, this was not a new concept and had already been stated in interwar doctrine, and by Army Co-operation Command and the WDAF. These two sections were to be 'an advanced (or operational) group headquarters and a rear (or administrative) group headquarters'.[19] Both of these headquarters were to be designed in such a way that they could be 'married to their equivalent army headquarters'.[20] The advanced headquarters was to be created in such a way that it was able to move quickly when required—it was not to be prevented from doing so by having to accommodate a large administrative staff. This staff would be placed within the rear headquarters organisation and would be responsible 'for the administration of all RAF units in the group area'. The squadrons' administration would be conducted through the 'headquarters at each airfield'. The advanced headquarters would be responsible for exercising 'operational control through control centres (Mobile Operations Room Units (MORU)). It was expected that the headquarters would be able to control three MORUs, but could, in exceptional circumstances, control up to four. A MORU would communicate with up to four separate airfields by R/T or landline and would be able to 'control further airfields by W/T'. These communications channels would allow a MORU to communicate also with 'adjacent MORUs and the Mobile Air Reporting Unit'. It would also be able 'to provide ground-to-air communications for the operational control of aircraft'.[21]

Further to this group headquarters structure, it had been suggested that an organisation on a mobile field force basis would require a headquarters for each individual airfield. This headquarters was to 'provide for all ground communications by wireless, to be augmented by landline when this can be provided by the Army'. This communications system, which was an extension of the AASC system, was required to provide the headquarters with the ability to communicate with aircraft whilst in the air, allowing localised flying control.[22] The formation of the four airfield headquarters for the exercise was nominally the responsibility of Fighter Command; however, No. 2 Group, Bomber Command, and Army Co-operation Command were to provide one of these units each from their own resources.[23] That personnel from within the Army Co-operation Command were required highlights two major points that have been overlooked in the literature available regarding the organisation.[24]

First, the work done by Army Co-operation Command had created a critical mass of thinkers that was simply unavailable in any other RAF

Command in Britain, and this knowledge was vital with preparations now being made to invade France. The delays that had been incurred due to the postponement of Roundup, and the lessons identified as a result of the Dieppe landings, had given the Air and General Staffs the time necessary to explore fully the composite group idea and to exploit the expertise of Army Co-operation Command. Second, with this new organisation under test, the role of Army Co-operation Command was starting to appear increasingly irrelevant. With this in mind, it appears unusual that personnel from this Command would be tasked to take part in an exercise such as this, but a partial explanation might be that shortages being experienced by the RAF account for it, as the Air Staff had been reluctant to involve Army Co-operation Command and its resources in exercises on this scale previously. Through this joint exercise, the personnel who would be conducting air support in the short-term at least (Fighter Command), would be able to gain valuable experience. Keeping at least a handful of Army Co-operation Command personnel fully versed in continuing and future army air support developments lends weight to the argument that very little would change in Britain if it were to be abolished. Whilst 2nd Tactical Air Force was not an upgraded, operational, Army Co-operation Command, the objectives of the two organisations were similar.

This proposed new organisation was an evolution of the Wann–Woodall system, which had been further refined by Army Co-operation Command. It advanced the concepts put forward in 1940, and allowed the command and communications system to evolve into one that was better designed to handle the fast-paced operations that it was hoped would be the result of a successful invasion of and breakout into the Continent. The evolution of doctrinal thinking encompassed first the solution to an operational problem at the theoretical level. The AASC was then further modified through the experience gained in experimentation and exported to an overseas theatre where it was further adapted to meet the specific operational conditions found there. The officers that were to form the staffs of the groups involved in Spartan were to be formed from the officers of Fighter, Bomber and Army Co-operation Commands. Barratt was tasked with giving 'all possible assistance' to the officer in charge of the whole exercise.[25] Barratt would not, however, be directing the air aspect of Spartan alone. Broadhurst stated that Barratt had the overall responsibility for the direction of the exercise so far as the RAF is concerned. Nevertheless, AOC-in-C Fighter Command as Commander designate of the RAF contingent to 'Roundup' is intimately concerned at all stages of the planning and execution of the exercise and will have the right to express such views as he may wish to the RAF Director ... with the object of ensuring that the forces to be placed at his disposal are economically and efficiently employed.[26]

This again demonstrates that Barratt had never been allowed overall control over any aspect of army co-operation training and development that the RAF felt could herald important developments, particularly if it involved training with the army. Despite Barratt being the most experienced person in Britain with regard to the thinking and development of both army air support and in fostering good relations with the army, he was not allowed free reign to conduct the air aspect of this exercise along the lines he saw fit. He would always have to take the opinion of another commander of a separate Command, with little practical experience of conducting air support, into account. Whilst this may give the commander of Fighter Command more experience in handling air support, especially on the scale envisaged in Spartan, it must be questioned why a joint directorship was not established. This would have allowed the future commander of air support during an invasion of north-west Europe to gain more detailed experience in this role, allowing him to actively work alongside Barratt. The new head of Fighter Command was Leigh-Mallory, and he had been promoted to this role from within the Fighter Command organisation.[27] Despite being well versed in army co-operation matters in general from his interwar experiences, Leigh-Mallory did not have Barratt's background both in the application of army air support in the field or in its theoretical development.[28] As was the case in the Western Desert command system, Barratt was to be an assistant director to the C-in-C Home Forces, who was overall director of the exercise.[29]

SPARTAN took place between 21 February and 3 March 1943 and the composite group allocated to the British side during the exercise 'was active on all days on which operations were possible'.[30] Paget was, however, also at pains to point out some of the difficulties that had been experienced by the RAF internally during the exercise. 'The internal RAF organisation was deliberately experimental and was handicapped by limitations in the availability of equipment and personnel.' The staffs assembled to conduct the support had little experience of working together with the army formation staffs to which they were responsible for providing support. This unfamiliarity, combined with 'constant communications difficulties confine[d] the possibilities of constructive criticism to the broader aspects'. Paget was, however, confident that despite the initial teething problems encountered during the exercise, 'sufficient experience was gained to confirm that this conception is sound and should be accepted for future training and operations'. He also believed that 'The main lesson to be drawn from Spartan is the clear recognition by both Services of the task which lies before them, and the urgent need to solve together the many outstanding problems of organisation, staff duties and procedure by practical means, as opposed to theory.'[31] The idea that the two Services should work together to resolve the problems inherently found in attempting to conduct successful tactical air support was not an original one, and was one of the fundamental principles behind the creation of Army Co-operation Command. Exercises on this scale, which would have allowed Army Co-operation Command to demonstrate its abilities to the fullest, could not have taken place without the work done and experience gained by it. The prevailing strategic situation between 1940 and 1943 had meant that the army did not have overseas operations to prepare for—now an assault on the continent was likely, an exercise on this scale was extremely useful. It is also doubtful whether the Air Staff would have allowed such exercises in a different strategic situation given the animosity between the two services prior to 1943. It did, however, show that the relations between them had improved to such an extent that exercises on the scale of Spartan could be conducted. Such a thing would have been impossible without the groundwork that had been laid by Army Co-operation Command in educating the army about the impact of tactical air power at the operational level of war.

Paget identified that the composite group, together with a joint, co-located, headquarters, would ensure 'that … Army and RAF resources are directed to the accomplishment of the common task'.[32] He was also concerned that exercises such as Spartan were not enough to allow the relationship between the army and RAF to develop to such an extent that they would be able to function as one unit effectively:

> the successful application of these principles is most likely when the respective commanders and staffs are given the opportunity of studying the mutual problems together and working in close harmony for some time before actual operations. *It was apparent from Spartan that there is much to be learnt by both Services before operational standards are reached in this direction* [emphasis added].[33]

The striking aspect of Paget's comments regarding operational standards and how best they could be improved was that he was critical of both services. This was a step change from how these problems had been approached previously when Paget had laid the blame for any problems in conducting effective air support at the RAF's door. This is indicative of Army Co-operation Command's work in two ways. First, it demonstrates the role Army Co-operation Command played in repairing relations between the two entities, particularly as Army Co-operation Command worked closely with Home Forces. Second, it shows that certain senior army commanders were beginning to understand the operational level impact of tactical air power.

As a result of Spartan, the future role of the AASC also came under consideration and the potential future of the composite group with its own communications system:

> Spartan showed that the Composite Group makes the A Air SC as an independent mixed unit illogical. Its functions, however, remain of prime importance.[34]

The AASC faced further change following the exercise. It was to be absorbed into the wider communications system, and it was argued that the functions it had performed previously could be done more efficiently if 'The Army ... provide[d] a separate W/T network for the rapid transmission of information affecting air action and requests for air support and reconnaissance'. This communications network was to consist of W/T tentacles 'working back from [the] headquarters of forward formations to the point at which the Army and RAF Headquarters meet normally corps and Army headquarters' as it had done previously. The RAF was to provide the communications system necessary for the AASC to execute the army's request as part of the general signals organisation of the composite group. It was noted that, 'These communications should include those to enable RAF sections at Corps Headquarters to exercise command on occasions.'[35] This system was emerging as a functional way of conducting air support on a joint basis whose impact would be felt at both the tactical and operational levels of war. A joint headquarters organisation would enhance the abilities of the AASC to work within the composite group system. This would be achieved through having those controlling the aircraft providing the support working alongside those who were receiving and prioritising requests for support from forward formations and reconnaissance flights conducted over the battlefield. This was a recommendation that had been reinforced by the work of Army Co-operation Command and was based upon interwar exercises. Further familiarisation through minor and major training exercises with the same formations would serve to further enhance the efficiency of the staff of these headquarters and provide greater experience of what constituted priority targets for each service and demonstrate the limitations of air support for land forces.

A recurring issue dealt with in Paget's comments about Spartan was the lead time between the identification of a fleeting target and its subsequent attack from the air.[36] As had been found during the Battle of France, this was prohibitively long. This is not surprising given the new and unfamiliar personnel combined with a new system that looked to integrate old formations into new ones. These long lead-times, however, represented a backwards step from the achievements of Wann and Woodall in Northern Ireland. Paget made his feelings on this issue clear:

> the heavy delays frequently experienced in Spartan ... would not be acceptable in operations and it is necessary to examine with the greatest care how they can be reduced by improved procedure and the highest standard of training and communications, before it is possible to lay down too rigidly that control of offensive air action must invariably be centralized. In this direction decentralization of effort must not be confused with decentralization of control.[37]

In their attempts to improve the communication and control procedures that would result in reduced lead-times for impromptu air support, both services had a vast wealth of experience upon which to base their subsequent training plans.

In Paget's opinion, the unrivalled success of Spartan was the utilisation of joint headquarters. That this was the case highlights how quickly improvements could have been made if it had been adopted during the interwar period or at the beginning of the Second World War. The reason that it had not lay in the animosity that had existed between the two services since the end of the First World War. The operational experience of the Western Desert had demonstrated the effectiveness of joint headquarters. Terraine has described the desert experience as the services in that theatre not having 'to struggle against the rigidities and dogmas of the functional Command system; the RAF [could be used] ... as a single unit'.[38] This point cannot be overstated when the developments in tactical air power in both Britain and overseas theatres are compared. Army Co-operation Command did not and never could have the freedom of action available to organisations in the Middle East who were far away from the central control of the Air Council and Air Ministry in Britain. They also faced active operations where co-operation was a must to stave off defeat and the devastating strategic consequences this would bring. There were still, however, areas where joint operations in Britain could be improved. Outside the joint operations headquarters establishment, 'separate RAF Operations and Army Operations sections' were to be set up, which would be responsible for the 'implementation of the decisions taken' in the joint operations headquarters.[39] The only exception to this splitting of headquarters was for the dissemination of intelligence material that was of use to both services.

Paget recommended that a combined intelligence organisation should be created to ensure both the RAF and the army received all intelligence that might be of use to both in another demonstration of the improved relations between the two services brought about in part by Army Co-operation Command.[40] In Spartan, the passage of information to RAF units had been described as poor and this, to a degree, accounted for the long-lead times in the engagement of impromptu targets:

> It is essential that a general up-to-date presentation of the military situation must be available for all squadrons. This should be supplemented by more precise information as may be necessary when attacks are ordered. The failure to achieve the requisite standard in this direction in Spartan may be attributed to inadequate communications and partly to a lack of joint intelligence cells at the point of the group organisation.[41]

The solution, as Paget saw it, to many of the problems that had been encountered during Spartan, was through greater integration at several levels of command. One reason why even greater problems had not been suffered was due to the army beginning to understand what the RAF required in terms of information in order to conduct an air support role with greater efficiency and effectiveness. The closest solution that had been tried prior to Spartan and the developments that emerged from it was in the creation of Army Co-operation Command, who had achieved a lot in educating Home Forces as to the limitations of air support and how it was best provided. Army Co-operation Command was not, however, given the support afforded to the composite group to allow it to fully embed itself with Home Forces. Without this necessary integration, it was unable to tackle fully many of the problems faced in developing air support in Britain. It was constrained by the functional command system present in Britain that did not exist in other theatres.[42]

Spartan also highlighted deficiencies in the collection and analysis of intelligence particularly that gained through aerial reconnaissance. One of the biggest issues revealed during the exercise was that 'the amount of work occasioned in dealing with information contained in reports of all operations—direct from Squadrons—congested the Section and restricted the G10's activities in the broader sphere'.[43] A report by Flying Officer R. A. Symonds argued that despite the teething problems experienced by the intelligence section during SPARTAN,

> There would not ... be any saving of time in Squadrons sending their reports direct to Group Headquarters by telephone. It became clear at once that this system failed owing to bad communications between Group and Advanced airfields. It is probably quicker for all reports to go via [the] MORU for one Intelligence Officer can be taking a report while another is passing an earlier one to the Group.[44]

It was recommended that through the use of a joint RAF/army headquarters, complete intelligence reports could be collected, collated and disseminated to all levels. The reliable communications system used in Spartan, which had been partly developed by Army Co-operation Command, allowed the system to flourish. To enable this system to be effective at higher levels of command, the Army Group Headquarters 'should be an "Information Centre" in which Army and RAF Intelligence staffs work together and into which information and intelligence from all Army and RAF sources is delivered'. This system 'should adjoin a Combined Operations Centre so that the complete air and ground situation can be jointly appreciated by the general and operations staff, together with their respective intelligence officers who will also be represented'.[45] It was determined that the minimum establishment for a continuous intelligence service should be 'one Flight Lieutenant as Senior Intelligence Officer, one Flight Officer to act as deputy, and two Pilot/Flying Officers'. In order to make the establishment work at maximum efficiency the Flight Lieutenant 'should be seated next to [the] Operations Brigadier'. Through this, the intelligence officer would be 'immediately aware of the contents of all Operations orders'. It would also ensure that if the intelligence officer was engaged in contacting a group headquarters, as had happened on a frequent basis during Spartan, he would be able to 'hand the telephone to [the] operations Brigadier or take down the message himself'. It was further suggested that 'an Air Liaison Officer [ALO] [should be employed to keep] the Situation Map [up-to-date], getting the necessary military information for this purpose from Army or Corps Headquarters and passing it to Squadrons'.[46] The effectiveness of the composite group relied heavily upon the timely dissemination of intelligence information to advanced group headquarters and required good co-operation. The despatch of reports from returning aircraft to the group or squadron intelligence officer responsible for them was to fall to the intelligence officers based at each airfield.[47] Both services were beginning to realise just how full and frank the co-operation between them would have to be to successfully prosecute operations on the continent.

The Air OP squadrons, developed under Army Co-operation Command, were also subject to test during Spartan. The result of this exercise was to alter how these units were to be used at the tactical level. A total of four Air OP squadrons took part with three being assigned to the German side and one to the British. It was seen that 'there are advantages in the Flight, rather than the Section being regarded as the Tactical unit'. To allow the Flight to function effectively as the tactical unit of the Air OP it was recommended that 'The flight should, wherever possible, move as a flight.' Where sections of the flight had been assigned to regiments for observation work, it was noted that 'they can often return at dusk to the Flight Advanced Landing Ground'. Briefing pilots whilst in the air was also seen to be easier if carried out by a Flight Commander and, as a result, there would be 'an economy of effort and minimum casualties'.[48] The chief umpire's report on Spartan gave the AIR OP glowing praise that deserves to be quoted at length:

> The exercise has taught us a lot as to the use of the AOP [Air OP]. Its value has recently been proved with First Army, was found to be immense. *This was the first time that many artillery commanders had had the chance to handle them. They did it well, and the AOP Flights did good work* ... It is now realised what an excellent weapon the AOP is, and it should not be misused, but retained for legitimate tasks. All Arty OPS should report everything they can about the battle and this applies to the AOP which can be used within our lines on various missions if they don't get taken off shooting the artillery when this is wanted. It should be used under the artillery commanders. AOPs

used for artillery observation are confined to the limit of visions from 2,000 yards behind our lines. It does not, therefore, replace Arty R[econnaissance]. Suggested that Arty R is not essential when the battle is fluid, but when it has been established and a fire plan is being made Arty R is valuable for the essential location of targets deeper within the enemy lines than can be seen from the AOP [emphasis added].[49]

The use of the Air OP in Spartan culminated the development in artillery observation that had begun in the First World War. Army Co-operation Command continued this development in conjunction with the School of Artillery. The comments of the Chief Umpire highlight one of the major problems faced by Army Co-operation Command—he noted that many artillery commanders had no experience of conducting shoots with Air OP aircraft, and it had in fact been an experimental organisation while its tactics and procedures were being refined. Very few large-scale exercises had been held to allow commanders to gain experience in using the Air OP. This was partly due to the squadrons being within Army Co-operation Command and its relative status within the RAF—this made it difficult to organise exercises and, as a result, artillery officers faced a steep learning curve in its use.

In order to identify and assimilate the lessons that emerged from the air aspect of Spartan a conference was held shortly after its conclusion so that the results and experiences of the exercise were 'still fresh in the participants' minds'.[50] The final report was not, in fact, written by Barratt, but by the senior air umpire, Thorold.[51] Barratt's conference attempted to answer several questions that had arisen as a result of the exercise, some that had been raised at army and corps commanders' headquarters, others about the proportion of effort devoted to attacking airfields during the exercise.[52] The answers to many of the questions put forward in a questionnaire devised by Barratt can be found in Thorold's reports on the exercise. Thorold identified that the army had 'accepted certain responsibilities for meeting the many needs of the RAF in the field'. This again marked a step change in the attitude of the army towards the RAF whilst they were conducting support in the field. The composite group also had to 'dovetail evenly into that of the Army [to ensure that] the machinery for obtaining [the RAF's] needs work smoothly'. To allow this to function with the least amount of friction it was 'essential … that the closest possible relationship be established from the outset between all branches of the staff and

Units of the Army and RAF wherever the two Services come into contact'. The third appendix is, however, the most important aspect of Thorold's report on Spartan—it deals with the composite group and concludes that many of the ideas tested during the exercise were found to be sound in principle but required more training in order to perfect. Of particular note was the use of advanced and rear headquarters and the MORU concept.[53]

The most significant development to emerge from Spartan was the creation of a fully operational composite group, although this was fraught with difficulties. Discussions regarding the establishment of such a force on a permanent basis began in early March 1943 whilst Spartan was still underway. The proposal originated at the COS level—they felt 'that immediate plans should be made for holding in constant readiness as from 1st May the strongest possible force to re-enter the Continent, as soon as German resistance weakens to the required extent'. The meeting was to look at 'what practical steps could be taken to implement this decision so far as the RAF was concerned'. DMC pointed out to the meeting that the headquarters of a composite group had been created to fulfil the requirements of Spartan and that 'the principal question to be decided ... was as to whether this organisation should be retained after the conclusion of Spartan'. This group would then be used as the training formation for squadrons who would be conducting the air support role during and, in the event of a successful landing attempt, the operations that would follow. It was pointed out that the creation of permanent composite group headquarters would cause difficulties as the units to form the headquarters for the exercise were in fact borrowed from other units, and 'would be returned to their respective Commands at the conclusion of the exercise'. If the composite group headquarters was to be established on a permanent basis, it was recommended that it should take over the training of No. 2 Group 'and possibly squadrons of Army Co-operation Command'.[54] The actual demise of Army Co-operation Command can be charted from this point as the success of the composite group had demonstrated it was no longer a necessity for the development of tactical air power in Britain.

The composite group also challenged the fundamental organisation of the RAF and blurred the lines on certain fundamental principles. The RAF in Britain had been organised on a functional basis and the composite group, containing a mixture of fighter, bomber, reconnaissance and army co-operation aircraft, was a radical step change in structure and reflected the WDAF set up. A unit organised along these lines could never have been contemplated when Army Co-operation Command was created due to the fractious relations between the two services, the mutual distrust and the RAF's unwillingness to compromise on the centralisation of air resources under an RAF commander. This lack of flexibility from both services hampered the work of Army Co-operation Command as neither side was willing to back down from what they saw as the correct way to conduct air support. Whilst the composite group would still be under an RAF commander it would be placed within the wider command framework and would work towards the wider military plan as set down by an army commander. To facilitate the training of units to the level where they would be able to conduct air support operations to the required standard, the meeting recommended that 'the group headquarters set up for Spartan should be retained as formed at present after the conclusion of the exercise'. Further to this, it was also decided that 'No. 2 Group and (as a first step) the wings of Army Co-operation Command should be transferred to Fighter Command'.[55] The idea to transfer Army Co-operation Command resources to Fighter Command was the logical conclusion to the discussions that had begun in 1942.

The recommendations put forward to retain the composite group headquarters permanently sparked discussions between the Deputy Chief of the Imperial General Staff, Lieutenant General Sir Ronald Weeks, Brooke and Portal. Weeks was of the opinion that the army 'should jump at the proposal, since it seems to meet the vital requirements for which we have been pressing'.[56] That the army was now in favour of the composite group is not surprising as it effectively gave them an operational force dedicated to army support. It also demonstrates the beginnings of their understanding of the impact of tactical air power at the operational level. Despite the composite group being under an RAF and not an army commander, the tactical level problems faced by ground forces would be targeted and aircraft could also be used to isolate the battlefield and act as a force multiplier for the army at the operational level. This would be achieved through a joint headquarters that was associated with the composite group—an army officer who worked in parallel to the air officer would have a degree of control over how the groups would be used and the targets engaged. In a memorandum from the ACAS responsible for policy, Air Vice-Marshal Douglas Coyler, it was argued that 'The immediate point at issue is not how a Composite Group shall be operated, but whether it is desirable to establish at once a Composite Group Headquarters.'[57] As a result of this issue being raised through Spartan, a conference was held by VCAS, Sir Douglas Evill, at which it was decided to recommend the following to Portal:

> That the immediate formation of a Composite Group Headquarters in Fighter Command should be authorised, and if possible that this should be done before the end of Exercise Spartan [and] that all existing Composite Group Units should be allotted to this Headquarters.[58]

This recommendation had major implications for the higher organisation of the RAF and the development of army co-operation in Britain. The conference highlighted that, as had been previously acknowledged during the discussions on the AASG in 1942, 'Army Co-operation Command ... will cease to exist'. It was, however, acknowledged that it would be required 'to maintain a formation ... which will be responsible for both Army Co-operation and Airborne forces training'. The Air Staff felt that the disbandment of Army Co-operation Command was a major issue and that it would 'raise a certain amount of protest' from the army. It was argued that despite the potential of these protests, it would be welcomed 'by [the] Commander-in-Chief Homes Forces ... in the interests of creating an effective force to support the Army in Continental operations'.[59] This demonstrates the split of opinion within the War Office with regard to the future development of air support in Britain and that the operational level impact of air power was not understood by all within the department.

With the acceptance of this recommendation, the days of Army Co-operation Command were numbered and the moves to establish a composite group headquarters proceeded rapidly. The issue was discussed between Portal and Leigh-Mallory in early March. At this meeting, Portal agreed to the formation of the group on a permanent basis, and that the temporary headquarters established for Spartan would be retained. Leigh-Mallory highlighted the difficulties this would cause as the majority of the staff officers that had formed the headquarters had been 'lent for Exercise purposes' only. As a result, there would be a period of disruption after the formation of the group while individuals were exchanged in order to bring the headquarters up to operational establishment. Portal further agreed that, in order to 'meet the requirements of Continental operations, No. 2 Group and the wings in Army Co-operation Command should be placed in Fighter Command'.[60]

That the transfer of units from Army Co-operation Command to Fighter Command was agreed to raises an interesting question over the status, not only of these units, but also of Army Co-operation Command itself. That these units were regarded as capable of being trained to perform as part of an operational Command within a reasonable time-frame questions the decision not to upgrade Army Co-operation Command to operational status, which would have aided its work during its existence. This non-operational status was part of the rationale for the development of the composite group once it had been established on a permanent basis. The VCAS argued that the hostility that might be expected from certain parts of the army would be quelled when it was seen that they would 'have trained for Continental operations a far larger number of squadrons of the types they require than they otherwise could expect, and that the squadrons will be trained in actual battle operations'.[61]

The reason why they would be trained in actual battle operations was due to the favourable strategic situation now confronting the Allies discussed earlier in this chapter, but such training could also have been accomplished within an upgraded, operational Army Co-operation Command. It was also argued that the creation of the composite group would remove the arguments over where the army air support unit should be placed.[62] The potential disbandment of Army Co-operation Command was also discussed by Hardman:

> I think that if the AOC-in-C's [Fighter Command] recommendations are adopted, and the Group remains in Fighter Command, we shall subsequently have to consider the whole question of the retention of Army Co-operation Command. I believe the Command has achieved a great deal since it was formed [a] little over two years ago, but now that so much of the work for which it was originally formed has been taken over by Fighter Command, and to some extent by Bomber Command, it is questionable whether it would be desirable any longer to retain it in its present form. This again need not interfere with the immediate issue, and if it is thought that Army Co-operation Command has now outlived its usefulness, this present proposal might be a convenient first step to its disbandment.[63]

The composite group was formed in May 1943 and placed within Fighter Command as No. 83 Composite Group.[64] This group was to 'provide facilities for training ground units and squadrons to work together under field conditions, and to provide a means of working out the full requirements and organisation of a Composite Formation'.[65] It was also decided to form a new larger tactical air force within Fighter Command, comprising No. 2 Group, No. 83 (Composite) Group, No. 38 Wing and No. 140 Squadron.[66] This was discussed at the COS Committee and Brooke stated that 'the War Office was in complete agreement'. He was at pains to point out, however, that there were still 'some points of detail … such as the Air OP squadrons and the provision for army staff officers at certain RAF headquarters, which would be for the Air Ministry and War Office to work out in consultation'.[67]

Spartan had demonstrated the efficiency of the composite group idea, which had been in development since 1942. The composite group required a fundamental change to the framework of the RAF and it was the first time that they were willing to contemplate such a change. This marked a fundamental shift in how air support was viewed within the RAF and how important it was to overall success on the battlefield. The trials and tribulations of Army Co-operation Command assisted, to a degree, this change in attitude and the creation of the composite group. Working with Army Co-operation Command also allowed the army to gain a greater understanding of the operational level impact of tactical air power.

With the creation of the first composite group and its placement within the wider tactical air force structure, work began to disband Army Co-operation Command. Its subordinate formations were placed elsewhere within the RAF's Command framework in order to retain the knowledge and expertise that had been gained.[68] Disbanding a Command organisation the size of Army Co-operation Command caused great administrative difficulties, as despite its non-operational status, it had a large staff and many resources that could be well used within the operational Commands of the RAF. To this end a conference was held on 13 May 'to discuss the administrative details arising out of the transfer of Army Co-operation Command and the transfer of its responsibilities'.[69] The other issue the Air Council faced with the disbanding of Army Co-operation Command was where to place its AOC-in-C Barratt, and how best to use the person who had been overseeing the development of army co-operation thinking and development with Home Forces in Britain.

The two major Army Co-operation Command formations that had to be disposed of were the headquarters of Nos. 70 and 72 Groups. There were, however, lower formations that contained experienced personnel who could develop the systems to be used once preparations for the invasion of the Continent were completed. The problems faced in this respect were further hampered by the fact that the units experienced in conducting air support in the Western Desert could not simply be transferred into the new tactical air force or composite group formations as they were being used in overseas theatres such as Italy. The training arm of Army Co-operation Command, No. 70 Group, 'with all its existing units is to be transferred to Fighter Command and will come directly under that Command Headquarters'.[70] When it was placed within Fighter Command, No. 70 Group was

> to retain its present function … [and] in addition, take over No. 13 (Light Bomber) OTU from No. 92 Group, Bomber Command. All anti-aircraft co-operation units at present in existing Groups of Fighter Command. Nos. 1 to 9 Anti-Aircraft practice camps from No. 72 Group.[71]

It had been decided originally that No. 72 Group should be disbanded as a headquarters organisation and part of its units and duties transferred to No. 70 Group. Those units that were not to be transferred were the 'RAF Regiment School, Department and Wing [which] are to be transferred to No. 20 Group, Technical Training Command'.[72] It had been decided that the date for closing down No. 72 Group should be decided between Army Co-operation Command and Technical Training Command.[73] After further discussion with Home Forces regarding the fate of No. 72 Group, however, Hardman decided 'to defer the closing down of 72 Group Headquarters'. It was now to 'be amalgamated [with No. 20 Group] and the new group thus formed entitled No. 22 Group'.[74] The wings that formed Army Co-operation Command, Nos. 32 to 37 and 39 Wings, were to be transferred to Fighter Command.[75] These wings had close relations with army commands with whom they had been training and it was decided that despite their transfer to another Command, the relationship that they had with their respective army commands should continue. The training of these wings would also continue and would now be administered by Fighter Command. They were also to 'exercise direct control of the squadrons for certain specific operations'. These operations were not specified at the time. The Fighter Command Groups that were now responsible for these Wings would now also 'assume the same responsibilities for the administration of the Wings and Squadrons as they have for their existing Fighter Command Stations and Squadrons'.[76]

There was also much discussion about the fate of the Air OP squadrons, which were the responsibility of Army Co-operation Command. It was decided, in the days leading up to the disbandment of Army Co-operation Command, that they

> will be under the composite group for the purpose of command and RAF administration, while they will be allocated to Corps in the appropriate Armies for training and operations in accordance with the present position. The remainder of the squadrons will remain in Army Co-operation Wings or formations appropriate to the Army formations with which these squadrons are working.[77]

The US VIII Air Support Command, which was under Army Co-operation Command for administration was also transferred to Fighter Command. The contentious issue of No. 2 Group, which had never been resolved fully during Army Co-operation Command's existence, was finally settled with the creation of 2nd Tactical Air Force. No. 2 Group was now to be transferred into this force from Bomber Command on a permanent basis.[78] Transferring No. 2 Group to a specialist tactical air force would allow it to receive the necessary specialist training that had been called for when it was first proposed to use the Group in an air support role. The only part of No. 2 Group that was to remain within Bomber Command was the 'unarmed Bomber Mosquito Squadrons'.[79] The major issue that had prevented this from occurring earlier was that No. 2 Group had a dual-role: that of strategic bombing and air support training. Army Co-operation Command had not been able to gain complete use of this Group due to the lack of aircraft available to conduct the strategic bombing campaign at that time. The subsequent loss of aircraft and trained personnel hampered the Command in its role to develop tactical air power in Britain.

There was also much discussion regarding the duties that would be transferred to Fighter Command when Army Co-operation Command was disbanded. The AVM that was to be responsible as the Air Officer for Training on air support matters was to have a staff that consisted of: 'A Group Captain—to be selected from among Army Co-operation Command, a Wing Commander—to be an expert in the flying side of Airborne Forces [and] a Squadron Leader'. With the transfer of No. 70 Group, it was agreed that 'the AOC 70 Group should be an Air Vice-Marshal, in order to compete with additions being made to 70 Group and his responsibilities in connection with the School of Army Co-operation, which he would have to discharge in place of the AOC-in-C Army

Co-operation Command'. Further to this, No. 70 Group was also to have 'an expert on Light Bombers' on their staff. Barratt was to forward a list 'of personnel to fill the establishment on TAF and AOT's [Air Officer Training] staff'.[80] This re-organisation of the role of No. 70 Group into 2nd Tactical Air Force, along with the transfer of responsibilities from Army Co-operation Command, was to involve not only the transfer of tasks, but also the people who would conduct them.

Army Co-operation Command's disbandment was, in real terms, a transferral or amalgamation of its resources to other areas of the RAF that had operational responsibilities. Barratt himself became AOC-in-C Technical Training Command.[81] Carrington has argued the Army Co-operation Command 'worked itself out of a job' and that this was the fundamental reason for its disbandment. Whilst the Command worked as well as it could, given the situation it faced when it was created, it is wrong to say, as Carrington does, that it simply 'faded out of existence'.[82] It is more correct to argue that events and developments in the Western Desert, combined with the increasingly favourable strategic situation, overtook Army Co-operation Command.[83] It was mostly for these reasons, along with the need to provide operational responsibilities for an army air support force, that 2nd Tactical Air Force was created. The majority of Army Co-operation Command's units were either reconfigured or transferred instead of being abolished completely, demonstrating the value of the work they had achieved. The knowledge and expertise gained were seen as being of vital importance to allow 2nd Tactical Air Force to flourish both during its training and its eventual deployment for overseas operations.[84] This was a necessity as the force that had been deployed in the Western Desert was now involved in conducting tactical air support operations during engagements in Italy.[85]

The tactical air force created at the same time as Army Co-operation Command's demise was designated 2nd Tactical Air Force following on from the first tactical air force that had been created under Tedder and Coningham in the Western Desert. The strategic situation had, by this time, turned the tide of the Second World War against the *Wehrmacht* and as noted by Murray and Millett, 'No matter how skilled their conduct of defensive battles, the weight of Allied military power was wearing away the Wehrmacht's tactical advantage.'[86] With the successes of the Red Army on the Eastern Front and pressure easing in the Battle of the Atlantic, the prospect of a successful invasion of France increased greatly, although there would still be great difficulty in launching the attack at operational and tactical levels.[87] 2nd Tactical Air Force force's headquarters were established at Bracknell, the previous home of Army Co-operation Command. The new force was to consist of various sections of other RAF Commands, transferred specially for this purpose. They were: No. 2 (Light Bomber) Group, which was in Bomber Command; No. 83 (Composite) Group, which was under Fighter Command; and No. 140 (Photo Reconnaissance) Squadron and No. 38 (Airborne Forces) Wing, which were both in Army Co-operation Command. No. 140 Squadron was also under the administration of No. 35 Wing, which would continue to administer it when it was part of 2nd Tactical Air Force. A second composite group, designated No. 84 (Composite) Group, would be added when it had been formed.[88] In order to ease the administrative difficulties and to allow the force to establish itself properly (something Army Co-operation Command had been unable to do when it was first created), 2nd Tactical Air Force was established in No. 11 Group, Fighter Command.[89]

The functions of 2nd Tactical Air Force were remarkably similar to those envisaged for Army Co-operation Command when it was created in 1940. The only real difference between the two was the operational nature of 2nd Tactical Air Force. It would be responsible for 'command[ing] the appropriate formations; study[ing] air aspects of Continental operations, [conducting] exercises with Army Group Headquarters, train[ing] the composite Groups, including tactical reconnaissance squadrons'. It was also to 'train light bomber squadrons with the fighters and fighter/bombers of the Tactical Air Forces and to exercise them in actual operations, to make detailed plans in conjunction with C-in-C Army group for the Continental operations when the outline cover plans have been issued'.[90]

The development of the Air OP squadron within the composite group organisation was subject to major discussion whilst 2nd Tactical Air Force was being created. One of the major points for discussion was 'the portion of Air OP Squadrons in the new organisation'.[91] In response to a note sent by the Director of Air at the War Office to Hardman, it was suggested that,

> it is not proposed to alter the basic operational and administration organisation of the Air OP squadrons in the re-organisation to which you refer. As far as can be foreseen the bulk of these squadrons will be under composite groups for purposes of command and RAF administration, while they will be allocated to corps in the appropriate Armies for training, and operations in accordance with the present practice. The remainder of the squadrons will remain in Army Co-operation Wings or formations appropriate.[92]

It was decided the Air OP should be allocated on the scale of 'one [squadron] per Corps and one per Army. It was felt that such a scale of allotment would not be permanent but would be effective for operations and necessary prior training only.' Further to this, the status of the troops that formed the Air OP was also subject to alteration and it was agreed the 'Air OP squadrons should be regarded as War Office troops which could be allotted to theatres as required by the general situation'.[93] This now made the Air OP an interesting functional construct.

That the RAF were willing to allow the transfer of resources away from their operational control highlights just how much the attitude towards army co-operation had changed. This change in attitude would lead to diminishing calls for an air arm under army operational control, something that had been the major fear of the Air Staff when Army Co-operation Command was created and which lasted throughout its existence. With offensive operations on the Continent being planned, the emphasis on development of air support shifted, and gave both the RAF and army something to concentrate on and a chance to work together to achieve a common aim. This ethos had been lacking while a return to the continent was unfeasible and led to increasing infighting between the two services. Army Co-operation Command, an RAF organisation, had been stuck in the middle of this infighting and its ability to fully develop tactical air power was hampered as a result. The experience in the Western Desert demonstrated what properly constituted air support could achieve and how important artillery observation was in supporting ground forces. This was combined with the theoretical work done by Army Co-operation Command to create a system that would act as a force multiplier in army co-operation.

Notes

1. TNA WO 199/334, Letter from the Director of Air (War Office) to Paget, 28 May 1943.
2. Further details of these refinements can be found at Gooderson, *Air Power at the Battlefront*.
3. TNA WO 32/10396, Letter from the Director of Air (War Office) to Paget, 13 January 1943.
4. Ibid.
5. TNA WO 32/10396, Letter from Paget to Under-Secretary of State for War and Director of Air (War Office) regarding Army Air Support Controls, 13 February 1943.
6. Ibid.

7. Ibid.
8. Ibid.
9. Ibid.
10. TNA AIR 19/318, Memorandum on Exercise Spartan March 1943, 12 December 1942. TNA AIR 16/559, Letter from Vice Chief of the Air Staff, Air Vice-Marshal Charles Broadhurst to AOCs-in-C Fighter, Bomber and Army Co-operation Commands, 12 December 1942.
11. TNA AIR 19/318, Memorandum on Exercise Spartan, 12 December 1942. TNA AIR 16/559, Letter from Broadhurst to AOCs-in-C Fighter, Bomber and Army Co-operation Commands, 12 December 1942.
12. TNA AIR 19/318, Memorandum on Exercise Spartan, 12 December 1942.
13. TNA AIR 16/821, RAF School of Army Co-operation Exercise, Employment of Air Forces with the Army, Exercise Instruction Foreword, undated, *c*.March 1943.
14. TNA AIR 39/91, Exercise Spartan—Preliminary Information, Object of RAF Participation, 12 January 1943.
15. TNA AIR 16/559, Agenda for Meeting on Spartan, 9 January 1943.
16. TNA WO 32/10396, Letter from the Chief of Combined Operations to the Director of Air (War Office) regarding Army Air Support Controls, 10 February 1943.
17. TNA AIR 39/91, Exercise Spartan—Preliminary Information, 12 January 1943.
18. TNA AIR 16/821, RAF School of Army Co-operation Exercise, undated, *c*.March 1943.
19. TNA AIR 39/91, Exercise Spartan—Preliminary Information, 12 January 1943. TNA AIR 16/821, RAF School of Army Co-operation Exercise, undated, *c*.March 1943.
20. TNA AIR 16/821, RAF School of Army Co-operation Exercise, undated, *c*.March 1943.
21. TNA AIR 39/91, Exercise Spartan—Preliminary Information, 12 January 1943.
22. Ibid.
23. TNA AIR 16/559, Memorandum on Exercise Spartan—RAF Participation and Allocation of Responsibility to Commands Organisation for Exercise, 21 January 1943.
24. Hall, *Strategy for Victory*; Hall, 'The Long Gestation'; Gooderson, *Air Power at the Battlefront*; Jacobs, 'Air Support'; Harvey, 'The Royal Air Force'.
25. TNA AIR 19/318, Memorandum on Exercise Spartan, 12 December 1942.
26. TNA AIR 16/559, Letter from Broadhurst. Recipient unknown and undated, *c*.January 1943.

27. Carrington, *Soldier at Bomber Command*, pp. 83, 110–11.
28. Leigh-Mallory, 'Air Co-operation', pp. 565–77.
29. TNA AIR 39/91, Exercise Spartan—Preliminary Information, 12 January 1943.
30. TNA AIR 39/128, GHQ Exercise Spartan, Narrative of Events, March 1943.
31. TNA AIR 39/128, GHQ Exercise Spartan, Comments by Paget, March 1943.
32. Ibid.
33. Ibid.
34. Ibid.
35. Ibid.
36. Ibid.
37. Ibid.
38. Terraine, *The Right of the Line*, p. 352.
39. TNA AIR 39/128, GHQ Exercise Spartan, Comments by Paget, March 1943.
40. Ibid.
41. Ibid.
42. Byford, 'Fair Stood', p. 122; Terraine, *The Right of the Line*, pp. 351–2.
43. TNA AIR 16/852, Brief Report on the Intelligence Report on Exercise Spartan, March 1943.
44. TNA AIR 16/852, Exercise Spartan Intelligence Aspect—Report by Flying Officer R. A. Symonds, 14 March 1943.
45. TNA AIR 12/852, Report on RAF Intelligence in Joint Army/Air Operations in the Field by Wing Commander C. W. B. Harrington, 21 March 1943.
46. TNA AIR 16/852, Report on Exercise Spartan (Intelligence Report) by Flying Officer R. A. Symonds, Senior Intelligence Officer, RAF, undated, c.March 1943.
47. TNA AIR 16/852 Spartan Intelligence Report—Report on Spartan—Spartan Reporting Instruction, undated, c.March 1943.
48. TNA AIR 39/128, Letter from Army Co-operation Command to Headquarters No. 70 Group, Nos. 32–39 Wings, No. 43 Operational Training Unit, School of Army Co-operation, Air Ministry (DMC), War Office (Director of Air), Headquarters Home Forces (Air), General Headquarters Home Forces, Royal Artillery, RAF General Headquarters, Home Forces School of Artillery, Larkhill, 17 April 1943.
49. TNA AIR 39/128, Exercise Spartan—Extract from the Chief Umpire's Report, Chapter VI, undated, c.May 1943.
50. TNA AIR 2/7808, Agenda for a Meeting to be held by Barratt (Director (Air) Spartan Exercise) at Army Co-operation Command, 19 March 1943.
51. TNA AIR 2/7808, GHQ Exercise Spartan, Report by Senior Administrative (Air) Umpire, Air Commodore H. K. Thorold, 25 March 1943.

52. TNA AIR 2/7808, Agenda for a Meeting to be held by Barratt, 19 March 1943.
53. TNA AIR 2/7808, Exercise Spartan Report by Thorold, 25 March 1943.
54. TNA AIR 20/2620, Minutes of a Meeting held under the Chairmanship of the VCAS, The Composite Group, 3 March 1943.
55. Ibid.
56. TNA WO 193/679, Letter from Weeks to Portal, 5 March 1943.
57. XXX
58. TNA AIR 20/2620, Memorandum from Evill to Portal, 4 March 1943.
59. Ibid.
60. TNA AIR 20/2620. Minutes of a Meeting on Roundup Preparations—Formation of a Composite Group, 5 March 1943.
61. TNA AIR 20/2620, Letter from Evill to Portal, 5 March 1943.
62. TNA AIR 20/2620, Letter from Hardman to Weeks, 27 February 1943.
63. Ibid.
64. TNA AIR 8/988. War Cabinet COS (43) 248 (0), Re-organisation of the Metropolitan Air Force for Cross-Channel Operations, Note by Evill, 10 May 1943.
65. TNA AIR 8/984, Memorandum on No. 83 (Composite) Group, Fighter Command—Formation of Group Headquarters and Allocation and Formation of Ground Units, 19 March 1943.
66. TNA AIR 8/988. War Cabinet COS (43) 248 (0), 10 May 1943.
67. TNA AIR 8/988, Minutes of COS (43) 99th Meeting, 11 May 1943.
68. TNA CAB 101/136, Unpublished Draft of Grand Strategy Narratives, undated. This section did not from part of the published Grand Strategy Series.
69. TNA AIR 39/94, Letter from ACI 1 (Air Ministry) to Air Officers in charge of Administration Fighter, Bomber and Army Co-operation Commands regarding the Disbandment of Army Co-operation Command, 10 May 1943.
70. TNA WO 32/10348, Memorandum on the Formation of Tactical Air Forces Headquarters. Disbandment of Army Co-operation Command. Closing Down of No. 72 Group Headquarters, 14 May 1943. TNA AIR 39/94, Draft Loose Minute—Formation of 2nd Tactical Air Force Headquarters and the Disbandment of Army Co-operation Command Headquarters. Disbandment of No. 72 Headquarters, undated, *c*.May 1943.
71. TNA AIR 39/94, Draft Loose Minute, undated, *c*.May 1943.
72. Ibid.
73. TNA WO 32/10348, Memorandum on the Formation of Tactical Air Forces Headquarters, 14 May 1943.
74. TNA WO 32/10348, Letter from Hardman to Director of Air (War Office), 28 May 1943.

75. TNA AIR 8/988, Memorandum on the Formation of Tactical Air Force Headquarters. Disbandment of Army Co-operation Command Headquarters. Closing Down of 72 Group Headquarters, 14 May 1943.
76. TNA WO 32/10348, Memorandum on the Formation of Tactical Air Force Headquarters, 14 May 1943.
77. TNA WO 32/10348, Letter from Director of Air (War Office) P. Browne to Paget, 20 May 1943.
78. TNA AIR 39/94, Letter from ACI 1 (Air Ministry) to Air Officers in Charge of Administration of Fighter, Bomber and Army Co-operation Commands, 10 May 1943.
79. TNA AIR 16/566, Letter from ACAS (Policy) Air Vice-Marshal O. E. H. Medhurst to Air Marshal Sir Arthur Harris, AOC-in-C Bomber Command, 24 May 1943.
80. TNA AIR 16/566, Minutes of a Meeting to Discuss Problems Arising out of the Transfer of Tasks Hitherto performed by Army Co-operation Command to Fighter Command, 19 May 1943.
81. TNA WO 32/10348, Air Ministry Communiqué, undated, c.June 1943.
82. Carrington, 'Army/Air Co-operation', p. 40.
83. Gooderson, *Air Power at the Battlefront*, p. 8; Jordan and Sheffield, 'The British Army and Air Power', p. 79.
84. Hall, *Strategy for Victory*, pp. 150–1; Hall, 'The Long Gestation', pp. 29–30.
85. More details on the use of air support and the developments that emerged from the theatre can be found in Gooderson, *Air Power at the Battlefront*.
86. Murray and Millett, *A War to be Won*, p. 374.
87. For details of the D-Day landings and the subsequent operations launched from the beachheads, see Max Hastings, *Operation Overlord: D-Day and the Battle for Normandy* (Pan Books: London, 1984); Murray and Millett, *A War to be Won*, pp. 411–45; Anthony Beevor, *D-Day: The Battle for Normandy* (Penguin: London, 2010 [Viking, 2009]).
88. TNA WO 199/334, Letter from Director of Air (War Office) to Paget, 28 May 1943.
89. Hall, 'The Long Gestation', pp. 29–30.
90. TNA WO 199/334, Letter from the Director of Air (War Office) to Paget, 28 May 1943.
91. TNA WO 32/10348, Note from Director of Air (War Office) to Hardman, 17 May 1943.
92. TNA WO 32/10348, Response to note from Director of Air (War Office) by Hardman, 20 May 1943.
93. TNA WO 193/679, Minutes of a Meeting to Discuss the Scale of Allotment of Air OP Squadrons and Future Training Policy for Pilots, 17 June 1943.

Conclusion

Army Co-operation Command was disbanded on 1 June 1943 and the sobriquet of the Cinderella Service which had been given to Coastal Command seemed to apply equally to this branch of the RAF that had played such an important and vital role in the development of tactical air power development in Britain between 1940 and 1943.

Given the interservice political situation that the RAF faced in the aftermath of the Battle of France, they were forced to create an organisation that would focus upon the future development of army co-operation. This organisation was to guide and influence the development of doctrinal thinking in ground force support. Its abilities to conduct this role were severely hampered by the way in which it was created by the RAF. Whilst this may not appear to be a major problem for a Command whose priorities were the development of ideas and procedures, and arranging the necessary training for both services, it was not the formation that the army had been expecting in 1940, and this caused much tension between the Air and General Staffs. Army Co-operation Command fell somewhere in the middle of what the War Office wanted and what the Air Ministry were trying to avoid providing. This is why it did not have the full support of the RAF and was, on the whole, mistrusted by the army. It was 'a child of uncertain paternity'.[1] That the army were willing to work with Army Co-operation Command speaks volumes for how desperately the army needed co-operation procedures pushed further up the RAF's list of priorities. It also demonstrates that there was no other part of the RAF that would take the development of army co-operation more seriously.

Although created primarily to develop ideas and test them on a theoretical basis, the Army Co-operation Command's greatest achievements were the codification of the signals experiments conducted by Wann and Woodall, the development of the Air OP and the education of the army in the operational level impact of tactical air power. The signals experiments, especially, were of vital importance not only to thinking in Britain, but as the theoretical basis for the development of a functioning close support doctrine in the Western Desert and North Africa. This doctrine was applied, after further refinement, in operations in Italy and north-west Europe. The signals system was transferred from Britain to the Western Desert through No. 2 AASC. It was through Army Co-operation Command's refinement of the original CSBC concept that gave the British forces in the Western Desert an operational level advantage over the *Wehrmacht* as they were able to conduct truly impromptu air support in the field. The Bartholomew Committee believed that the *Wehrmacht* possessed this capability, but in actual fact all close support operations during the Battle of France had been pre-planned. This misreading of German capabilities drove the development of a system that the Allies were to exploit to the full in operations in Europe from 1944 onwards.

Due to its non-operational status and experimental undertakings, it is difficult to assess where Army Co-operation Command sits in the levels of war. The actual work done by the Command sat at the tactical level, as it dealt in the main with tactical refinement and technological development. Its work, in areas such as the CSBC/AASC concept and the development of the Air OP, however, had major implications for the conduct of war at the operational level. The CSBC/AASC allowed the signals framework available in Fighter Command to be exploited to the full in the conduct of an operational air battle. The Air OP allowed artillery to also operate at the operational level. As the impact of its work affected both tactical and operational levels, it is fair to conclude that Army Co-operation Command sat in between the two.

Army Co-operation Command's development of the Air OP transformed army co-operation within Britain and overseas theatres, demonstrating that the Command was able to forge good relations with certain parts of the army and could develop ideas in theory and then refine them through extensive testing in exercises. Army Co-operation Command achieved much within its operational constraints and might have achieved so much more if it had been established in a slightly different form and received greater support from the Air Staff and the Air Ministry.

Barratt was highly suited to the development of artillery observation ideas as he had been a gunner in the Royal Artillery prior to his transfer to the RFC in the First World War. A greater insight into Barratt as a commander can be gained during the initial testing period of the Air OP. The experience of sending squadrons of Fairey Battles to attack the bridgeheads over the Meuse several days after the initial German crossings had a profound effect on him. To begin with his doubts about the Air OP concept and the risks to aircrew could be viewed as arguments to deliberately block a promising army co-operation idea, but his experience, both within the artillery and in France, and the proposals he put forward for further tests of the idea stand great scrutiny. He felt that the first tests had not been rigorous enough upon which to form conclusions, but that the idea had promise—further experimentation established just how this role was to be performed and what aircraft and tactics were required to allow it to function at maximum effectiveness and with increased safety.

The Air OP, after much experimentation and refinement, was one of the greatest developments of the Second World War, not just for Army Co-operation Command, but in the field of army co-operation as a whole. Further procedural development of this idea and a roll-out on a larger scale was hampered by the other major problem Army Co-operation Command faced during its existence: a shortage of aircraft. During training exercises conducted with the army, Army Co-operation Command were not able to field as many Air OP squadrons as requested. Despite the potential of the Air OP squadron, it was always a low priority on exercises, with other forms of tactical reconnaissance taking precedent. However, the Air OP was to be used with great success in the Western Desert and North Africa, as well in operations on the Continent after Army Co-operation Command's disbandment.

A major factor that prevented Army Co-operation Command from developing tactical air power in Britain further was the way in which the organisation was created. As Carrington stated, 'It seems hard to escape the conclusion that the Air Ministry had invented the Command in order to rid themselves at the same time of a very irksome problem and of a very senior officer who was held to be a dangerous man.'[2] Whilst Carrington's assessment of where the original idea for Army Co-operation Command emerged is misguided, his assessment of the Air Staff's intentions when they created it are not. The make-up of the Command, particularly its non-operational status and the motivations of the Air Staff in its creation, has been vastly overlooked in the literature currently available on this subject.

When criticisms are made of Army Co-operation Command, they are usually in comparison to the work done in the Western Desert, particularly by Tedder and Coningham. The literature on the RAF's development of tactical air power has focused on the Western Desert to a greater extent than Army Co-operation Command. This is a direct reflection of how Army Co-operation Command was seen by contemporaries. It was viewed as a necessary evil to be endured only as long as was necessary, created to placate the army at a time of difficulty for the RAF as a whole. It was never intended to upgrade the status of the Command.

Army Co-operation Command found itself isolated within the RAF as a whole due to the service's feelings towards army co-operation. It was also useful for the RAF to be able to point the army in the direction of the Army Co-operation Command whenever any army co-operation matters arose so that the RAF were able to give their full attention to the strategic offensive against Germany and avoid discussions about tactical air power. With no operations for the army to prepare for, the ideas developed by Army Co-operation Command remained in the realm of theory. Whilst this may make for good theoretical doctrine, the rigorous testing of ideas against an enemy is required to iron out teething problems and enhance basic ideas. Without an operational status, other RAF Commands tested any ideas that were developed by Army Co-operation Command. This status also meant that they were always at the bottom of the list in the scrabble for resources. At times there were, in fact, more staff officers than aircraft within the Army Co-operation Command framework.[3]

The Command would always find the role it was tasked with difficult to fulfil, given the situation it faced when it was created. It was further hampered in this by the attitudes of other RAF Commands and the Air Staff who wanted to avoid involvement in this area as much as possible while still pleasing the army. The work Army Co-operation Command did do, however, led to the creation of an operational tactical air force that was able to deliver air support effectively and learn from operational experience. It fostered better relations between the RAF and army that would have hampered the creation of such a tactical air force. This was achieved from a low starting point in the wake of the Battle of France. With greater freedom and responsibility, Army Co-operation Command could have achieved so much more, but it was prevented by the interservice rivalry in Britain. If this had not been the case, the history of tactical air power development in Britain might not have experienced as many problems and disputes as it did.

Notes

1. TNA WO 233/60, Draft of The Development of Air Support to the Army, 25 May 1945.
2. IWM Carrington Papers, 8/11/6.
3. IWM Carrington Papers, 8/11/4.

Appendix: Directive to AOC-in-C Army Co-operation Command

1. You are appointed Air Officer Commanding-in-Chief, Army Co-operation Command.
2. Your Command will be organised into two groups:-
   (a) *An Operational group*, comprising those squadrons allotted to Army formations in Great Britain.

   The Commander of the group will act in the capacity of an AOC, Air Component as laid down in AP 1300 Chap. XI, para. 7. An appropriate proportion of the Air Branch of the Staff of this Group will be located with GHQ, Home Forces.
   (b) *A Training group*, comprising:-
   The Army Co-operation Schools.
   The Central Landing Establishment.
   The Air OP Flight.
   Anti-Aircraft and Searchlight Co-operation Units.
3. The Operational and Training Groups will be under your command, except that the Operational Group, being equivalent to an Air Component, will be under the operational control of GHQ Home Forces. These two groups will comprise all RAF units specifically engaged in Army Co-operation duties in Great Britain.
4. Your primary duties will be to implement the policy decided upon by the Air Ministry and War Office, to foster the development of all aspects of Army Co-operation and to further mutual co-operation between the

Army and the Royal Air Force. You are responsible in these matters to the Air Ministry and will be adviser to the Air Ministry on all Army Co-operation matters.
5. You will be charged:-
    (a) With the supervision of all training in co-operation with the Army, within the terms of the policy communicated to you from time to time by the Air Ministry; and
    (b) With the development of the tactics and technique of Army Co-operation, including close support.
        You will co-operate as necessary with Commanders-in-Chief of other RAF Commands, and Commanders-in-Chief, Home Forces and Northern Ireland, on these matters.
6. Your responsibility towards the Commander-in-Chief, Home Forces will consist solely in ensuring the efficiency of the air forces in the Operational Group. During active operations, you will not be responsible for the operational employment of the Army Co-operation squadrons, nor for air forces provided by other Commands to act in support of Home Forces.
7. In addition to your responsibilities for the two Groups in your Command, you will direct the policy in training and development to be followed by the Officer Commanding No. 75 Wing, whose squadrons are under GOC-in-C Northern Ireland for operations and operational training. You will therefore establish close liaison with the GOC-in-C. You will have the right to inspect No. 75 Wing generally, and to supervise and initiate training exercises in particular. You will not have any other responsibility for No. 75 Wing, which is under the AOC, RAF in Northern Ireland, for administration. The Officer Commanding No. 75 Wing will act in the capacity of an OC Air Component as laid down in AP 1300m Chap. XI, para. 7. Instructions covering the GOC's responsibilities in this connection will be issued by the War Office.
8. Your Command and Group Headquarters staffs will be composed of Army and RAF officers in suitable proportions.

Bibliography

Primary Sources (Unpublished)

Government Records, The National Archives (Public Records Office) of the United Kingdom, Kew

Royal Air Force Papers
AIR 2 – Air Ministry and Ministry of Defence: Registered Files
AIR 5 – Air Historical Branch Papers (Series II)
AIR 8 – Chief of the Air Staff
AIR 9 – Director of Plans
AIR 10 – Air Publications
AIR 14 – Bomber Command
AIR 16 – Fighter Command
AIR 19 – Air Department: Private Office Papers
AIR 20 – Unregistered Papers
AIR 23 – RAF Overseas Commands: Reports and Correspondence
AIR 24 – Operations Record Books: Commands
AIR 29 – Operations Record Books: Miscellaneous Units
AIR 30 – Submission Papers to Sovereign
AIR 32 – Flying Training Command and Technical Training Command: Registered Filed and Reports
AIR 35 – Air Ministry: British Air Forces in France
AIR 39 – Army Co-operation Command
AIR 40 – Directorate of Intelligence

AIR 41 – Air Historical Branch (AHB) Narratives and Monographs
AIR 75 – Marshal of the Royal Air Force (RAF) Sir John Slessor: Papers

Cabinet Office Papers

CAB 2 – Committee of Imperial Defence: Minutes and Memoranda
CAB 5 – Committee of Imperial Defence: Colonial Defence Memoranda (C Series)
CAB 24 – War Cabinet and Cabinet: Memoranda
CAB 53 – Chiefs of Staff Committee: Minutes and Memoranda (1924–1939)
CAB 65 – War Cabinet Minutes and Conclusions (1939–1945)
CAB 66 – War Cabinet Memoranda
CAB 80 – War Cabinet and Cabinet: Chiefs of Staff Committee: Memoranda
CAB 92 – Miscellaneous
CAB 101 – War Cabinet and Cabinet Office: Historical Section: War Histories
CAB 106 – War Cabinet and Cabinet Office: Historical Section

Prime Minister's Papers

PREM 3 – Prime Minister's Office: Operational Correspondence and Papers
PREM 4 – Prime Minister's Office: Confidential Correspondence and Papers

War Office Papers

WO 32 – War Office Registered Files (General Series)
WO 33 – 'O' and 'A' Papers
WO 101 – Meritorious Service Awards
WO 106 – Directorate of Military Operations and Intelligence
WO 190 – Directorate of Military Operations: Appreciation Files
WO 193 – Directorate of Military Operations: Collation Files
WO 199 – Home Forces: Military Headquarters Papers
WO 216 – Office of the Chief of the Imperial General Staff
WO 233 – Directorate of Air Papers
WO 277 – Department of the Permanent Under-Secretary of State, C.3 Branch: Historical Monographs

Private Papers

Christ Church, Oxford
Papers of Marshal of the Royal Air Force Viscount Portal

Department of Documents, Imperial War Museum, London

Papers of Lieutenant Colonel Charles E Carrington

Liddell Hart Centre for Military Archives, King's College London

Papers of Field Marshal Viscount Alanbrooke
Papers of Major-General Sir Robert Laycock

Royal Air Force Museum, Hendon

Papers of Air Chief Marshal Sir Douglas Evill
Papers of Marshal of the Royal Air Force Lord Trenchard

Official Manuals

AP 3000, British Air and Space Power Doctrine, (Fourth Edition, Directorate of the Air Staff, MoD, 2009).

Hansard (Parliamentary Debates)

HC Deb 4 March 1942, vol.378, cols.656–749. Available at http://hansard.millbanksystems.com/commons/1942/mar/04/sir-archibald-sinclairs-statement. Accessed 24 November 2012.

Primary Sources (Published)

Contemporary Articles

Carrington, C.E., 'Army/Air Co-operation, 1939–1943', *JRUSI*, 115 (December, 1970), pp. 37–41.
Coningham, Arthur 'The Development of Tactical Air Forces', *JRUSI*, 91 (February/November, 1946), pp. 211–226.
Everett, M., 'Fire Support from the Air', *JRUSI*, 83 (February/November, 1938), pp. 587–591.
Foster, W.F. MacNeece, 'Air Power and its Application', *JRUSI*, 73 (February/November, 1928), pp. 247–261.
Gossage, E.L., 'Air Co-operation with the Army', *JRUSI*, 72 (February/November, 1927), pp. 561–579.

Leigh-Mallory, Wing Commander, T.L., 'Air Co-operation with Mechanized Forces', *JRUSI*, 75 (February/November, 1930), pp. 565–577.
Pile, F.A., 'The Army's Air Needs', *JRUSI*, 71 (February/November, 1926), pp. 725–727.
Portal, Air Commodore C.F.A., 'Air Force Co-operation in Policing the Empire', *JRUSI*, 82 (February/November, 1937), pp. 343–358.
Samson, Air Commodore C.R., 'Aeroplanes and Armies', *JRUSI*, 75 (February/November, 1930), pp. 676–680.
Stewart, Oliver, 'Air Forces in the Great War: Some Strategical Lessons', *JRUSI*, 79 (February/November, 1934), pp. 289–293.
Trenchard, Hugh, 'Aspects of Service Aviation', *The Army Quarterly*, 2: 1 (April, 1921), pp. 10–21.

Secondary Sources (Published Works)

Official Histories

Butler, J.R.M., *Grand Strategy Vol. II: September 1939–June 1941*, Her Majesty's Stationery Office: London, 1957.
Collier, Basil, *The Defence of the United Kingdom*, Her Majesty's Stationery Office: London, 1957.
Ellis, L.F., *The War in France and Flanders 1939–1940*, Imperial War Museum Department of Printed Books: London, 1996.
Gibbs, N. H., *Grand Strategy Vol. I: Rearmament Policy*, Her Majesty's Stationery Office: London, 1976.
Hornby, William, *Factories and Plant*, Her Majesty's Stationery Office: London, 1958.
Inman, P., *Labour in the Munitions Industries*, Her Majesty's Stationery Office: London, 1957.
Jones, H.A., *The War In The Air: Being the Story of The part played in the Great War by the Royal Air Force Vol. IV*, The Imperial War Museum: London, 1928.
Playfair, I.S.O., *The Mediterranean and Middle East Vol. I: The Early Successes against Italy*, Her Majesty's Stationery Office: London, 1954.
 – *Vol. II: The Germans Come to the Help of their Ally*, Her Majesty's Stationery Office: London, 1956.
 – *Vol. III: British Fortunes reach their Lowest Ebb*, Her Majesty's Stationery Office: London, 1960.
 – *Vol. IV: The Destruction of the Axis Forces in Africa*, Her Majesty's Stationery Office: London, 1966.
Postan, M. M., *British War Production*, Her Majesty's Stationery Office: London, 1952.

Webster, Charles, and Noble Frankland, *The Strategic Air Offensive against Germany, 1939–1945 Vol. 1, Preparation*, Her Majesty's Stationery Office: London, 1961.

Autobiographical and Biographical Studies

Connell, John, *Auchinleck: A Biography of Field Marshal Sir Claude Auchinleck*, (Cassell: London, 1959.
Orange, Vincent, *Coningham: A Biography of Air Marshal Sir Arthur Coningham*, New Edition, Center for Air Force History: Washington, D.C., 1992.
 – *Dowding of Fighter Command: Victor of the Battle of Britain*, Grub Street: London, 2008.
 – *Slessor: Bomber Champion The Life of Marshal of the RAF Sir John Slessor*, Grub Street: London, 2006.
 – *Tedder: Quietly in Command*, Frank Cass: Oxon, 2004.
Richards, Denis, *Portal of Hungerford*, Heinemann: London, 1977.

Diaries, Memoirs, Journals and Accounts

Carrington, Charles, *Soldier at Bomber Command*, Leo Cooper: London, 1987.
Churchill, Winston, *Their Finest Hour*, Cassell: London, 1949.
Danchev, Alex and Daniel Todman (eds), *War Diaries 1939–1945: Field Marshal Lord Alanbrooke*, Phoenix: London, 2002 [Weidenfeld & Nicolson: London, 2001].
Edmonds, Charles, *A Subaltern's War*, Anthony Mott: London, 1984.
Guderian, Heinz, *Panzer Leader*, Penguin Books: London, 2000 [Michael Joseph: London, 1952].
Ironside, Sir Edmund, *Time Unguarded: The Ironside Diaries 1937–1940*, Constable: London. 1962.
Lord Tedder, *With Prejudice: The War Memoirs of Marshal of the Royal Air Force Lord Tedder*, Cassell: London, 1966.
Douglas, Sholto, W., *Years of Command* Collins: London, 1966.
Slessor, J.C., *The Central Blue*, Cassell: London, 1956.

General Works: Books

Armitage, Michael, *The Royal Air Force: An Illustrated History*, Arms and Armour Press: London, 1993.
Barker, Ralph, *A Brief History of the Royal Flying Corps in World War I*, Constable and Robinson: London, 2002 [Constable & Co.: London, 1995].
Beevor, Anthony, *D-Day: The Battle for Normandy*, Penguin: London, 2010 [Viking, 2009].

– *Stalingrad*, Penguin Books: London, 1999 [Viking: London, 1998].
Biddle, Tami Davis, *Rhetoric and Reality in Air Warfare: The Evolution of British and American Ideas about Strategic Bombing, 1914–1945* Princeton University Press: Princeton, New Jersey, 2002.
Bidwell, Shelford and Dominick Graham, *Fire-Power: British Army Weapons and Theories of War 1904–1945*, George Allen & Unwin: London, 1982.
Bingham, Victor F., *Blitzed: The Battle of France May-June 1940*, Air Research Publications: New Malden, Surrey, 1990.
Bond, Brian, *Britain, France and Belgium 1939–1940*, Second Edition, Brassey's (UK) London, 1990 [first edition 1975].
– *British Military Policy between the Two World Wars*, Clarendon Press: Oxford, 1980.
– *Survivors of a Kind: Memoirs of the Western Front*, Continuum: London, 2008.
Bowyer, Chaz, *Fighter Command 1936–1968*, J.M. Dent & Sons Ltd: London, Toronto and Melbourne, 1980.
Bryant, Arthur, *The Turn of the Tide 1939–1945*, Collins: London, 1957.
Buckley, John, *Air Power in the Age of Total War*, University College London Press: London, 1999.
Bungay, Stephen, *The Most Dangerous Enemy: A History of the Battle of Britain*, Aurum Press: London, 2000.
Caffrey, Kate, *Combat Report: The RAF and the Fall of France*, The Crowood Press: Swindon, 1990.
Campbell, John P., *Dieppe revisited: a documentary investigation*, Frank Cass: London, 1993.
Cawthorne, Nigel, *Steel Fist: Tank Warfare 1939–45*, Arcturus Publishing: London, 2003.
Citino, Robert M., *Quest for Decisive Victory: From Stalemate to Blitzkrieg in Europe, 1899–1940*, University Press of Kansas: Kansas, 2002.
– *The Wehrmacht Retreats: Fighting a Lost War, 1943*, University Press of Kansas: Kansas, 2012.
– *The Path to Blitzkrieg: Doctrine and Training in the German Army, 1920–1939*, Lynne Reinner Publishers: Boulder, Colorado and London, 1999.
Clayton, Anthony, *The British Empire as a Superpower, 1919–39*, Macmillan: London, 1986.
Cooper, Malcolm, *The Birth of Independent Air Power: British Air Policy in the First World War*, Allen & Unwin: London, 1986.
Cooper, Matthew, *The German Air Force 1933–1945: An Anatomy of Failure*, Janes: London, New York and Sydney, 1981.
Corum, James S., *The Luftwaffe: Creating the Operational Air War, 1918–1940*, University Press of Kansas: Kansas, 1997.

– *The Roots of Blitzkrieg: Hans von Seeckt and German Military Reform*, University Press of Kansas: Kansas, 1992.

Cull, Brian, and Bruce Lander with Heinrich Weiss, *Twelve Days in May: The Air Battle for Northern France and the Low Countries, 10–21 May 1940, As Seen Through the Eyes of the Fighter Pilots Involved*, Grub Street: London, 1995.

Dancey, Peter G., *British Aircraft Manufacturers since 1909*, Fonthill: London, 2014.

Dean, Sir Maurice, *The Royal Air Force and Two World Wars*, Cassell: London, 1979.

Deichmann, Paul, *Spearhead For Blitzkrieg: Luftwaffe Operations in Support of the Army, 1939–1945*, Greenhill Books: London, 1996.

Delaney, John, *The Blitzkrieg Campaigns: Germany's 'Lightning War' Strategy in Action*, Caxton Publishing Group: London, 2000.

Diamond, Hanna, *Fleeing Hitler: France 1940*, Oxford University Press: New York, 2007.

Dixon, Jack, *Dowding and Churchill: The Dark Side of the Battle of Britain*, Pen and Sword: Barnsley, 2008.

Doughty Robert Allan, *The Seeds of Disaster: The Development of French Army Doctrine 1919–1939*, Archon Books: Connecticut, 1985.

Douhet, Giulio, *The Command of the Air*, Natraj Publishers: Dehradun, India, 2003.

Edgerton, David, *Britain's War Machine: Weapons Resources and Experts in the Second World War*, Penguin Books: London, 2012 [Allen Lane: 2011].
– *England and the Aeroplane: Militarism, Modernity and Machines*, Penguin Books: London, 1991.
– *Warfare State: Britain, 1920–1970*, Cambridge University Press: Cambridge, 2006.

Ellis, John, *Brute Force: Allied Strategy and Tactics in the Second World War*, Andre Deutsch: London, 1990.

Ferris, John, *The Evolution of British Strategic Policy, 1919–1926*, Macmillan Press: London, 1989.

Ford, Ken, *Dieppe 1942: prelude to D-Day*, Osprey: Oxford, 2003.

Forty, George and John Duncan, *The Fall of France: Disaster in the West 1939–1940*, Guild Publishing: London, 1990.

French, David, *Raising Churchill's Army: The British Army and the War against Germany 1919–1945*, Oxford University Press: New York, 2000.

Frieser, Karl-Heinz, *The Blitzkrieg Legend: The 1940 Campaign in the West*, trans. John T. Greenwood, Naval Institute Press: Annapolis, Maryland, 2005.

Fuller, J.F.C., *Tanks in the Great War*, John Murray: London, 1920.
– *The Foundations of the Science of War*, Hutchinson: London, 1925.

Gardner, W.J.R. (ed.), *The evacuation from Dunkirk: Operation Dynamo, 26 May – 4 June 1940*, Cass: London, 2000.
Gilbert, Martin, *Winston S. Churchill vol. VI: Finest Hour, 1939–1941*, London: Heinemann, 1983.
Gladman, Brad, *Intelligence and Anglo-American Air Support in World War Two: The Western Desert and Tunisia, 1940–43*, Palgrave MacMillan: Basingstoke and New York, 2009.
Gollin, Alfred, *The Impact of British Air Power on the British People and their Government, 1909–1914*, Stanford University Press: Stanford, California, 1989.
Gooderson, Ian, *Air Power at the Battlefront: Allied Close Air Support in Europe 1943–45*, Frank Cass: London and Portland Oregon, 1998.
Goulter, Christina J.M., *A Forgotten Offensive: Royal Air Force Coastal Command's Anti-Shipping Campaign, 1940–1945*, Frank Cass: London and Portland, Oregon, 1995.
Gray, Peter, W., *The Leadership, Direction and Legitimacy of the RAF Bomber Offensive from Inception to 1945*. Continuum: London, 2012.
Guedalla, Philip, *Middle East 1940–1942: A Study in Air Power*, Hodder and Stoughton: London, 1944.
Hall David Ian, *Learning how to Fight Together: The British Experience with Joint Land-Air Warfare*, Air Force Research Institute: Maxwell Air Force Base, Alabama, 2009.
– *Strategy for Victory: The Development of British Tactical Air Power, 1919–1943*, Praeger Security International, Westport, Connecticut and London, 2008.
Hallion, Richard P., *Strike from the Sky: the history of battlefield air attack, 1911–1945* Smithsonian Institute Press: Washington, D.C. and London, 1989.
Hart, B.H. Liddell, *Strategy: The Indirect Approach* (4th Edition), Faber and Faber Ltd: London, 1967.
Harvey, A.D., *Collision of Empires: Britain in Three World Wars, 1793–1945*, Phoenix: London, 1994 [The Hambledon Press: London, 1992].
Hastings, Max, *Bomber Command*, Pan Books: London, 1981.
- *Overlord: D-Day and the Battle for Normandy*, Pan Books: London, 1984
Hendrie, Andrew W.A., *The Cinderella Service: Coastal Command 1939–1945*, Pen & Sword Aviation: Barnsley, 2006.
Higham, Robin, *Air Power: A Concise History*, St. Martin's Press: New York, 1972.
Horne, Alistair, *To Lose a Battle: France 1940*, Macmillan: London, 1990 [1969].
Howard, Michael, *The Continental Commitment: The Dilemma of British Defence Policy in the Era of Two World Wars*, Pelican Books: Harmondsworth, Middlesex, 1974 [Temple Smith, 1972].

Hyde, H. Montgomery, *British Air Policy Between the Wars 1918–1939*, Heinemann: London, 1976.
Jackson, Robert, *Air War over France 1939–1940*, Ian Allan: London, 1974.
Jeffrey, Keith, *The British army and the crisis of empire 1918–22*, Manchester University Press: Manchester, 1984.
Johnson, J.E., *Full Circle: The Story of Air Fighting*, Cassell Military Paperbacks: London, 2001.
Kaufmann, J.E. and H.W. Kaufmann, *Hitler's Blitzkrieg Campaigns: The Invasion and Defense of Western Europe, 1939–1940*, Combined Books: London, 1993.
Kennedy, Paul, *Strategy and Diplomacy 1870–1945: Eight Studies*, George Allen and Unwin: London, Boston and Sydney, 1983.
Knight, Darrell, *Artillery Flyers at War: A History of the 664, 665 and 666 'Air Observation Post' Squadrons of the Royal Canadian Air Force*, Merriam Press: Bennington, Vermont, 2010.
Larson, Robert H., *The British Army and the Theory of Armored Warfare, 1918–1940*, University of Delaware Press: Newark, New York, 1984.
Marwick, Arthur, *The Deluge: British Society and the First World War*, 2nd Edition, Macmillan: Basingstoke, 1991.
Masefield, John, *The nine days wonder: (Operation Dynamo)*, Heinemann: London, 1941.
Mason, R.A., *Air Power: A Centennial Appraisal*, (Revised Edition) Brassey's: London, 2002 [Brassey's: London, 1994].
Air Power: An Overview of Roles, Brassey's: London, 1987.
May, Ernest R., *Strange Victory: Hitler's Conquest of France*, I.B. Tauris: London and New York, 2000.
Mead, Peter, *The Eye in the Air: History of Air Observation and Reconnaissance for the Army 1785–1945*, Her Majesty's Stationery Office: London, 1983.
Messenger, Charles, *The Art of Blitzkrieg*, Ian Allan: London, 1976.
Meilinger, Philip S., *Airwar: Theory and Practice*, Frank Cass: London and Portland, Oregon, 2003.
Moorehead, Alan, *The Desert War*, Hamish Hamilton: London, 1965 [Sphere: London, 1989].
Mosier, John, *The Blitzkrieg Myth: How Hitler and the Allies Misread the Strategic Realities of World War II*, Harper Collins: New York, 2003.
Murray Williamson, *Luftwaffe: Strategy for Defeat*, The Nautical and Aviation Publishing Company of America: Baltimore, Maryland, 1985.
– and Alan R. Millett, *A War to be Won: Fighting the Second World War*, Belknap University Press: Cambridge, Massachusetts and London, 2001.
Naveh, Shimon, *In Pursuit of Military Excellence: The Evolution of Operational Theory*, Frank Cass: London and Portland, Oregon, 1997.

O'Malley, Michael C., *Military Aviation in Ireland 1921–45*, University College Dublin Press: Dublin, 2010.
Oddone, Patrick, *Dunkirk 1940: French ashes, British deliverance: the story of Operation Dynamo*, Tempus Publishing: Stroud, 2000.
Omissi, David, *Air Power and Colonial Control: The Royal Air Force 1919–1939*, Manchester University Press: Manchester and New York, 1990.
Overy, Richard J., *The Air War 1939–1945*, Potomac Books: Washington D.C., 1980.
Parham, H.J. and E.M.G. Belfield, *Unarmed Into Battle: The Story of the Air Observation Post*, 2nd Edition, Picton Publishing: Chippenham, Wiltshire, 1986 [The Wykeham Press: London, 1956].
Peden, G.C., *Arms, Economics and British Strategy: from Dreadnoughts to Hydrogen Bombs*, Cambridge University Press: New York, 2007.
– *British Rearmament and the Treasury: 1932–1939*, Scottish Academic Press: Edinburgh, 1979.
Perrett, Bryan, *A History of Blitzkrieg*, Stein and Day: New York, 1983.
Posen, Barry R., *The Sources of Military Doctrine: France, Britain, and Germany Between the World Wars*, Cornell University Press: Ithaca, New York and London, 1984.
Powaski, Ronald E., *Lightning War: Blitzkrieg in the West, 1940*, John Wiley and Sons: Hoboken, New Jersey, 2006.
Powers, Barry D., *Strategy Without Slide-Rule: British Air Strategy 1914–1939*, Croom Helm: London, 1976.
Ray, John, *The Battle of Britain: Dowding and the First Victory, 1940*, Cassell Military Paperbacks: London, 2000 [Arms and Armour Press: London, 1994].
Richards, Denis, *Royal Air Force 1939–1945 Vol. 1: The Fight At Odds 1939–1941*, Her Majesty's Stationery Office: London, 1953.
Richardson, Dick, *The Evolution of British Disarmament Policy in the 1920s*, Pinter: London, 1989.
Ritchie, Sebastian, *Industry and Air Power: The Expansion of British Aircraft Production, 1935–1945*, Frank Cass: London and Portland, Oregon, 1997.
– *The RAF, Small Wars and Insurgencies in the Middle East, 1919–1939*, Air Historical Branch: London, 2011.
Robertson, Scot, *The Development of RAF Strategic Bombing Doctrine, 1919–1939*, Praeger: Westport, Connecticut and London, 1995.
Saunders, Hilary St. George, *Per Ardua: The Rise of British Air Power 1911–1939*, Oxford University Press: London, New York and Toronto, 1944.
Sheehan, William, *A Hard Local War: The British Army and the Guerrilla War in Cork 1919–1921*, The History Press: Stroud, 2011.
Sheffield, Gary, *Forgotten Victory: The First World War Myths and Realities*, Review: London [Headline Book Publishing, 2001], 2002.

Shay Jr., Robert Paul, *British Rearmament in the Thirties: Politics and Profits*, Princeton University Press: Princeton, New Jersey, 1977.

Shirer, William L., *The Collapse of the Third Republic: An Inquiry into the Fall of France in 1940* (2nd Edition), The Literary Guild: London, 1970 [1st Edition 1969].

Simkins, Peter, *Air Fighting 1914–18: The Struggle for Air Superiority over the Western Front*, Imperial War Museum: London, 1978.

Sinnott, Colin, *The Royal Air Force and Aircraft Design: Air Staff Operational Requirements 1929–1939*, Frank Cass: London and Portland, Oregon, 2001.

Slessor, J.C., *Air Power and Armies*, University of Alabama Press: Tuscaloosa, Alabama, 2009 [Oxford University Press: London, 1936].

Smith, Malcolm, *British Air Strategy between the Wars*, Clarendon Press: Oxford, 1984.

Smith, Peter C., *Close Air Support: An Illustrated History, 1914 to the Present*, Orion Books: New York, 1990.

– *Dive Bomber: Aircraft, Technology, and Tactics in WWII*, Stackpole Books: Mechanicsburg, Pennsylvania, 2008.

Sprigg, T. Stanhope, *Wings of the Army*, Collins: London and Glasgow, 1942.

Strachan, Hew, *European Armies and the Conduct of War*, Routledge: London and New York, 1983.

Terraine, John, *To Win a War: 1918, the year of victory*, Sidgwick and Jackson: London, 1978.

– *The Right of The Line: The Royal Air Force in the European War 1939–1945*, Sceptre: London, 1985.

Warden, John A. III, *The Air Campaign: Planning For Combat*, Excel Press: San Jose, New York, Lincoln and Shanghai, 2000.

Warner, Philip, *The Battle of France, 1940*, Cassell Military Paperbacks: London, 2001.

Watt, Donald Cameron, *Too Serious a Business: European Armed Forces and the Approach to the Second World War*, University of California Press: Berkeley, California and Los Angeles, 1975.

Weinberg, Gerhard L., *A World At Arms: A Global History of World War II*, New Edition, Cambridge University Press: New York, 2005 [1995].

General Works: Chapters

Alexander, Martin S., '"Fighting to the last Frenchman?" Reflections on the BEF Deployment to France and the Strains in the Franco-British Alliance, 1939–1940', in Joel Blatt (ed.), *The French Defeat of 1940: Reassessments*, Berghahn Books: Providence, Rhode Island and Oxford, 1998.

- 'In Defence of the Maginot Line: security, policy, domestic politics and the economic depression in France', in Robert Boyce (ed.), *French Foreign and Defence Policy, 1918–1940*, Routledge: London, 1998.
- 'The Fall of France', in John Gooch (ed.), *Decisive Campaigns of the Second World War*, Frank Cass: London and Portland, Oregon, 1990.

Belich, Jamie, 'Air Support, Close' in Richard Holmes (ed.), *The Oxford Companion to Military History*, Oxford University Press: Oxford, 2001.

Bond, Brian, 'The Army Between the Two World Wars' in David G. Chandler (ed.), *The Oxford History if the British Army*, Oxford University Press: New York, 1994.
- and Williamson Murray, 'The British Armed Forces, 1918–1939', in Allan R. Millett and Williamson Murray (eds), *Military Effectiveness Vol. II: The Interwar Period*, New Edition, Cambridge University Press: New York, 2010 [Unwin Hyman: 1988].

Buckley, John, 'The Air War in France', in Brian Bond and Michael D. Taylor (eds), *The Battle for France and Flanders 1940: Sixty Years On*, Pen & Sword: Barnsley S. Yorkshire., 2001.

Coningham, Simon, 'The Battle of Amiens: Air-Ground Co-operation and its Implications for Imperial Policing', in Gary Sheffield and Peter Gray (eds), *Changing War: The British Army, The Hundred Days Campaign and the Birth of the Royal Air Force*, Bloomsbury: London and New York, 2013.

Corum, James S., 'The *Luftwaffe* and Lessons Learned in the Spanish Civil War', in Sebastian Cox and Peter Gray (eds), *Air Power History: Turning Points From Kitty Hawk to Kosovo*, Frank Cass: London and Portland, Oregon, 2002.
- 'The Luftwaffe and the Coalition Air War in Spain, 1936–1939', in John Gooch, (ed.), *Airpower Theory and Practice*, Frank Cass: London, 1995.

Cox, Sebastian, 'Setting the Historical Agenda: Webster and Frankland and the Debate over the Strategic Bombing Offensive against Germany, 1939–1945', in Jeffrey Grey (ed.), *The Last Word? Essays on Official History in the United States and British Commonwealth*, Praeger: Westport, Connecticut and London, 2003.

Doughty, Robert A., 'The illusion of security: France 1919–1940', in Williamson Murray, MacGregor Knox and Alvin Bernstein (eds), *The Making of Strategy: Rulers, states and war*, Cambridge University Press: Cambridge, New York and Melbourne, 1994.

Fearon, P., 'Aircraft Manufacturing', in Neil K. Buxton and Derek H. Aldcroft (eds), *British industry between the wars: Instability and industrial development 1919–1939*, Scholar Press: London, 1979.

Gladman, Brad, 'The Development of Tactical Air Doctrine in North Africa', in Sebastian Cox and Peter Gray (eds), *Air Power History: Turning Points from Kitty Hawk to Kosovo*, Frank Cass: London and Portland, Oregon, 2002.

Glove, P.D.L., 'Air Supremacy – The Enduring Principle', in R.A. Mason (ed.), *War in the Third Dimension: Essays in Contemporary Air Power*, Brassey's: London, 1986.

Goulter, Christina, 'British Official Histories of the Air War', in Jeffrey Grey (ed.), *The Last Word? Essays on Official History in the United States and British Commonwealth*, Praeger: Westport, Connecticut and London, 2003.

Greenhous, Brereton, 'The Israeli Experience', in Benjamin Franklin Cooling (ed.), *Case Studies in the Development of Close Air Support*, Office of Air Force History, United States Air Force: Washington, D.C., 1990.

Griffith, P. G., 'British Armoured Warfare in the Western Desert', in J.P Harris and F.H. Toase (eds), *Armoured Warfare*, B.T. Batsford Ltd: London, 1990.

Hall, David, 'Lessons Not Learned: The Struggle between the Royal Air Force and Army for the Tactical Control of Aircraft and the Post-mortem on the Defeat of the British Expeditionary Force in France in 1940', in Gary Sheffield and Geoffrey Till (eds), *The Challenges of High Command: The British Experience*, Macmillan: London, 2003.

Hallion, Richard P., 'The Second World War as a Turning Point in Air Power', in Sebastian Cox and Peter Gray (eds), *Air Power History: Turning Points from Kitty Hawk to Kosovo*, Frank Cass: London and Portland, Oregon., 2002.

Harris, J.P., 'British Armour 1918–40: Doctrine and Development', in J.P Harris and F.H. Toase (eds), *Armoured Warfare*, B.T. Batsford Ltd: London, 1990.

Heinemann, W, 'The Development of German Armoured Forces 1918–40', in J.P Harris and F.H. Toase (eds), *Armoured Warfare*, B.T. Batsford Ltd: London, 1990.

Jacobs, Will A., 'The Battle for France, 1944', in Benjamin Franklin Cooling (ed.), *Case Studies in the Development of Close Air Support*, Office of Air Force History, United States Air Force: Washington, D.C., 1990.

Jordan, David, 'War in the air: the fighter pilot', in John Bourne, Peter Liddle and Ian Whitehouse (eds), *The Great World War 1914–45 Vol. I; Lightening Strikes Twice*, Harpers Collins: London, 2000.

– and Gary Sheffield, 'The British Army and Air Power', in Peter W. Gray (ed.), *British Air Power*, The Stationery Office: London, 2003.

Kennet, Lee, 'Developments to 1939', in Benjamin Franklin Cooling (ed.), *Case Studies in the Development of Close Air Support*, Office of Air Force History U.S. Air Force: Washington D.C., 1990.

McCluskey, Alistair, 'The Battle of Amiens and the Development of British Air-Land Battle, 1918–1945', in Gary Sheffield and Peter Gray (eds), *Changing War: The British Army, The Hundred Days and the Birth of the Royal Air Force*, Bloomsbury: London and New York, 2013.

Mason, R.A., 'The British Dimension' in Mark K. Wells (ed.), *Air Power: Promise and Reality*, Imprint Publications: Chicago, 2000.

Meilinger, Phillip S., 'Trenchard, Slessor, and Royal Air Force Doctrine before World War II' in Phillip S. Meilinger (ed.), *The Paths of Heaven: The Evolution of Air Power Theory* Air University Press: Maxwell Alabama, 1997.

Melvin, Mungo, 'The Land/Air Interface: An Historical Perspective', in Peter W. Gray (ed.), *Air Power 21: Challenges for the New Century*, The Stationery Office: Norwich, 2000.

Mets, David R., 'A Glider in the Propwash of the Royal Air Force?: Gen. Carl A. Spaatz, the RAF and the Foundation of American Tactical Air Doctrine', in Daniel R. Mortensen (ed.), *Airpower and Ground Armies: Essays in the Evolution of Anglo-American Air Doctrine, 1940–43*, University Press of the Pacific: Honolulu, Hawaii, 2005.

Messerschmidt, Manfred, 'German Military Effectiveness between 1919 and 1939', in Allan R. Millett and Williamson Murray (eds), *Military Effectiveness Vol. II: The Interwar Period*, New Edition, Cambridge University Press: New York, 2010 [Unwin Hyman: 1988].

Millett, Allan R., 'Korea, 1950–1953', in Benjamin Franklin Cooling (ed.), *Case Studies in the Development of Close Air Support*, Office of Air Force History, United States Air Force: Washington, D.C., 1990.

Moradiellos, Enrique, 'Appeasement and Non-Intervention: British policy during the Spanish Civil War', in Peter Catterall with C.J. Morris (eds), *Britain and the Threat to Stability in Europe, 1918–45*, Leicester University Press: London, 1993.

Moran, Daniel, 'Doctrine, military', in Richard Holmes (ed.), *The Oxford Companion to Military History*, Oxford University Press: Oxford, 2001.

Muller, Richard, R., 'Close air support: The German, British, and American experiences, 1918–1941', in Williamson Murray and Alan R. Millett (eds), *Military Innovation in the Interwar Period*, Cambridge University Press: New York, 1996.

Murray, Williamson, 'The Collapse of Empire: British Strategy, 1919–1945', in Williamson Murray, MacGregor Knox and Alvin Bernstein (eds), *The Making of Strategy: Rulers, states and war*, Cambridge University Press: Cambridge, New York and Melbourne, 1994.

– 'The Influence of Pre-War Anglo-American Doctrine on the Air Campaigns of the Second World War', in Horst Boog (ed.), *The Conduct of the Air War in the Second World War: An International Comparison*, Berg Publishers: New York and Oxford, 1992.

– 'The *Luftwaffe* Experience', in Benjamin Franklin Cooling (ed.), *Case Studies in the Development of Close Air Support*, Office of Air Force History U.S. Air Force: Washington, D.C., 1990.

Omissi, David, 'The Mediterranean and the Middle East in British Global Strategy, 1935–1939', in Michael J. Cohen and Martin Kolinsky (eds), *Britain and the Middle East in the 1930s: security Problems, 1935–1939*, St Martin's Press: New York, 1992.

Orange, Vincent, 'Getting Together: Tedder, Coningham, and Americans in the Desert and Tunisia, 1940–43', in Daniel R. Mortensen (ed.), *Airpower and Ground Armies: Essays on the Evolution of Anglo-American Air Doctrine, 1940–43*, University Press of the Pacific: Honolulu, Hawaii, 2005.
— 'World War II: Air Support for Surface Forces', in Alan Stephens (ed.), *The War in the Air 1914–1994* (American Edition), Air University Press: Maxwell Air Force Base, Alabama, 2001.
Overy, Richard J., 'Air Power and Warfare: A Historical Overview', in Mark K. Wells (ed.), *Air Power: Promise and Reality*, Imprint Publications: Chicago, 2000.
Peach, Stuart W., 'A Neglected Turning Point in Air Power History: Air Power and the Fall of France', in Sebastian Cox and Peter Gray (eds), *Air Power History: Turning Points From Kitty Hawk to Kosovo*, Frank Cass: London and Portland, Oregon., 2002.
Probert, Robert A., 'The Determination of R.A.F. Policy in the Second World War', in Horst Boog (ed.), *The Conduct of the Air War in the Second World War: An International Comparison*, Berg Publishers: New York and Oxford, 1992.
Richardson, Dick and Carolyn Kitching, 'Britain and the World Disarmament Conference', in Peter Catterall with C.J. Morris (eds), *Britain and the Threat to Stability in Europe, 1918–45*, Leicester University Press: London, 1993.
Sabin, Philip A.G., 'Air Power in Joint Warfare', in Stuart Peach (ed.), *Perspectives on Air Power: Air Power in its Wider Context*, The Stationary Office: London, 1998.
Sbrega, John J., 'Southeast Asia', in Benjamin Franklin Cooling (ed.), *Case Studies in the Development of Close Air Support*, Office of Air Force History, United States Air Force: Washington, D.C., 1990.
Sheffield, G.D., '*Blitzkrieg* and Attrition: Land Operations in Europe 1914–45', in Colin McInnes and G.D. Sheffield, *Warfare in the Twentieth Century: Theory and Practise*, Unwin Hyman: London, 1988.
Syrett, David, 'The Tunisian Campaign, 1942–1943', in Benjamin Franklin Cooling (ed.), *Case Studies in the Development of Close Air Support*, Office of Air Force History U.S. Air Force: Washington D.C., 1990.
Taylor, Joe Gray, 'American Experience in the Southwest Pacific', in Benjamin Franklin Cooling (ed.), *Case Studies in the Development of Close Air Support*, Office of Air Force History, United States Air Force: Washington, D.C., 1990.
Whiting, Kenneth R., 'Soviet Air-Ground Coordination, 1941–1945', Benjamin Franklin Cooling (ed.), *Case Studies in the Development of Close Air Support*, Office of Air Force History, United States Air Force: Washington, D.C., 1990.
Wilt, Alan F., 'Allied Cooperation in Sicily and Italy, 1943–1945', in Benjamin Franklin Cooling (ed.), *Case Studies in the Development of Close Air Support*, Office of Air Force History, United States Air Force: Washington, D.C., 1990.

Journal Articles

Armstrong, Brian, 'Through a Glass Darkly: The Royal Air Force and the Lessons of the Spanish Civil War 1936–1939', *Air Power Review*, 12: 1 (Spring, 2009), pp. 32–55.

Barua, Pardeep, 'Strategies and Doctrines of Imperial Defence: Britain and India, 1919–45', *The Journal of Imperial and Commonwealth History*, 25: 2 (May, 1997), pp. 240–266.

Bechtold, B. Michael, 'A Question of Success: Tactical Air Doctrine and Practise in North Africa, 1942–43', *Journal of Military History*, 68: 3 (July, 2004), pp. 821–851.

Betts, Richard K., 'Despite Warning: Why Sudden Attacks Succeed', *Political Science Quarterly*, 95: 4 (Winter, 1980–1981), pp. 551–572.

Blunt, Raymond S., and Thomas O. Cason, 'Realistic Doctrine: Basic Thinking Today', *Air University Review*, (May – June 1973). Available at http://www.airpower.au.af.mil/airchronichles/aureview/1973/may-jun/blunt.html. Accessed 14 March 2011.

Boff, Jonathan, 'Air/Land Integration in the 100 days: The case of Third Army', *Air Power Review*, 12: 2 (Summer, 2009), pp. 77–88.

Buckley, John, 'Air Power and the Battle of the Atlantic, 1939–45', *Journal of Contemporary History*, 28:1 (January, 1993), pp. 143–161.

Byford, Alistair, 'Fair Stood the Wind for France? The Royal Air Force's experience in 1940 as a case study of the relationship between policy, strategy and doctrine', *Air Power Review*, 14: 3 (Autumn/Winter, 2011), pp. 35–60.

– 'False Start: the Enduring Air Power Lessons of the Royal Air Force's Campaign in Norway, April-June 1940', *Air Power Review*, 13: 3 (Spring, 2011), pp. 119–142.

– 'The Battle of France, May 1940: Enduring, combined and joint lessons', *Air Power Review*, 11: 2 (Summer, 2008), pp. 60–73.

Cooper, Malcolm, 'Blueprint for Confusion: The Administrative Background to the Formation of the Royal Air Force', *Journal of Contemporary History*, 22: 3 (July, 1987), pp. 437–453.

Corum, James S., 'From Biplanes to Blitzkrieg: The Development of German Air Doctrine between the Wars', *War In History*, 3: 1 (January, 1996), pp. 85–101.

– 'The *Luftwaffe's* Army Support Doctrine, 1918–1941', *Journal of Military History*, 59: 1 (January, 1995), pp. 53–76.

– 'The Myth of Air Control: reassessing the History', *Aerospace Power Journal*, (Winter, 2000). Available at http://www.airpower.au.af.mil/airchronicles/apj/apj00/win00/corum.pdf. Accessed 17 February 2011.

– 'The Spanish Civil War: Lessons Learned and Not Learned by the Great Powers', *Journal of Military History*, 62: 2 (April, 1998), pp. 313–334.

Cox, Sebastian, 'The Air/Land relationship – an historical perspective 1918–1991', *Air Power Review*, 11: 2 (Summer, 2008), pp. 1–11.

Darwin, John, 'Imperialism in Decline? Tendencies in British Imperial Policy between the Wars', *The Historical Journal*, 23: 3 (September, 1980), pp. 657–679.

Danchev, Alex, 'Liddell Hart and the Indirect Approach', *Journal of Military History*, 63: 2 (April, 1999), pp. 313–337.

DiNardo, R.L., 'German Armour Doctrine: Correcting the Myths', *War In History*, 3: 4 (November, 1996), pp. 384–397.

Drew, Dennis M., 'Informal Doctrine and the Doctrinal Process: A Response', *Air University Review*, (September- October 1984). Available at http://www.airpower.maxwell.af.mil/airchronicles/aureview/1984/sep-oct/drew.html. Accessed 14 March 2011.

Fearon, Peter, 'The British Airframe Industry and the State, 1918–35', *The Economic History Review*, 27: 2 (May, 1974), pp. 236–251.

– 'The Formative Years of the British Aircraft Industry, 1913–1924', *The Business History Review*, 43: 4 (Winter, 1969), pp. 476–495.

Fedorowich, Kent, 'Axis prisoners as sources of British military intelligence', *Intelligence and National Security*, 14: 2 (1999), pp. 156–178.

Ferris, John, "Far Too Dangerous a Gamble?' British Intelligence and policy during the Chanak crisis, September-October 1922', *Diplomacy and Statecraft*, 14: 2 (2003), pp. 139–184.

– 'Fighter Defence Before Fighter Command: The Rise of Strategic Air Defence in Great Britain, 1917–1934', *Journal of Military History*, 63: 4 (October, 1999), pp. 845–884.

– 'The Theory of the French Air Menace: Anglo-French Relations and the British Home Defence Air Force Programmes of 1921–1925', *The Journal of Strategic Studies* 10: 1 (March 1987), pp. 62–83.

– 'Treasury Control, the Ten Year Rule and British Service Policies, 1919–1924', *The Historical Journal*, 30. 4 (December, 1987), pp. 859–883.

Gat, Azar, 'British Influence and the Evolution of the Panzer Arm: Myth or Reality? Part I', *War In History*, 4: 2 (April, 1997), pp. 150–173.

– 'British Influence and the Evolution of the Panzer Arm: Myth or Reality? Part II', *War In History*, 4: 3 (July, 1997), pp. 316–338.

Gollin, Alfred M., 'England is No Longer an Island: The Phantom Airship Scare of 1909', *Albion: A Quarterly Journal Concerned with British Studies*, 13: 1 (Spring, 1981), pp. 43–57.

Gooderson, Ian, "Doctrine from the crucible: The British air-land experience in the Second World War', *Air Power Review*, 9: 2 (Autumn, 2006), pp. 1–14.

Gray, Peter W., 'Air Power and Joint Doctrine: An RAF Perspective', *Air Power Review*, 3: 4 (Winter, 2000), p. 1–14.
— 'The Gloves Will Have to Come Off: A Reappraisal of the Legitimacy of the RAF Bomber Offensive Against Germany', *Air Power Review*, 13: 3 (Autumn/Winter, 2010), pp. 9–40.
— 'The Myths of Air Control and the realities of Imperial Policing', *Air Power Review*, 4: 2 (Summer, 2000), pp. 37–52.
Greenhous, Brereton, 'Evolution of a Close-Ground-Support Role for Aircraft in World War I', *Military Affairs*, 39: 1 (February, 1975), pp. 22–28.
Gunsburg, Jeffrey A., 'The Battle of the Belgian Plain, 12–14 May 1940: The First Great Tank Battle', *Journal of Military History*, 56: 2 (April, 1992), pp. 207–244.
Hall, David Ian, 'Creating the 2nd Tactical Air Force: Inter-Service and Anglo-Canadian Cooperation in World War II', *Canadian Military Journal*, 3: 4 (Winter, 2002–2003), pp. 39–45.
— 'Ruling the Empire out of the Central Blue: The Royal Air Force and Counter-Insurgency (COIN) Operations in the Inter-War Period', *Air Power Review*, 10: 2 (Summer, 2007), pp. 68–79.
— 'The Long Gestation and Difficult Birth of the 2nd Tactical Air Force (RAF)', *Air Power Review*, 5: 3 (Autumn, 2002), pp. 32–34.
Hallion, Richard P., 'Battlefield Air Support: A Retrospective Assessment', *Air Power Journal*, (Spring 1990). Available at http://www.airpower.au.af.mil/airchronicles/apj/apj90/spr90/2spr90.htm. Accessed 2 December 2011.
Harris, J.P., 'The Myth of Blitzkrieg', *War In History*, 2: 3 (November, 1995), pp. 335–352.
Harvey, A.D., 'The French Armée de l'Air in May –June 1940: A Failure of Conception', *Journal of Contemporary History*, 25: 4 (October, 1990), pp. 447–465.
— 'The Royal Air Force and Close Support, 1918–1940', *War In History*, 15: 4 (November, 2008), pp. 462–486.
Higham, Robin, 'Government, Companies and National Defense: British Aeronautical Experience, 1918–1945 as the Basis for a Broad Hypothesis', *The Business History Review*, 39: 3 (Autumn, 1965), pp. 323–347.
— 'Quantity vs. Quality: The Impact of Changing Demand on the British Aircraft Industry, 1900–1960', *The Business History Review*, 42: 4 (Winter, 1968), pp. 443–466.
Holley, I.B., 'Concepts, Doctrines, Principles: Are You Sure You Understand These Terms?', *Air University Review*, (July/August, 1984). Available at http://www.airpower.maxwell.af.mil/airchronicles.aureview/1984/jul-aug/holley.html. Accessed 22 February 2011.

Holman, Brett, 'World Police for World Peace: British Internationalism and the Threat of a Knock-out Blow from the Air, 1919–1945', *War In History*, 17: 3 (July, 2010), pp. 313–332.

Horne, Paul, 'The RAF in Command: The Policing of Mesopotamia from the Air', *Air Power Review*, 13: 2 (Summer, 2010), pp. 33–41.

Hughes, Thomas Alexander, 'Air Lines: Anglo-American Tactical Air Operations in World War II', *Air and Space Power Journal*, XVIII: 4, (Winter, 2004), pp. 34–49. Available at http://www.airpower.maxwell.af.mil/airchronicles/apj/apj04/win04/hughes.html. Accessed 14 April 2010.

Jacobs, W.A., 'Air Support for the British Army, 1939–1943', *Military Affairs*, 46: 4 (December, 1982), pp. 174–182.

Jordan, David, 'The Royal Air Force and Air/Land integration in the 100 days, August-November 1918', *Air Power Review*, 11: 2 (Summer, 2008), pp. 12–29.

Kiesling, Eugenia C., 'If It Ain't Broke Don't Fix It: French Military Doctrine Between the World Wars', *War In History*, 3: 2 (April, 1996), pp. 208–223.

Killingray, David, "A Swift Agent of Government': Air Power in British Colonial Africa', *Journal of African History*, 25: 4 (1984), pp. 429–444.

Kirkland, Faris R., 'The French Air Force in 1940: Was it Defeated by the Luftwaffe or by Politics?', *Air University Review*, XXXVI: 6 (September/October, 1985). Available at http://www.airpower.au.af.mil/airchronicles/aureview/1985/sep-oct/kirkland.html. Accessed 2 December 2011.

Meilinger, Phillip S., 'Clipping the Bomber's Wings: The Geneva Disarmament Conference and the Royal Air Force, 1932–1934', *War In History*, 6: 3 (July, 1999), pp. 302–330.

— 'The Historiography of Airpower: Theory and Doctrine', *Journal of Military History*, 64: 2 (April, 2000), pp. 467–501.

— 'Trenchard and "Morale Bombing": The Evolution of Royal Air Force Doctrine Before World War II', *Journal of Military History*, 60: 2 (April, 1996), pp. 243–270.

Murray, Williamson, 'British and German Air Doctrine Between The Wars', *Air University Review*, XXX: 3, (March/April, 1980), pp. 39–85. Available at http://www.airpower.au.af.mil/airchronicles/aureview/1980/mar-apr/murray.html. Accessed 18 May 2009.

Overy, Richard, 'Doctrine Not Dogma: Lessons from the Past', *Air Power Review*, 3: 1 (Spring, 2000), pp. 32–47.

Parton, Neville, 'The Development of Early RAF Doctrine', *The Journal of Military History*, 72: 4 (October, 2008), pp. 1155–1178.

Pauly, John W., 'The Thread of Doctrine', *Air University Review*, (May-June, 1976). Available at http://www.airpower.maxwell.mil/airchronichles/aureview/1976/may-jun/pauly/html. Accessed 10 March 2011.

Place, T. Harrison, 'British Perceptions of the Tactics of the German Army, 1938–40', *Intelligence and National Security*, 9: 3 (July, 1994), pp. 495–519.

Peden, G.C., 'The Burden of Imperial Defence and the Continental Commitment Reconsidered', *The Historical Journal*, 27: 2 (1984), pp. 405–423.

Powell, Matthew, 'A Forgotten Revolution? Army Co-operation Command and Artillery Co-operation, 1940–1942', *Canadian Military History*, 23: 1 (Winter, 2014), pp. 71–88.

– 'Re-discovering the Operational Level: Army Co-operation Command and Tactical Air Power Development in Britain, 1940–1943', *British Journal for Military History*, 2: 1 (October, 2015), pp. 72–86.

– 'The Battle of France, Bartholomew and Barratt: The Creation of Army Co-operation Command', *Air Power Review*, 18: 1 (Spring, 2015), pp. 90–107.

– 'The RAF Must Fly the Flag: The British Army's Interpretation of Tactical Air Power during the Battle of France 1940', *The University of Sussex Journal of Contemporary History*, 16 (2015), pp. 63–74.

Price, Alfred, 'The Rise and Demise of the Stuka', *Air Power Review*, 3: 4 (Winter, 2000), pp. 39–54.

Roe, Major Andrew, 'Friends in high places: air power on the North-West Frontier of India', *Air Power Review*, 11: 2 (Summer, 2008), pp. 30–44.

Ryan, W. Michael, 'The Influence of the Imperial Frontier on British Doctrines of Mechanized Warfare', *Albion: A Quarterly Journal Concerned with British Studies*, 15: 2 (Summer, 1983), pp. 123–142.

Satiya, Priya, 'The Defense of Inhumanity: Air Control and the British idea of Arabia', *The American Historical Review*, 111: 1 (February, 2006), pp. 16–51.

Simonson, G.R., 'The Demand for Aircraft and the Aircraft Industry, 1907–1958', *The Journal of Economic History*, 20: 3 (September, 1960), pp. 361.382.

Smith, Malcolm, 'A Matter of Faith: British Strategic Air Doctrine before 1939', *Journal of Contemporary History*, 15: 3 (July, 1980), pp. 423–442.

– 'The Royal Air Force, Air Power and British Foreign Policy, 1932–37', *Journal of Contemporary History*, 12: 1 (January, 1977), pp. 153–174.

Strachan, Hew, 'The British Way in Warfare Revisited', *The Historical Journal*, 26: 2 (June, 1983), pp. 447–461.

Tjepkema, Andy, 'Coningham: The Architect of Ground-Air Doctrine', *Air Clues*, 45: 6 (June, 1991), pp. 204–211.

Watts, Barry D., and James O. Hale, 'Doctrine: Mere Words or a Key to War-Fighting Competence?', *Air University Review*, (September/October, 1984). Available at http://www.airpower.maxwell.af.mil/aichronicles/aureveiw/1984/sep-oct/watts.html. Accessed 22 February 2011.

Whitmarsh, Andrew, 'British Army Manoeuvres and the Development of Military Aviation, 1910–1913', *War In History*, 14: 3 (July, 2007), pp. 325–346.

Young, Robert J., 'The Strategic Dream: French Air Doctrine and the Inter-War Period, 1919–39', *Journal of Contemporary History*, 9: 4 (October, 1974), pp. 57–76.

Unpublished Theses and Manuscripts

Gray, Peter William, *The Strategic Leadership and Direction of the Royal Air Force Strategic Air Offensive Against Germany from Inception to 1945*, PhD Thesis, University of Birmingham, Great Britain, 2009.

Jordan, David, *The Army Co-operation Missions of The Royal Flying Corps/Royal Air Force 1914–1918*, PhD Thesis, University of Birmingham, Great Britain, 1997.

Mahoney, Ross, *The Forgotten Career of Air Marshal Sir Trafford Leigh-Mallory. 1892–1937: A Social and Cultural History of Leadership Development in the Inter-War Royal Air Force*, PhD Thesis, University of Birmingham, 2015.

Parton, Neville, *The Evolution and Impact of Royal Air Force Doctrine: 1919–1939*, PhD Thesis, University of Cambridge, Great Britain, 2009.

Pugh, James, *The Conceptual Origins of the Control of the Air: British Military and Naval Aviation, 1911–1918*, PhD Thesis, University of Birmingham, 2012.

Sinnot, Colin Sydney, *RAF Operational Requirements*, PhD Thesis, King's College London, Great Britain, 1998.

Waldie, Derek J.P., *Relations between the Army and Royal Air Force 1918–1939*, PhD Thesis, Kings College London, Great Britain, 1980.

Television

The World At War: France Falls, 1939–1940, Thames Television, 1973.

Index

A

Advanced Air Headquarters, 168
Advanced Air Striking Force, 43, 46–54, 57, 68, 69
Aircraft Industry, 29, 48
Aircraft Requirements, xiv, 121
Air Historical Branch, 49, 93, 188
Air Ministry, xiii, 19, 28, 32, 47–52, 54, 57, 58, 69, 84, 85, 91, 94, 95, 103, 104, 122, 124, 127, 129–32, 138, 145–50, 163, 167, 179, 229
Air Observation Post, xiv, 59, 136, 161, 178, 189–91, 197, 211–12, 217, 218, 221–2, 228, 229
Air Staff, 5–8, 12, 19, 22, 23, 69, 71, 101–2, 104–5, 107–8, 110–11, 120, 122, 124–9, 131, 135, 140, 149–51, 161, 173, 174, 178, 184, 198
Air Support Signals Unit, 57, 71, 165–6
Alam el Halfa, Battle of, 165

Allied Central Air Bureau, 55–8, 70–1, 97, 98, 102
Anti-Invasion Measures, xiv, 122, 147
Ardennes, 61–2, 66
Armeé de l'Air, 47, 60, 68
Army Air Arm, 31, 32, 47, 48, 71, 84, 91, 94, 104, 121, 122, 124, 125, 133, 149, 177–8, 185
Army Air Support, xv, 142–5, 151, 179, 183–4, 198, 201, 204, 205, 216, 220
Army Air Support Control, 144–6, 165, 168, 169, 172, 176, 198–201, 204, 207, 228
Army Air Support Group, xv, 169, 173, 178–89, 215
Army Co-operation, 2–4, 6, 11, 13–17, 24, 90, 104, 107–8, 111, 120–1, 129, 144, 146, 148, 170
Army Co-operation Command, xi–xii, 3, 12, 44, 55, 59, 71, 84–5, 94, 103–11, 119–42, 146, 148–53, 161–5, 173–91, 197–222, 227–30

INDEX

A
Army Co-operation Exercises, 2, 11–13, 15, 16, 90, 98, 99, 134, 143, 148, 164, 200
Army Co-operation Squadrons, 5, 7, 11, 14, 15, 26, 29, 105, 127, 137, 144, 147, 150, 152, 162, 173
Artillery Observation, 59, 135, 145, 212, 229
Artillery Reconnaissance, 58, 59, 120, 134–6, 189
Auftragstaktik, 61

B
Barratt, Air Marshal Sir Arthur 'Ugly,' xiii
Bartholomew Committee, 86, 92, 103, 133, 134, 228
Bartholomew, General William, 86
Battlefield Air Interdiction, xii, vii, 10, 12, 27
Battle of Britain, 91, 106, 120, 129–30, 138, 183
Battle of France, 1940, 12, 22, 44, 51, 55, 62, 71, 83–5, 103, 106, 121, 122, 132, 140, 145, 147, 164, 184
Blitzkrieg, 45, 61, 89
Blount, Air Vice-Marshal C.H.R, 49
Bomber Command, 4, 52–3, 57, 108, 109, 138, 139, 141, 142, 147–9, 198, 219, 221
Bristol Blenheims, 59, 67, 151
British Air Forces in France, 52–5, 57, 62, 66–71, 86, 89, 92–3, 95, 110, 175, 177
British Army of the Rhine, 12
British Expeditionary Force, vii, 8, 44, 49–51, 57, 59–62, 66, 83, 86–90, 94, 142
Brooke, General Sir Alan, 121

C
Chief of the Air Staff, 20, 47, 111, 124–5, 129
Chief of the Imperial General Staff, 6, 127, 131, 214
Chiefs of Staff Committee, 236
Churchill, Winston, 5, 69
Clock Code System, 58, 135–7
Close Air Support, viii, 2, 12, 15, 21, 22, 24–30, 55, 62, 96, 138, 141
Close Support Bombing Control, 96, 97, 100, 109
Coastal Command, 52, 104, 108, 180, 227
Command and Control, 1, 3, 12, 20, 25, 31, 44, 164, 183, 200
Command, Control and Communications, 45
Committee of Imperial Defence, 6, 17
Composite Group, 165, 175–7, 197, 200–3, 206, 207, 209–10, 213–19, 221
Coningham, Air Vice-Marshal Sir Arthur 'Mary,' xi

D
Dieppe, 164, 183, 187, 2047
Dill, Field Marshal Sir John, 92
Directorate of Military Co-operation, 92, 111, 126, 128, 131, 167–9, 213
Dive-bomber, 86, 90–1, 94, 95, 99, 148
Doctrine, x, 21–3, 31, 54, 63, 86, 111, 167, 228
Douglas, Air Marshal Sir W. Sholto, 172
Dowding, Air Marshal Sir Hugh, 69
Dyle River, 61, 63

INDEX 259

E
Eden, Anthony, 91
El-Alamein, Second Battle of, 166
Empire, xiii, 2, 17–20, 22, 25–7, 31, 132, 163
Exercises
  BUMPER, 138, 144–6
  DRAGON, 138
  SPARTAN, 197, 201–2, 204–15, 217
  VICTOR, 123

F
Fairey Battle, 47, 94, 229
Festing, Lieutenant-Colonel F.W., 48
Fighter Command, 69, 120, 129, 135, 150, 161–3, 170, 172–3, 180, 183, 185, 186, 188, 191, 204, 205, 214, 216–19, 221
First World War, vii–viii, x, xii, xiii, 1–4, 9, 13, 17, 28, 45, 55, 58, 65, 70, 84, 89, 135, 137, 171, 189
Flying Observation Posts, 59
France, xiii, 32, 43–5, 49, 51, 54, 56, 59, 65, 69–71, 83–8, 90–102, 120, 132, 135, 164, 181, 201, 208
Fraser, Group Captain H., 92
Freeman, Air Chief Marshal Sir Wilfrid, 124–5

G
Garrod, Air Marshal Sir Alfred, 130
Geddes, Sir Eric, 5
General Staff, 8, 48, 91, 95, 97, 99–5, 107–10, 119, 121–3, 125, 130, 139, 141, 144, 149–50, 161, 169, 171, 173–6, 178, 180, 186, 188, 204, 214

Geneva Disarmament Conference, 29
Germany, 7, 12, 28, 30, 31, 49, 54, 62, 106, 141, 146, 165, 175, 230
Goddard, Air Commodore R.V., 124
Gort, Lord, 49
Grey Book, 26–7
Guderian, Lieutenant-General Heinz, 62

H
Hardman, Air Commodore J.D.I., 167
Headquarters
  co-location of, 12, 13, 16, 22, 63, 66, 70, 164
Heer, 54, 61, 66, 90, 95, 100, 101
Home Forces, 104–8, 110, 121–6, 149, 173, 174, 176–7, 190, 200–1, 209–10

I
Imperial Policing, 19–20
Impromptu Support, 21, 97
Independent Force, 1, 3, 9, 12, 19, 30, 104
India, 17–21, 24, 27, 181

J
Joint Planning Staff, 178, 179
Ju-87 Stuka, 64

L
Land Observation Post, 136
League of Nations, 18
Leigh-Mallory, Air Marshal Sir Trafford, 34
Limited Liability, 46

Luftwaffe, 22, 24, 44, 45, 49, 50, 61, 63–6, 69, 87–8, 90–2, 95, 100, 101, 133, 135, 170, 173, 201
Lysander, 50, 59, 94, 110, 135, 151

M
Manual of Army Co-operation, 10
McNeil, Major-General J.M., 165
Medhurst, Air Marshal M.E.H., 169
Middle East, xiv, 134, 162, 163, 165, 168–70, 177, 181, 182, 209
Mobile Operations Rooms Units, 203, 210, 213

N
Newall, Air Chief Marshal Sir Cyril, 47
No.2 Army Air Support Control, 144, 145, 165, 228
No. 2 (Light Bomber) Group, 221
No. 22 (Army Co-operation) Group, 95, 104
North-West Frontier, 20–2, 25, 26
No. 257 Squadron, 170–1
No.3 (Indian) Wing, 21, 24

O
Operations
  BATTLEAXE, 121, 132, 133, 164
  CRUSADER, 164
  DYNAMO, 44
  ROUND-UP, 178, 180, 183, 204
  TORCH, 178, 198

P
Paget, General Charles, 130, 151, 176, 178, 179, 181, 198, 205–9, 227
Peirse, Air Marshal Richard, 130
Phantom, 56, 57, 69, 95, 100, 102
Photographic Reconnaissance Group, 105
Portal, Air Marshal Sir Charles, 108

R
Radio Telegraphy, 21, 189
Reconnaissance, vii–viii, 24–6, 50, 55–62, 66, 67, 89, 95, 103, 109, 110, 120, 134–7, 143–5, 149–51, 169, 173, 176–8, 187–8
Rommel, Major-General Erwin, 64
Royal Air Force (RAF)
  Component, 46, 49–51, 53, 60, 69
  83 Composite Group, 216
  2 Group, 141–3, 145, 146, 150, 170, 171, 174, 175, 178–9, 213–15, 217, 219
  20 Group, 218
  70 Group, 218–20
  71 Group, 103, 122–3, 125–7, 147
  72 Group, 218
Royal Artillery, 135, 229
Royal Flying Corps, vii–viii, 13, 30, 58, 137, 229
Royal Naval Air Service, xiii, 3, 30

S
School of Artillery, 135, 137, 189–91, 212
Schwerpunkt, 61, 62
Second World War, xi, 2, 4, 9, 12, 15, 27, 58, 84, 93, 119, 140, 145, 172, 186, 208
Sedan, 44, 45, 61–9, 87, 88
Senior Air Staff Officer, 123, 126, 163, 173, 181
Slessor, Air Vice-Marshal John, xv
Somaliland, 18–19
Spanish Civil War, 22–3, 62

Spitfire, 58
Strategic Bombing, x, 43, 219
Symonds, Flying Officer R.A., 210

T
Tactical Air Force
  2nd Tactical Air Force, xv, 197, 198, 204, 219–221
Tactical Air Power, viii, xi, xiv, 11, 13, 24, 27, 45, 84, 87, 95–7, 105, 119, 130, 162, 174, 197, 214, 230
Technical Training Command, 218, 220
Tedder, Air Marshal Sir Arthur, xi
Ten Year Rule, 4, 5
Thorold, Air Commodore Henry 'Thorold Paper,' xv
Treasury, 29
Trenchard, Major-General Sir Hugh, ix

U
United States, 95, 151, 175, 181

V
Vachell, Air Commodore J.L., 126

W
Wann, A., 94, 100–3, 111, 134, 137, 139, 141–5, 147, 164–6, 170, 200, 202, 204, 208, 228
Wann/Woodall Experiments, 94, 111, 137, 139, 144, 145, 147, 166
War Cabinet, 47, 48, 52, 69, 86, 93, 104, 187
War Office, 236
Wehrmacht, xiv, 44, 45, 60–5, 69, 87, 100, 165, 170, 220, 288
Western Desert, 103, 111, 132–4, 162–4, 166–7, 170, 198, 200, 208, 220, 228, 230
Western Desert Air Force, xi, 12, 133, 164, 182, 203, 213
Williams, Air Commodore T.W., 181
Wireless Telegraphy, 21
Woodall, Lieutenant-Colonel J.D., 55